COMPUTER SECURITY FUNDAMENTALS

Nastaran Nazar Zadeh

Toronto Academic Press

COMPUTER SECURITY FUNDAMENTALS

Nastaran Nazar Zadeh

Toronto Academic Press
4164 Lakeshore Road
Burlington ON L7L 1A4
Canada
www.tap-books.com

Email: orders@arclereducation.com

ISBN: 978-1-77956-281-4

ABOUT THE AUTHOR

Nastaran Nazar Zadeh is a highly experienced computer engineer, researcher, and advisor in the fields of robotics, artificial intelligence and computer science. She holds a Master of Science in Computer Engineering from Mapua University of the Philippines and pursed her Ph.D. in Electronic Engineering at the same institution. With over seven years of teaching experience, Nastaran has taught electronic and computer engineering programs at several reputable academic institutions, where she has also led numerous thesis studies. Her research focuses on developing robotics systems with A.I. and machine learning, which enables her to stay up-to-date with the latest advancements in the field and implement cutting-edge technologies.

Table of Contents

List of Figures

List of Tables

PREFACE

In today's digital world, the significance of safeguarding computer systems against malicious intrusions and vulnerabilities cannot be overstated. The landscape of computing and information technology has evolved exponentially since its inception, presenting both remarkable opportunities and complex challenges in equal measure. Computer security fundamentals encompass a range of principles, practices, and technologies aimed at protecting computer systems, networks, and data from unauthorized access, attacks, damage, or theft. These fundamentals form the bedrock of a robust security posture and are essential in maintaining the confidentiality, integrity, and availability of information in digital environments.

This book comprises of eight-chapters;the first chapter discusses the fundamental concepts of computer security such as the CIA (confidentiality, integrity, and availability) Triad with emphasis onten security principles. The second chapter discusses the common threats to computer systems such as fraud, theft, malicious code, hackers, and employee sabotage.

The third chapter is about computer viruses containing the details of different viruses, their propagation methods, and mitigation strategies. Physical Security, often overlooked yet undeniably vital, is discussed in the fourth chapter, emphasizing the significance of tangible safeguards in conjunction with digital protections.

The fifth chapter describes theconcept of cryptography with emphasis on the basic types, uses, and implementation issues of this technique.The sixth chapter deals with operating system security, elucidating the methodologies to fortify the very core of computing environments. Network Security, an indispensable facet in today's interconnected world, is thoroughly examined in chapter seven, encompassing protocols, intrusion detection, and preventive measures against network-based threats.The final chapter, Web Applications Security, navigates through the intricacies of securing web-based platforms, addressing vulnerabilities, and implementing defenses to mitigate potential risks.

This book is intended as a comprehensive resource for students, researchers, and professionals in the field of computer security. It provides a solid foundation for understanding the potential threats to computer systems along with the importance and possible solutions for securing the computer systems.

—*Author*

CHAPTER 1

Introduction to Computer Security

LEARNING OBJECTIVES

After studying this chapter, you will be able to:

- Familiarize yourself with the concepts of confidentiality, integrity, and availability in terms of computer security.
- Comprehend key concepts such as assurance, authenticity, and anonymity.
- Identify different types of threats that pose risks to computer systems and networks.
- Interpret the ten fundamental security principles in designing secure systems.

INTRODUCTORY EXAMPLE

Ensuring information system security is critical in today's digital environment. Digitech Corporation, a multinational enterprise specializing in financial services, encountered a significant computer security breach that exposed sensitive customer information. The repercussions were immediate and severe. The malware swiftly propagated through the corporate infrastructure, compromising login credentials, financial databases, and confidential client data. The breach resulted in financial losses, damage to the company's reputation, and regulatory investigations. This incident serves as a stark reminder of the vulnerabilities inherent in contemporary computing environments. As technology continues to advance, so do the tactics employed by malicious actors seeking to exploit weaknesses in security defenses. Consequently, understanding and implementing effective computer security measures are imperative for organizations to safeguard their assets, maintain the trust of clients, and adhere to regulatory requirements.

UNIT INTRODUCTION

Current computer systems may contain legacy features from previous versions, such as when the Internet was primarily used by military labs and academic researchers. For instance, the functioning of the Internet is still based on assumptions that were reasonable in the early 1980s, such as the absence of hostile behavior among devices connected to the network. These assumptions have contributed to the increase in online criminal activity (Gollmann, 2010).

The identification of vulnerabilities in computer systems is crucial for ensuring computer security, as they can potentially grant hostile users access to personal information and even enable device takeover. Numerous attacks are made possible through these vulnerabilities. By analyzing these attacks, one can assess the potential damage that can be inflicted and the likelihood of further attacks. It is necessary to identify compromised devices, eliminate malicious code, and patch systems to address vulnerabilities in order to combat these attacks (Landwehr, 2001).

Secure models are a first step toward having a secure computer system. It is critical to identify the security attributes that need to be guaranteed, predict the kinds of assaults that might be made, and create tailored responses. The design should also take into account usability issues. Security measures that are challenging to comprehend and difficult to implement are likely to fail. Next, the hardware and software implementation of a system needs to be rigorously tested to detect programming errors that introduce vulnerabilities. Following system deployment, protocols should be established to track system behavior, identify security breaches, and take appropriate action. Finally, security-related patches to the system must be applied as soon as they become available (Bishop, 2003).

1.1. CONFIDENTIALITY, INTEGRITY, AND AVAILABILITY

→Learning Objectives

- Understand the concepts of confidentiality, integrity, and availability.
- Comprehend the importance of maintaining a balance between the three principles of the CIA Triad.

The misuse of computers and networks is becoming more common. Spam, phishing, computer viruses, and identity theft, which endanger people's finances and expose businesses to liability, are all becoming multibillion-dollar issues. Therefore, there is an increasing demand for information technology professionals to have more experience and a deeper understanding of computer security. More security-savvy computer experts who can effectively counter and prevent cyber-attacks are needed by society, as are security-savvy computer users who can securely handle their data and the systems they use (Samonas & Coss, 2014). C.I.A. (Confidentiality, Integrity, and Availability) has traditionally been used to describe information security (*See* Figure 1.1).

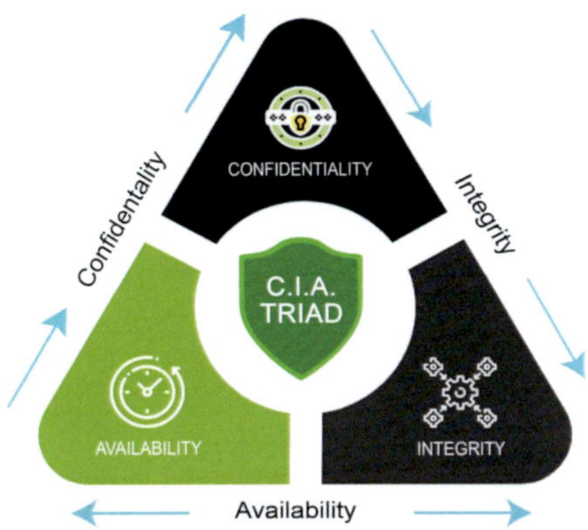

Figure 1.1. Illustration of confidentiality, integrity, and availability (Source: Digicert, Creative Commons License).

1.1.1. Confidentiality

Confidentiality in computer security refers to the prevention of unauthorized disclosure of information. In other words, maintaining confidentiality involves safeguarding data, granting access only to authorized individuals, and preventing unauthorized parties from gaining knowledge about its contents.

The concept of maintaining information confidentiality has been present long before the advent of computers. For instance, Julius Caesar employed a basic cipher to communicate orders to his generals, marking one of the earliest known uses of cryptography. Caesar's method involved replacing each letter in his message with a different letter in his code, such as substituting D for A, E for B, and so on. While this encryption method is easily deciphered and not suitable for maintaining confidentiality in the modern world, it was likely secure during Caesar's time, considering that most of his competitors were illiterate in Latin (Kelly & McKenzie, 2002).

Maintaining confidentiality has become more challenging in contemporary times. With computers being ubiquitous, they possess the capability to carry out tasks that may pose a threat to confidentiality. In response to the numerous risks to information confidentiality, computer security researchers and system designers have developed various techniques to safeguard sensitive data. These techniques incorporate the following ideas:

Did you know?

The idea of encryption has a long history, with notable examples such as the Caesar cipher, which was developed by Julius Caesar to ensure the secrecy of military messages.

a) **Encryption:** Information is changed using a secret known as an encryption key, making it inaccessible without using a second secret known as a decryption key (which, in certain circumstances, may be the same as the encryption key). An encryption technique must make it very difficult for someone to decrypt the original data without the decryption key for it to be considered secure (Kerievsky, 1976).

b) **Access control:** Rules and regulations are in place to restrict access to private information only to individuals and systems that have a legitimate authority to access it. Information can be discovered based on an individual's identity, such as their name or a computer's serial number, or by their function, such as being a manager or a computer security professional (Arockiam & Monikandan, 2014).

c) **Authentication:** The procedure of establishing an individual's identification or position. The process of ascertaining someone's identity can be achieved through various approaches, usually relying on a blend of possession (such as a smart card or secret keys), knowledge (such as a password), and inherent characteristics (such as a human's fingerprint). Figure 1.2 presents a visual depiction of the authentication principle.

d) **Authorization:** Access control determines whether a person or system can access resources according to an access control policy. These authorizations should effectively hinder an attacker from deceiving the system into granting them access to safeguarded resources (Chavez et al., 2005).

e) **Physical Security:** Corporations implement physical barriers to restrict access to protected computing resources. These barriers include installing locks on cabinets and doors, locating computers in rooms without windows, utilizing sound-absorbing materials, and constructing buildings or rooms with walls containing copper meshes (known as Faraday cages) to prevent the transmission of electromagnetic signals (Cowan, 2005).

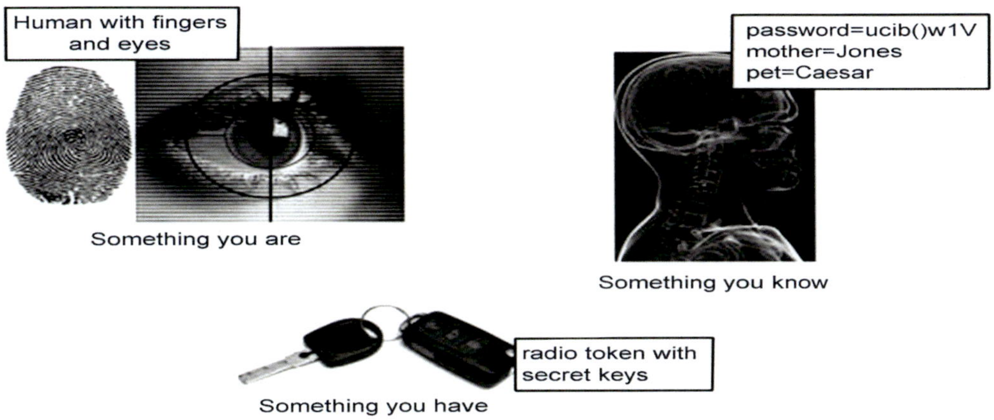

Figure 1.2. Illustration of three foundations for authentication (Source: Shutterstock, Creative Commons License).

1.1.2. Integrity

Integrity, a crucial element of information security, is a characteristic that ensures information remains unchanged without authorization. The significance of integrity is frequently demonstrated to school students through the Telephone game (Chinese whisper). In this game, a cohort of children forms a circular arrangement where the one designated as "it" quietly transmits a message by whispering it into the ear of the next neighbor on the right. Each child in the circle awaits the word from the neighbor on the left. After receiving the message, the child whispers it to a neighbor on the right (Clark & Wilson, 1987).

This message-passing process occurs until the message completes a full circuit and returns to the individual who initiated it. Subsequently, the final individual to receive the message vocalizes it to make it audible to everybody. Usually, the message has become so disorganized at this stage that it becomes a source of entertainment for all the children, and the game is then restarted with a different individual as the "it" role. Furthermore, through each subsequent play, the game consistently emphasizes that this whispering process rarely maintains the transmitted information's accuracy. Could this perhaps explain why rumors are frequently described as "whispers"? (Limoges et al., 1994).

Data integrity in computer systems and networks can be compromised in various ways, and these threats can be either malicious (harmful) or benign (harmless). An example of a benign threat is when a random message like "Peace on Earth" flashes on the screen or the computer beeps with each keystroke. Fortunately, the majority of viruses are benign. On the other hand, a malicious threat can occur when a computer virus infiltrates and modifies certain operating system files. The virus then replicates within the computer and spreads to other systems. Therefore, computer systems must include capabilities to ensure data integrity (Burow et al., 2017).

Did you know?

Physical barriers intended to stop fires from spreading are the roots for the word "firewall," and this idea served as an inspiration for creating network firewalls in computer networks.

1.1.3. Availability

In addition to confidentiality and integrity, availability is crucial to information security. It refers to the capacity for information to be promptly accessed and modified by authorized individuals.

Even if information is stored securely in a highly protected location and monitored by a dedicated team, it does not guarantee security from an information security perspective. The availability of information directly impacts its usefulness and effectiveness.

For instance, imagine the potential harm if a credit card is stolen and it takes weeks for the credit card company to notify anyone because retailers cannot access the list of stolen numbers (Naidu et al., 2021). Therefore, similar to integrity and confidentiality, availability can be ensured through various methods developed by computer security researchers and system designers.

These methods include:

a) **Physical Protections**: Infrastructure must be designed to maintain information accessibility even in the case of technical difficulties. Buildings holding vital computer systems may be designed to survive bomb blasts, earthquakes, and hurricanes. They may also have generators and other electrical equipment to withstand power outages and surges (Kumar & Bhatia, 2020).

b) **Computational Redundancies:** Computers and storage units must have backups in case of a security breach. For example, storage redundancies are used by redundant arrays of independent disks (RAID) to maintain data availability for their clients. Additionally, web servers are sometimes set up in groups so that any computer failure may be handled without compromising the website's availability.

Due to the importance of availability, an attacker may target its availability rather than its confidentiality or integrity. For example, a credit card hacker with many stolen cards may want to target the major company's publicly available list of stolen credit cards. Availability constitutes the third pillar supporting the crucial C.I.A. triad of information security (Hassan & Azam, 2014).

1.2. ASSURANCE, AUTHENTICITY, AND ANONYMITY

→Learning Objectives

- Recognize the significance of providing assurance in security measures to users.
- Understand the methods employed to establish and verify the authenticity of users, devices, or data.
- Identify the importance of anonymity in online transactions.

In addition to the traditional concepts of confidentiality, reliability, and accessibility covered in the previous section, several additional principles are crucial in contemporary computer security applications. The three-letter abbreviation A.A.A., which stands for assurance, authenticity, and anonymity in this context, can also describe these ideas (Cherdantseva & Hilton, 2015) (Figure 1.3).

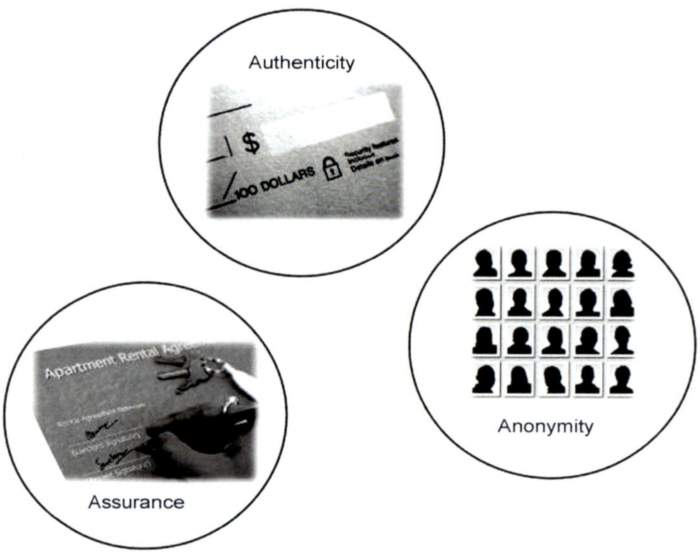

Figure 1.3. Representation of the concepts of assurance, authenticity, and anonymity (Source: Melissa King, Creative Commons License).

1.2.1. Assurance

Assurance, within the field of computer security, pertains to how trust is established and controlled in computer systems. Undeniably, quantifying trust is challenging, although people understand that it encompasses the extent to which one possesses faith in the conformity of individuals or systems to expectations (Bacon & Tikekar, 2003).

Moreover, trust involves the interaction of the following factors:

a) Policies establish explicit guidelines for the expected behavior of individuals or systems, both towards themselves and others. For example, the creators of an online music store may establish guidelines that outline how users can obtain and duplicate songs.

b) Permissions refer to the actions which users are authorized to perform while interacting with a person or systems. For example, an online music store may grant limited access and copying privileges to individuals who have bought specific songs.

c) Protections refer to the measures implemented to enforce permissions and policies. Continuing with the ongoing example of an online music store, it is conceivable that this system would incorporate safeguards to deter individuals from gaining unlawful access and duplicating its audio tracks (Shukla et al., 2022).

Assurance is not limited to the transfer of information from systems to users. When users share their credit card information with an online music store, they anticipate that the store will adhere to its publicly stated policies regarding the handling of credit card numbers. Additionally, they may authorize the store to make automatic payments from their card for music acquisitions. Furthermore, they may have signed an agreement with their credit card company to ensure the company will not be held responsible for any unauthorized charges made on the card. In computer systems, assurance refers to managing trust in two ways: from users toward systems and from systems toward users (Koopman, 1998).

1.2.2. Authenticity

Given the abundance of online service providers offering materials, resources, and computational services, these service providers need to have the capability to enforce their policies. From a legal perspective, it is necessary to possess an electronic mechanism for ensuring contract compliance. Specifically, when an individual expresses their intention to purchase a song from an online music store, there must be a mechanism in place to ensure compliance with this commitment. Similarly, when an online movie store guarantees a customer the ability to rent and view a movie within the next 30 days, there should be a reliable method for the consumer to verify that the movie will indeed be accessible for the full duration (Gordon & Jeffrey, 2003).

Authenticity refers to the capacity to determine the genuineness of claims, policies, and approvals granted by individuals or corporations. If such phenomena are counterfeited, it becomes impossible to maintain the implicit agreements that individuals and corporations enter into during online transactions involving the purchase and sale of goods. Furthermore, an individual or a company may argue that they did not undertake such a commitment, contending that it was carried out by a person impersonating those individuals (Naeem et al., 2019).

1.2.3. Anonymity

As previously mentioned, there are several advantages to users engaging with computer systems in ways that incorporate their true identities. However, utilizing personal identities in computerized transactions has an unfavorable side effect. Personal information eventually becomes dispersed among various digital platforms, connecting it to past health issues, purchases, legal proceedings, emails, work, etc. As a result, anonymity is required—the quality that allows some information or transactions to be linked to no specific person (Wright, 2004).

Organizations should be expected to use some of the following tools to protect privacy when publishing information about their members or clients:

a) **Data Aggregation:** This involves the collection of data from multiple sources so that averages or reported sums are not personally identifiable. For example, the U.S. Census frequently releases population breakdowns of zip-code regions according to factors like age, salary, and ethnicity. However, it only does so when doing so would not reveal personal information about any individual.

b) **Data Mixing:** Mixing is the process of combining conversations, transactions, or information in a way that prevents them from being linked to a specific individual. This technique utilizes systems that can blend data in a quasi-random manner, allowing searches or transactions to take place without revealing personal information (Armstrong & Forde, 2003).

c) **Proxies:** Proxies are trustworthy intermediaries who are willing to perform tasks on behalf of an individual in a manner that cannot be traced back to that person. Internet searching proxies provide an Internet browser interface, enabling individuals to access websites that may be restricted based on their location.

d) **Pseudonyms:** False identities are used as substitutes for real identities in communications and transactions, but they are only known to a trusted entity. For instance, various online social networking platforms allow users to interact with each other using pseudonyms, facilitating communication and the creation of an online persona while keeping their true identity concealed.

Ensuring privacy should be a primary objective, accompanied by relevant and feasible protective measures (Shmatikov, 2004).

PRACTICE PROBLEM

1. In an online banking system, how can the assurance of security measures be enhanced to build customer trust? Explain with practical steps.

SOLUTION TO PRACTICE PROBLEM

i. Implement two-factor authentication to strengthen user verification.

ii. Regularly conduct security audits and penetration testing to identify vulnerabilities.

iii. Use SSL/TLS encryption to secure data transmitted between the user's device and the banking server.

iv. Provide clear and transparent privacy policies and security practices to customers.

1.3. THREATS AND ATTACKS

→Learning Objectives

- Identify and classify various types of threats that can compromise computer systems or data.

After considering the various objectives of computer security, it is important to address the potential risks and attacks that can undermine these objectives.

1.3.1. Eavesdropping

Eavesdropping is the act of intercepting data meant for someone else while it is being transmitted over a communication link. Common examples are packet sniffers, which monitor local Internet activity at a wireless access point. This is an attack on confidentiality.

1.3.2. Alteration

Man-in-the-middle attacks and computer viruses are two examples of alteration assaults. In man-in-the-middle attacks, a network stream is intercepted, altered, and transferred. On the other hand, computer viruses alter critical system files to carry out destructive actions and multiply with time. In short, data integrity is attacked through alteration (Amara et al., 2017).

1.3.3. Denial-of-Service

It is the decline or suspension of an information access or data service. Examples include email spam which is designed primarily to clog mail servers and increase queue size. A denial-of-service attack targets the availability of data.

1.3.4. Masquerading

A masquerade attack occurs when a cyber attacker impersonates a genuine device or user to gain unauthorized entry into a network or system. Masquerade threats include phishing and spoofing. Phishing attacks are confidence tricks in which a threat actor sends out bulk generic messages, typically by email, to deceive people into clicking on harmful links. The goal is usually to steal login credentials or private data, such as social security numbers. On the other hand, spoofing attacks involve threat actors disguising themselves as trustworthy sources in an attempt to deceive the victim. A spoofing attack aims to target a victim with malware and use the obtained information or access to plan further crimes. Masquerading is an attempt to establish credibility; in the case of phishing, it is an effort to compromise privacy and anonymity (Sinha et al., 2019).

1.3.5. Repudiation

A repudiation attack occurs when a system or application fails to provide measures to accurately monitor and record user behavior, allowing for malicious manipulation or falsifying verification of new actions.

1.3.6. Correlation and TraceBack

Correlation and TraceBack involves penetrating information flows and data sources to identify the source of a specific information stream. This threat is an attack on anonymity.

In addition, there are various kinds of attacks, such as military-grade attacks (designed to crack cryptography secrets) and composite attacks (which integrate multiple categories of attacks mentioned before into a single attack). However, the attacks mentioned above are some of the most prevalent ones (Ruiz et al., 2012).

1.4. SECURITY PRINCIPLES

→Learning Objectives

- Comprehend each of the ten fundamental security principles.
- Understand how fundamental security principles contribute to establishing a robust and comprehensive security posture.

To conclude the introductory chapter, this section discusses ten security principles established in a seminal work by Saltzer and Schroeder (1975). Despite their age, these ideas remain relevant today for safeguarding computer networks and systems.

1.4.1. Economy of Mechanism

This philosophy emphasizes the importance of keeping the design and execution of security measures simple. The principle of simplicity applies to most engineering projects, but it holds particular significance in the field of security. A straightforward security framework facilitates understanding for developers and users and enables an efficient design and implementation of cybersecurity techniques (Bella & Vasundra, 2022).

1.4.2. Fail-Safe Defaults

According to this theory, a system's default configuration must include a robust security framework. For example, the default group of newly added users in an operating system needs to have restricted access to files and services. Unfortunately, default settings in operating systems and programs frequently prioritize usability over security. Several widely used programs, including web browsers that allow the execution of code downloaded from the web server, have historically operated in this manner. A fail-safe permission default is the foundation of several widely used access control mechanisms. Specifically, all access to an object (function) is prohibited for a subject if no explicit access rights are defined for a given subject-object pair (Thomas, 2020).

1.4.3. Complete Mediation

This principle states that each time a resource is used, it must be verified that it complies with the protection plan. Because permissions can vary over time, one should be cautious when using performance improvement strategies that save the outcomes of prior authorization checks. For example, users should be required to re-login on an online banking website after a predetermined period, such as fifteen minutes. File systems differ in their methods of performing access checks by an application. For example, there is a potential risk when permissions are only verified upon a program's initial request for file access. However, future attempts to access the same file are not re-evaluated while the application remains active (Abomhara & Koien, 2015).

1.4.4. Open Design

As per this concept, a system's security structure and blueprint should be openly accessible. Security should primarily rely on the confidentiality of cryptographic keys. The open design of a system allows for examination by different entities, facilitating the prompt identification and rectification of security vulnerabilities resulting from design shortcomings. Enabling the examination of the system's implementation (as seen in open-source software) allows for a thorough evaluation of security attributes and a more streamlined approach to resolving software defects. The open design principle competes with the ineffective practice of relying on invisibility to create security by concealing cryptographic techniques. It is important to understand that while it is relatively easy to replace a compromised cryptographic key, it is typically difficult to change a system that has been compromised due to a disclosure of its architecture (Kumar et al., 2016).

1.4.5. Separation of Privilege

The notion of Separation of Privilege (SoP) entails the allocation of system privileges or access rights in a manner that prevents any single entity from having all the required permissions to compromise system security or access essential resources (Thabit et al., 2020).

1.4.6. Least Privilege

Every application and user of a computer system should run with the absolute minimum privileges required for proper functioning. Applying this approach limits privilege abuse and reduces the harm resulting from the breach of a specific application or user account. The military concept of 'necessary information' exemplifies this approach. Failure to adhere to this concept can lead to increased vulnerability to security breaches, resulting in potential additional harm. For instance, if an attacker injects malicious code into a web server operating with complete administrator credentials, it could cause significant damage to the system. Therefore, by adhering to the concept of least privilege, the web server program should only possess the essential rights required for its functioning (Igure & Williams, 2008).

1.4.7. Least Common Mechanism

In multi-user systems, it is advisable to minimize the utilization of methods that enable resource sharing among numerous users. For example, when several users need to access a file or application, it is essential to provide distinct channels for each user to access these resources. This measure is necessary to avoid potential security issues arising from unintended resource sharing (Kettani & Wainwright, 2019).

1.4.8. Psychological Acceptability

According to this principle, all security-related settings should align with what a typical user could expect, and user interfaces should be well-designed and intuitive. This approach aims to reduce gaps between program behavior and user expectations, as these discrepancies can lead to security issues, including potentially harmful software setups. While many email apps use cryptographic techniques to sign and encrypt emails digitally, these strong features are rarely used in real-world scenarios, despite their wide range of use. This situation is partly caused by the awkward and confusing user interfaces that email apps now use for utilizing cryptographic capabilities (Sibi et al., 2018).

1.4.9. Work Factor

This idea states that when creating a security plan, the expense of circumventing a security measure should be evaluated in relation to an attacker's resources. A system designed to protect students' grades in a university database requires less complex security measures compared to a system designed to safeguard military secrets. Saltzer and Schroeder acknowledge that the work factor principle does not apply well to electronic systems, as it is difficult to estimate the amount of work required to breach security. Additionally, with the rapid advancement of technology, intrusion techniques that were once deemed impossible may become easily accessible within a few years (Seeam et al., 2019).

1.4.10. Compromise Recording

This principle asserts that it is preferable to document and address the specifics of an incursion on certain occasions rather than implementing more advanced safeguards on the entire system. Internet-connected security cameras are a common and efficient alternative to strengthening doors and windows for protecting a building. They serve as an excellent compromise record system. The servers within an office network can retain logs for each file access event, email transmission and reception, and web browsing activity. On personal computer systems, the compromise recording principle is not as effective because it can be challenging to identify unauthorized access, and skilled attackers can erase evidence of their presence on the compromised machine by deleting log entries (Humayun et al., 2020).

1.5. ILLUSTRATION OF SECURITY PRINCIPLES

Figure 1.4 provides a graphic representation of ten security principles. As previously stated, these concepts have consistently proven to be essential for computer security. Furthermore, as the diagram shows, these principles safeguard computers and information. For example, the efficiency of a mechanism inherently supports open design and an open system publicly exhibits the security derived from such simplicity (Adlakha et al., 2019).

Figure 1.4. Representation of the ten security principles (Source: Saltzer, Creative Commons License).

SUMMARY

- This chapter provides a comprehensive introduction to the fundamentals of computer security. The cornerstone of computer security lies in the CIA Triad—Confidentiality, Integrity, and Availability. These three interrelated elements of the CIA Triad form the foundation of a robust security framework. Confidentiality ensures that information is accessible only to authorized entities, integrity guarantees the accuracy and reliability of data, and availability ensures that systems and data are consistently accessible.
- Assurance, a critical aspect of computer security, involves instilling confidence in the reliability and trustworthiness of systems. This is achieved through rigorous testing, auditing, and adherence to best practices. Availability, as a component of the CIA Triad, focuses on ensuring that information and services are accessible when needed, without compromise. Anonymity, while not always a primary concern, plays a role in certain security contexts where the protection of user identity is paramount.
- As this chapter explores the landscape of computer security, understanding the spectrum of potential threats becomes essential. Threats encompass a broad range of malicious activities, from unauthorized access to data breaches, and they pose significant challenges to the integrity of systems. Attacks, the manifestations of threats, exploit vulnerabilities in systems or networks to compromise security. Recognizing and mitigating these attacks is essential to maintaining a secure computing environment.
- Ten essential security concepts provide a foundation for creating strong security solutions. These security measures encompass the lowest level of privilege, division of duties, defense in depth, control of access, and work factor, among others. Every principle is essential for creating a thorough and robust security stance.

MULTIPLE CHOICE QUESTIONS

1. **Which of the following best defines Confidentiality in computer security?**
   a) Ensuring data is unchanged and reliable.
   b) Protecting data from unauthorized access.
   c) Ensuring data is available when needed.
   d) Verifying the legitimacy of users.
2. **Which aspect of the CIA Triad ensures data remains accurate and unaltered?**
   a) Confidentiality
   b) Integrity
   c) Availability
   d) Assurance

3. **What does Authenticity refer to in computer security?**
   a) Protecting sensitive information from unauthorized access.
   b) Ensuring data remains accurate and unaltered.
   c) Verifying the legitimacy of users or data.
   d) Ensuring data is available when needed.
4. **What is the main difference between a Threat and an Attack in computer security?**
   a) Threats exploit vulnerabilities, while Attacks are deliberate actions.
   b) Threats always cause damage, while Attacks are preventive measures.
   c) Attacks occur internally, while Threats come from external sources.
   d) Threats are intentional, while Attacks are accidental.
5. **Which principle emphasizes employing multiple layers of security controls to mitigate risks?**
   a) Least Common Mechanism
   b) Defense in Depth
   c) Security by Design
   d) Fail-Safe Defaults

REVIEW QUESTIONS

1. Define Confidentiality, Integrity, and Availability in the context of computer security. Provide examples of each.
2. What methods can ensure the Authenticity of users and data in an online environment?
3. Provide examples of various types of threats and corresponding potential attacks on computer systems.
4. Explain the principle of "Least Privilege" and its significance in maintaining system security.
5. Discuss the importance of Anonymity in specific scenarios and how it relates to privacy and security.

Answers to Multiple Questions

1. (b) 2. (b) 3. (c) 4. (b) 5. (b)

REFERENCES

1. Abomhara, M., & Køien, G. M., (2015). Cyber security and the internet of things: Vulnerabilities, threats, intruders, and attacks. *Journal of Cyber Security and Mobility, 1*(1), 65–88.

2. Adlakha, R., Sharma, S., Rawat, A., & Sharma, K., (2019). Cyber security goal's, issue's, categorization & data breaches. In: *2019 International Conference on Machine Learning, Big Data, Cloud and Parallel Computing (COMITCon)* (Vol. 1, No. 1, pp. 397–402).
3. Amara, N., Zhiqui, H., & Ali, A., (2017). Cloud computing security threats and attacks with their mitigation techniques. In: *2017 International Conference on Cyber-Enabled Distributed Computing and Knowledge Discovery (CyberC)* (Vol. 1, No. 1, pp. 244–251).
4. Armstrong, H. L., & Forde, P. J., (2003). Internet anonymity practices in computer crime. *Information Management & Computer Security, 11*(5), 209–215.
5. Arockiam, L., & Monikandan, S., (2014). Efficient cloud storage confidentiality to ensure data security. In: *2014 International Conference on Computer Communication and Informatics* (Vol. 1, No. 1, pp. 1–5).
6. Bacon, T., & Tikekar, R., (2003). Experiences with developing a computer security information assurance curriculum. *Journal of Computing Sciences in Colleges, 18*(4), 254–267.
7. Bella, H. K., & Vasundra, S., (2022). A study of security threats and attacks in cloud computing. In: *2022 4th International Conference on Smart Systems and Inventive Technology (ICSSIT)* (Vol. 1, No. 1, pp. 658–666).
8. Bishop, M., (2003). What is computer security? *IEEE Security & Privacy, 1*(1), 67–69.
9. Blanchet, B., (2002). From secrecy to authenticity in security protocols. In: *International Static Analysis Symposium* (Vol. 1, No. 1, pp. 342–359).
10. Burow, N., Carr, S. A., Nash, J., Larsen, P., Franz, M., Brunthaler, S., & Payer, M., (2017). Control-flow integrity: Precision, security, and performance. *ACM Computing Surveys (CSUR), 50*(1), 1–33.
11. Chavez, M. L., Rosete, C. H., & Henriquez, F. R., (2005). Achieving confidentiality security service for can. In: *15th International Conference on Electronics, Communications and Computers (CONIELECOMP'05)* (Vol. 1, No. 1, pp. 166–170).
12. Cherdantseva, Y., & Hilton, J., (2015). Understanding information assurance and security. *J. Organ. End User Comput., 16*(3), 1–20.
13. Clark, D. D., & Wilson, D. R., (1987). A comparison of commercial and military computer security policies. In: *1987 IEEE Symposium on Security and Privacy* (Vol. 1, No. 1, pp. 183–184).
14. Cowan, D. F., (2005). Security and confidentiality on laboratory computer systems. In: *Informatics for the Clinical Laboratory: A Practical Guide* (Vol. 1, No. 1, pp. 59–86).
15. Gautam, S., Malik, A., Singh, N., & Kumar, S., (2019). Recent advances and countermeasures against various attacks in IoT environment. In: *2019 2nd International Conference on Signal Processing and Communication (ICSPC)* (Vol. 1, No. 1, pp. 315–319).
16. Ghorbani, A. A., Lu, W., Tavallaee, M., Ghorbani, A. A., Lu, W., & Tavallaee, M., (2010). Network attacks. *Network Intrusion Detection and Prevention: Concepts and Techniques, 1*, 1–25.

17. Gollmann, D., (2010). Computer security. *Wiley Interdisciplinary Reviews: Computational Statistics, 2*(5), 544–554.

18. Gordon, A. D., & Jeffrey, A., (2003). Authenticity by typing for security protocols. *Journal of Computer Security, 11*(4), 451–519.

19. Gordon, A. D., & Jeffrey, A., (2003). Typing correspondence assertions for communication protocols. *Theoretical Computer Science, 300*(1–3), 379–409.

20. Hassan, S., & Azam, F., (2014). Analysis of cloud computing performance, scalability, availability, & security. In: *2014 International Conference on Information Science & Applications (ICISA)* (Vol. 1, No. 1, pp. 1–5).

21. Humayun, M., Niazi, M., Jhanjhi, N. Z., Alshayeb, M., & Mahmood, S., (2020). Cyber security threats and vulnerabilities: A systematic mapping study. *Arabian Journal for Science and Engineering, 45*, 3171–3189.

22. Igure, V. M., & Williams, R. D., (2008). Taxonomies of attacks and vulnerabilities in computer systems. *IEEE Communications Surveys & Tutorials, 10*(1), 6–19.

23. Kates, J., Nickson, S., Greisiger, M., & Taffea, P. R., (2001). The reality of hackers. *Risk Management, 48*(7), 50.

24. Kelly, G., & McKenzie, B., (2002). Security, privacy, and confidentiality issues on the Internet. *Journal of Medical Internet Research, 4*(2), e861.

25. Kerievsky, B., (1976). Security and confidentiality in a university computer network. *ACM SIGUCCS Newsletter, 6*(3), 9–11.

26. Kettani, H., & Wainwright, P., (2019). On the top threats to cyber systems. In: *2019 IEEE 2nd International Conference on Information and Computer Technologies (ICICT)* (Vol. 1, No. 1, pp. 175–179).

27. Koopman, P., (1998). Toward a scalable method for quantifying aspects of fault tolerance, software assurance, and computer security. In: *Proceedings Computer Security, Dependability, and Assurance: From Needs to Solutions (Cat. No. 98EX358)* (pp. 103–131).

28. Kumar, M., Kaur, N., Kaur, S., & Singh, R., (2016). Different security threats and its prevention in computer networks. *International Journal of Advanced Research in Computer Science, 7*(6), 1–20.

29. Kumar, R., & Bhatia, M. P. S., (2020). A systematic review of the security in cloud computing: Data integrity, confidentiality, and availability. In: *2020 IEEE International Conference on Computing, Power and Communication Technologies (GUCON)* (Vol. 1, No. 1, pp. 334–337).

30. Landwehr, C. E., (2001). Computer security. *International Journal of Information Security, 1*(1), 3–13.

31. Limoges, C. G., Nelson, R. R., Heimann, J. H., & Becker, D. S., (1994). Versatile integrity and security environment (VISE) for computer systems. In: *Proceedings of the 1994 Workshop on New Security Paradigms* (Vol. 1, No. 1, pp. 109–118).

32. Naeem, R. Z., Abbas, H., Shafqat, N., Saleem, K., & Iqbal, W., (2019). A framework to determine applications' authenticity. *Procedia Computer Science, 155*, 268–275.

33. Naidu, P. R., Guruprasad, N., & Gowda, V. D., (2021). A high-availability and integrity layer for cloud storage, cloud computing security: From single to multi-clouds. In: *Journal of Physics: Conference Series* (Vol. 1921, No. 1, p. 012072). IOP Publishing.
34. Ruiz, J. F., Harjani, R., Mana, A., Desnitsky, V., Kotenko, I., & Chechulin, A., (2012). A methodology for the analysis and modeling of security threats and attacks for systems of embedded components. In: *2012 20th Euromicro International Conference on Parallel, Distributed and Network-Based Processing* (Vol. 1, No. 1, pp. 261–268).
35. Saltzer, J. H., & Schroeder, M. D., (1975). The protection of information in computer systems. *Proceedings of the IEEE, 63*(9), 1278–1308.
36. Samonas, S., & Coss, D., (2014). The CIA strikes back: Redefining confidentiality, integrity, and availability in security. *Journal of Information System Security, 10*(3), 1–20.
37. Seeam, A., Ogbeh, O. S., Guness, S., & Bellekens, X., (2019). Threat modeling and security issues for the internet of things. In: *2019 Conference on Next-Generation Computing Applications (NextComp)* (Vol. 1, No. 1, pp. 1–8).
38. Shmatikov, V., (2004). Probabilistic analysis of an anonymity system. *Journal of Computer Security, 12*(3, 4), 355–377.
39. Shukla, A., Katt, B., Nweke, L. O., Yeng, P. K., & Weldehawaryat, G. K., (2022). System security assurance: A systematic literature review. *Computer Science Review, 45*, 100496.
40. Sibi, C. S., Sangeetha, D., Venkata, R. M., Srinithi, K., & Vaidehi, V., (2018). Futuristic cyber-attacks. *International Journal of Knowledge-based and Intelligent Engineering Systems, 22*(3), 195–204.
41. Sinha, P., Kumar, R. A., & Bhushan, B., (2019). Information security threats and attacks with conceivable counteraction. In: *2019 2nd International Conference on Intelligent Computing, Instrumentation and Control Technologies (ICICICT)* (Vol. 1, pp. 1208–1213.
42. Thabit, F., Alhomdy, S. A. H., Alahdal, A., & Jagtap, S. B., (2020). Exploration of security challenges in cloud computing: Issues, threats, and attacks with their alleviating techniques. *Journal of Information and Computational Science, 12*(10), 1–20.
43. Thomas, C., (2020). Introductory chapter: Computer security threats. In: *Computer Security Threats* (Vol. 1, No. 1, pp. 1–20).
44. Wright, T., (2004). Security, privacy, and anonymity. *XRDS: Crossroads, The ACM Magazine for Students, 11*(2), 1–5.

CHAPTER

2

Common Threats to Computer Systems

LEARNING OBJECTIVES

After studying this chapter, you will be able to:

- A broad view of the risky environment in which computer systems operate.
- The threat of errors, omissions, fraud, and theft to the integrity of the system and data.
- The concept of employee sabotage.
- How do hackers breach the computer system's security?
- Concept of viruses in computer systems.

INTRODUCTORY EXAMPLE

In today's digital landscape, the protection of computer systems from various threats is paramount for organizations across various industries. Understanding the common threats to computer systems is crucial to fortifying defenses against potential risks and vulnerabilities. One example that highlights the significance of these threats occurred within a reputable software house, Octet.

Octet, a renowned company catering to thousands of clients, encountered a critical security breach due to an employee's unintentional error. During routine system maintenance, an employee mistakenly misconfigured a firewall, leaving a critical network segment exposed to external access. This error led to unauthorized access to sensitive customer data, posing a severe threat to the firm's integrity and customer privacy.

This incident highlights the fact that even well-established organizations can be vulnerable to threats resulting from errors and omissions. In addition to this example, computer systems face a wide range of other threats, including fraud, theft, employee sabotage, malicious hackers, and the infiltration of malicious code. Each threat presents unique challenges, requiring comprehensive security measures to mitigate potential risks and protect sensitive information.

Understanding these common threats is essential for developing robust security strategies and protocols to safeguard computer systems against evolving risks. This ensures the resilience and integrity of organizational assets in an increasingly interconnected digital environment.

UNIT INTRODUCTION

Computer systems are susceptible to a wide variety of threats, each of which has the potential to cause a unique kind of damage. Common types of damages that can occur include errors that compromise the integrity of databases and fires that destroy entire computer centers. Losses can be caused by a variety of factors, including the actions of apparently trustworthy personnel who commit fraud against a system, the actions of hackers from the outside, or the carelessness of data input clerks. When it comes to assessing losses related to computer security, precision is not attainable because many losses are never found, and others are "moved under the carpet" to avoid unwanted publicity. The effects of the numerous cyber threats are quite different from one another: Some of them impact the availability of a system, while others impact the confidentiality or integrity of the data (Schmidt et al., 2007).

This chapter presents a comprehensive overview of the risky environment in which systems are currently operating. The dangers and associated losses discussed in this chapter were chosen due to their prevalence and significance in the existing computer environment. The following list is not exhaustive, and certain dangers may encompass aspects from multiple domains. Businesses seeking to avoid risky environments may find this review of today's typical threats helpful; however, the perspective provided in this chapter is somewhat broad (Thomas, 2020).

Managers and users of an information system need to be aware of the vulnerabilities of the system, as well as the threats that could exploit those flaws, in order to effectively control the risks associated with the system. Understanding the threat environment enables the system manager to adopt the most cost-efficient security measures. In certain circumstances, managers may discover that instead of avoiding the risks, it is more cost-effective to accept the anticipated loss. Such judgments should align with the findings of a risk assessment report (Loch et al., 1992).

2.1. ERRORS AND OMISSIONS

→Learning Objectives

- Understand errors and omissions in computer systems.
- Comprehend how errors and omissions are a threat to data and system integrity.
- nderstand the bugs in computer systems.

Errors and omissions seriously threaten data and the integrity of the system. These errors are caused not only by data entry clerks processing hundreds of transactions per day, but also by users who create and edit data. Quality control methods are absent from many programs, particularly the ones created by users for personal computers. Even the most advanced programs cannot simultaneously identify every kind of input error or deletion. A well-planned awareness and training program can assist an organization in reducing both the number and the quality of errors and omissions (Overhage et al., 1997).

Errors made by users, data-entry clerks, system operators, and programmers often result in security issues, directly or indirectly. Sometimes, the error poses a serious threat—for example, a programming error can cause a system to crash. In other scenarios, the errors create vulnerabilities. Errors can happen at any stage of the system's life cycle. Robert Courtney, a computer security expert and a former member of the Computer Systems Security and Privacy Advisory Board, undertook a long-term analysis of computer-related economic losses, and discovered that errors and omissions accounted for 65% of enterprise losses. This number remained constant across public and private sector organizations (Baird, 2001).

Errors in programming and development, commonly called "bugs," can vary in severity from minor to disastrous. The legal team of the Subcommittee on Investigations and Oversight provided the following summary of the extent and gravity of this issue in terms of governmental systems in a 1989 report for the House Committee on Science, Space, and Technology, titled "Bugs in the Program" (Chapman, 1990):

As expenditures grow, so do concerns about the reliability, cost, and accuracy of ever-larger and more complex software systems. These concerns are heightened as computers perform more critical tasks, where mistakes can cause financial turmoil, accidents, or in extreme cases, death.

Did you know?

About 95% of cyber security breaches are the result of human error.

2.2. FRAUD AND THEFT

→Learning Objectives

- Understand how computer systems can be misused for theft and fraud.
- Identify who commits computer fraud and theft.

Computer systems can be exploited for both fraud and theft, both by "automating" traditional methods of fraud and by using new methods. For instance, individuals may utilize computers to steal small amounts of money from numerous bank accounts, assuming that insignificant differences will not be scrutinized. Fraud and theft in cyberspace are not only a risk to financial systems, but also to other areas such as time and attendance, inventory, school grading, and long-distance communication systems (Haugen & Selin, 1999).

Both outsiders and insiders are capable of committing computer fraud and theft. Insiders, who are authorized users of a system, are often to blame for fraud. According to a 1993 InformationWeek/Ernst and Young research, 90% of chief information officers considered employees *who do not need to know* information as a threat. The Computer Crime Unit of the U.S. Department of Justice also states that insiders pose the biggest threat to computer systems. Insiders have access to and knowledge of the target computer system, including its resources and vulnerabilities, making them more likely to commit crimes. Insiders can be technical staff members or common users, such as clerks. Former employees of a company may also pose a threat if their access is not immediately suspended, as they are familiar with its internal workings (Smith, 2013).

Furthermore, computer hardware and software may be vulnerable to theft for the purpose of conducting fraudulent and criminal activities. According to a survey conducted by Safeware Insurance, $882 million worth of personal computers were lost in 1992 due to theft (Guttman & Roback, 1995).

Remember

In the 1830s, a talented mathematician who collaborated with Charles Babbage committed the first known cybercrime by utilizing his analytical engine to engage in fraud and manipulate punch cards for personal gain.

2.3. EMPLOYEE SABOTAGE

→Learning Objectives

- Understand the concept of employee sabotage.
- Identify examples of computer-related employee sabotage.

Employees possess extensive knowledge of their employer's computer systems and software, enabling them to identify actions that could result in a severe data breach. The reduction in the size of organizations, whether in public or private sectors, has resulted in a cohort of individuals possessing organizational expertise who may still be able to access the system (for example, if their system identities are not promptly erased). The frequency of employee sabotage is considered far lower than theft occurrences; however, the financial implications of such actions might be substantial (Nahrstadt, 2009).

According to Martin Sprouse, the author of Sabotage in the American Workplace, the reasons behind sabotage can vary from selflessness to retaliation (Ambrose et al., 2002):

"As long as individuals experience feelings of being deceived, disinterested, harassed, threatened, or betrayed in their workplace, sabotage will continue to be used as a direct method of attaining job satisfaction without requiring clearance from superiors."

2.4. LOSS OF PHYSICAL AND INFRASTRUCTURE SUPPORT

→Learning Objectives

- Understand the loss of supporting infrastructure along with examples.
- Learn about the consequences of infrastructure loss.

The loss of supporting infrastructure includes power failures (outages, spikes, and brownouts), loss of communications, water leaks, sewer problems, lack of transportation services, fire, flood, civil unrest, and strikes. These losses encompass significant incidents like the Chicago tunnel flood, and more ordinary occurrences such as damaged water pipes. Infrastructure loss frequently leads to system outages, occasionally in unforeseen manners. During a snowstorm, employees may encounter difficulties commuting to work, although the computer system may remain operational (Ali, 2013).

PRACTICE PROBLEMS

1. Identify three examples of errors and omissions that can lead to security vulnerabilities in a computer system.
2. Discuss three preventive measures organizations can implement to mitigate the risks associated with insider threats or employee sabotage.

SOLUTIONS TO PRACTICE PROBLEMS

1. Three examples of errors and omissions are:

a) Failure to apply security patches and updates regularly.

b) Using default passwords for system accounts.

c) Misconfiguring firewall rules.

2. Preventive measures which organizations can implement are:

a) Restrict access to sensitive data or critical systems only to employees who require it for their roles.

b) Educate employees about security risks, emphasizing the consequences of malicious actions.

c) Implement robust monitoring systems to detect suspicious activities and maintain detailed logs for forensic analysis.

2.5. MALICIOUS HACKER

→Learning Objectives

- Understand the term hacker.
- Comprehend how a hacker poses a threat to the security of a computer system.

Malicious hackers, often referred to as crackers, are individuals who gain unauthorized access to systems. They can include individuals who are external to the organization as well as those within it. The increase in hacker activity is often attributed to the growing interconnectedness of government and industry sectors. In a 1992 investigation, it was observed that hackers attempted to breach the security of a specific Internet site or computer system at least once every other day.

The threat posed by hackers should be considered in terms of both past and potential future damage. While the financial impact of hacker attacks is currently smaller compared to losses caused by insider theft and sabotage, the issue of hacking is widespread and serious. One example of malicious hacker activity is their targeting of the public telephone system (Sen et al., 2020).

Research conducted by the National Research Council and the National Security Telecommunications Advisory Committee reveals that hacker activity extends beyond toll theft. It also includes the ability to infiltrate telecommunications systems, leading to the degradation or interruption of system accessibility. Although these investigations do not definitively determine the level of threat or risk, they highlight the hackers' capacity to cause significant harm (Furnell, 2013).

The threat posed by hackers often receives more attention than other types of threats. The Computer Crime Unit of the US Department of Justice provides three explanations for this phenomenon.

a) Firstly, the hacker threat is relatively new. Employers have long been concerned about the behavior of their staff members, and they can mitigate that risk by implementing disciplinary actions. However, these actions are ineffective against external individuals who are not bound by the employer's policies and procedures.

b) Secondly, companies are unaware of the intentions of hackers. Some hackers engage in theft, some cause damage, and others simply browse. This inability to pinpoint their goals suggests that hacker attacks are unrestricted (Shakarian et al., 2016).

c) Thirdly, people feel exposed due to cyber-attacks, especially when the identity of the hackers is unknown. Consider the scenario where a painter gets paid to paint a house and, while inside, steals some valuables. It is possible that other neighborhood homeowners will be alarmed by this crime and will defend themselves by refusing to work with that painter. However, if a burglar enters the same home and takes an identical item of jewelry, the neighborhood as a whole might feel threatened and victimized (Marin et al., 2016).

2.6. INDUSTRIAL ESPIONAGE

→Learning Objectives

- Understand the concept of industrial espionage.
- Comprehend the basics of economic espionage.

Industrial espionage involves the acquisition of confidential information from government agencies or private enterprises for the benefit of another organization. Governments and businesses engage in industrial espionage to safeguard economic secrets and gain a competitive advantage. When carried out by a government, it is often referred to as economic espionage. While computer security can help protect against these threats, it is ineffective in mitigating the risk of authorized personnel selling such information (Thonnard et al., 2012).

There has been a notable increase in industrial espionage. According to a 1992 research study funded by the American Society for Industrial Security (ASIS), theft of confidential company information has risen by 260%. The data indicates that foreign activity accounted for thirty percent of reported losses in 1991 and 1992. The study also revealed that current or former employees were responsible for 58% of the thefts. The most affected categories of stolen information were product development, specification, price, and manufacturing process data. Additionally, customer lists, basic research, sales data, personnel data, pay data, cost data, proposals, and strategic plans were among the other types of information that were compromised (Glitz & Meyersson, 2020).

The Central Intelligence Agency has declared that technological information is the primary goal of economic espionage. However, it also aims to gather intelligence on commodities, interest rates, and other economic factors. While acknowledging that technology-related data is the primary goal, the Federal Bureau of Investigation also identifies corporate private data (including contracting data and negotiation terms) as a target (Crane, 2005).

2.7. MALICIOUS CODE

→Learning Objectives

- Understand different types of malicious codes and computer viruses.
- Comprehend the exponential growth of computer viruses.

Malicious code includes worms, Trojan horses, logic bombs, viruses, and other unauthorized software. Malicious code can also target other systems when linked to personal computers.

A study conducted on viruses revealed that although the quantity of identified viruses is growing exponentially, the frequency of virus attacks remains unchanged. The study also determined that the number of new virus attacks is increasing, albeit at a slow pace (Bayer et al., 2006).

The direct expenses associated with the existence of malicious code have mostly arisen from system disruptions and the human resources required to restore the systems. These expenses can be quite substantial (Cui et al., 2018).

Keyword

Virus: A virus is a component of a code that propagates by attaching copies of itself to pre-existing executable files. Upon execution of the newly infected host program, a new instance of the virus is initiated. It is possible for the virus to contain an additional "payload" that becomes active under specific conditions. For example, certain viruses display a text string on a particular day. There are various types of viruses, including resident, overwrite, multiparticle, network, and web-scripting viruses.

2.8. FOREIGN GOVERNMENT ESPIONAGE

→Learning Objectives

- Comprehend how foreign intelligence agencies target unclassified information.

There may occasionally be threats from the intelligence agencies of foreign governments. Foreign intelligence services may target unclassified information to accomplish their intelligence operations, ultimately conducting economic espionage. Unclassified information material that could be useful includes official travel schedules, disaster preparedness, civil defense plans, manufacturing technologies, satellite data, payroll data, law enforcement, investigation, and security files. The responsible security office should be consulted for advice on such threats (Hyde, 1918).

Keyword

Trojan Horse: It is a malicious program that achieves a specific purpose along with other unintended consequences. For example, it is possible to modify files of a multiuser system's editing tool in a manner that results in random deletion of user's files whenever an operation is performed.

2.9. THREATS TO PERSONAL PRIVACY

→Learning Objectives

- Understand how the personal privacy of an individual is compromised.
- Learn about the sources causing a threat to personal privacy.

Individual privacy is currently at risk due to the vast amount of electronic data collected by governments, credit bureaus, and private businesses. Furthermore, the lack of computer capabilities to track, analyze, and collect extensive personal data further compromises privacy. One of the major concerns in the information age is the potential integration of all this data and technology, often referred to as "Big Brother." In an effort to prevent such intrusions, Congress has enacted laws over the years, such as the Computer Matching and Privacy Protection Act of 1988, which imposes limitations on the government's collection of personal data (Ziegeldorf et al., 2014).

There are numerous ways in which privacy can be threatened. In the past, employees of federal and state governments have sold personal data to private investigators and other information brokers. One such incident came to light when the Justice Department revealed in 1992 that over twenty individuals had been arrested for purchasing and reselling data from the Social Security Administration (SSA) computer databases. Auditors discovered during their investigation that more than 130 million job records were freely accessible to SSA staff members. Further inquiry revealed that five percent of the employees in one IRS region had accessed the tax returns of their friends, family members, and even celebrities. While some employees were merely curious, others used the information to create fraudulent tax returns (Strickland & Hunt, 2005).

Many people are growing increasingly concerned about threats to their privacy as more of these situations come to light. According to survey data from Louis Harris and Associates, included in a special MacWorld study published in July 1993, only 33% of respondents in 1970 expressed concern about personal privacy. However, that percentage skyrocketed to 79% by 1990. In 2024, the concerns have grown exponentially.

Although it is difficult to measure the extent and societal cost of the danger to personal privacy, it is evident that information technology has become powerful enough to warrant concerns from corporate and governmental "Big Brothers." Therefore, it is imperative to raise awareness of this issue (Al-Charchafchi et al., 2020).

SUMMARY

- This chapter provides an overview of the common threats to computer security that pose unique challenges to computer systems.
- Errors and omissions can result in incorrect implementations, vulnerabilities, or configurations, which may create loopholes that hackers can exploit to gain unauthorized access or steal confidential information.
- Attempts to deceive users or systems for financial gain or access to information can result in identity theft, financial losses, or compromised data integrity, affecting both individuals and companies.
- Hackers may exploit system vulnerabilities to gain unauthorized access, compromise data, manipulate or destroy data, or disrupt services, causing significant harm to systems.
- Various types of malware can infect systems, leading to data loss, system errors, and service disruptions.

MULTIPLE CHOICE QUESTIONS

1. **How can errors and omissions impact computer systems?**
   a) Strengthen system security
   b) Create intentional vulnerabilities
   c) Enhance data encryption
   d) None of the above
2. **What is employee sabotage in computer security?**
   a) Enhancing system security protocols
   b) Deliberate actions by insiders to compromise security or operations.
   c) Regular system maintenance
   d) None of the above
3. **What characterizes malicious code?**
   a) Software designed to enhance system performance
   b) System updates provided by trusted sources
   c) Harmful software intended to infiltrate systems and cause damage.
   d) None of the above
4. **What are the primary risks related to threats to personal privacy?**
   a) Unauthorized access or misuse of personal data
   b) Strengthened data protection laws
   c) Open access to personal information on social media
   d) None of the above

REVIEW QUESTIONS

1. What are the common causes of errors and omissions in computer systems?
2. How do fraud and theft impact both individuals and organizations in terms of security and financial risks?
3. How can organizations detect and prevent insider threats or malicious activities by employees?
4. Explain the motivations and methods of successful hacker attacks on systems and organizations.

Answers to Multiple Questions

1. (b) 2. (b) 3. (c) 4. (a)

REFERENCES

1. Al-Charchafchi, A., Manickam, S., & Alqattan, Z. N., (2020). Threats against information privacy and security in social networks: A review. In: *Advances in Cyber Security: First International Conference, ACeS 2019, Penang, Malaysia, Revised Selected Papers 1* (Vol. 1, No. 1, pp. 358–372). Springer Singapore.
2. Ali, S. M., (2013). Challenges and security issues in future IT infrastructure components. *International Journal of Computers & Technology, 8*(2), 845–847.
3. Ambrose, M. L., Seabright, M. A., & Schminke, M., (2002). Sabotage in the workplace: The role of organizational injustice. *Organizational Behavior and Human Decision Processes, 89*(1), 947–965.
4. Baird, L., (2001). The detection of crimes and errors and omissions. *EDP Audit Control Secur. Newsl., 20*(3), 1–8.
5. Bayer, U., Moser, A., Kruegel, C., & Kirda, E., (2006). Dynamic analysis of malicious code. *Journal in Computer Virology, 2*, 67–77.
6. Chapman, G., (1990). Bugs in the program. *Communications of the ACM, 33*(3), 251–253.
7. Clifton, D. A., Clifton, L., Sandu, D. M., Smith, G. B., Tarassenko, L., Vollam, S. A., & Watkinson, P. J., (2015). 'Errors' and omissions in paper-based early warning scores: The association with changes in vital signs—A database analysis. *BMJ Open, 5*(7), e007376.
8. Crane, A., (2005). In: The company of spies: When competitive intelligence gathering becomes industrial espionage. *Business Horizons, 48*(3), 233–240.
9. Cui, Z., Xue, F., Cai, X., Cao, Y., Wang, G. G., & Chen, J., (2018). Detection of malicious code variants based on deep learning. *IEEE Transactions on Industrial Informatics, 14*(7), 3187–3196.

10. Demarest, G. B., (1995). Espionage in international law. *Denv. J. Int'l L. & Pol'y, 24*, 321.
11. Furnell, S., (2013). Hackers, viruses, and malicious software. In: *Handbook of Internet Crime* (Vol. 1, No. 1, pp. 173–193). Willan.
12. Glitz, A., & Meyersson, E., (2020). Industrial espionage and productivity. *American Economic Review, 110*(4), 1055–1103.
13. Goutas, L., Hess, B., & Sutanto, J., (2020). If erring is human, is system use divine? Omission errors during post-adoptive system use. *Decision Support Systems, 130*, 113225.
14. Guttman, B., & Roback, E. A., (1995). Sp 800-12. *An Introduction to Computer Security: The NIST Handbook* (Vol. 1, pp. 1–22).
15. Haugen, S., & Selin, J. R., (1999). Identifying and controlling computer crime and employee fraud. *Industrial Management & Data Systems, 99*(8), 340–344.
16. Hyde, C. C., (1918). The espionage act. *American Journal of International Law, 12*(1), 142–146.
17. Jacsó, P., (2009). Errors of omission and their implications for computing scientometric measures in evaluating the publishing productivity and impact of countries. *Online Information Review, 33*(2), 376–385.
18. Kozlov, D., Veijalainen, J., & Ali, Y., (2012). Security and privacy threats in IoT architectures. In: *BODYNETS* (Vol. 1, No. 1, pp. 256–262).
19. Li, Y., Ma, R., & Jiao, R., (2015). A hybrid malicious code detection method based on deep learning. *International Journal of Security and Its Applications, 9*(5), 205–216.
20. Lindorfer, M., Di Federico, A., Maggi, F., Comparetti, P. M., & Zanero, S., (2012). Lines of malicious code: Insights into the malicious software industry. In: *Proceedings of the 28th Annual Computer Security Applications Conference* (Vol. 1, No. 1, pp. 349–358).
21. Loch, K. D., Carr, H. H., & Warkentin, M. E., (1992). Threats to information systems: Today's reality, yesterday's understanding. *MIS Quarterly, 1*(1), 173–186.
22. Marin, E., Diab, A., & Shakarian, P., (2016). Product offerings in malicious hacker markets. In: *2016 IEEE Conference on Intelligence and Security Informatics (ISI)* (Vol. 1, No. 1, pp. 187–189). IEEE.
23. Nahrstadt, B. C., (2009). Former employee sabotage? Invoke the computer fraud and abuse act. *Journal of Internet Law, 1*(1), 17–26.
24. Overhage, J. M., Tierney, W. M., Zhou, X. H., & McDonald, C. J., (1997). A randomized trial of "corollary orders" to prevent errors of omission. *Journal of the American Medical Informatics Association, 4*(5), 364–375.
25. Pedreschi, D., Bonchi, F., Turini, F., Verykios, V. S., Atzori, M., Malin, B., & Saygin, Y., (2008). Privacy protection: Regulations and technologies, opportunities, and threats. *Mobility, Data Mining and Privacy: Geographic Knowledge Discovery, 1*(1), 101–119.

26. Schmidt, G., Tanner, M., & Hayes, T., (2007). Computer security threats: Student confidence in their knowledge of common threats. *Journal of Business & Leadership: Research, Practice, and Teaching (2005–2012), 3*(1), 211–215.
27. Sen, R., Verma, A., & Heim, G. R., (2020). Impact of cyberattacks by malicious hackers on the competition in software markets. *Journal of Management Information Systems, 37*(1), 191–216.
28. Shabtai, A., Moskovitch, R., Elovici, Y., & Glezer, C., (2009). Detection of malicious code by applying machine learning classifiers on static features: A state-of-the-art survey. *Information Security Technical Report, 14*(1), 16–29.
29. Shakarian, J., Gunn, A. T., & Shakarian, P., (2016). Exploring malicious hacker forums. *Cyber Deception: Building the Scientific Foundation, 1*(1), 259–282.
30. Smith, R. G., (2013). Identity theft and fraud. In: *Handbook of Internet Crime* (Vol. 1, No. 1, pp. 273–301). Willan.
31. Solberg, S. K., (2016). Economic and industrial espionage at the start of the 21st century–status quaestionis. *Journal of Intelligence Studies in Business, 6*(3), 51–64.
32. Strickland, L. S., & Hunt, L. E., (2005). Technology, security, and individual privacy: New tools, new threats, and new public perceptions. *Journal of the American Society for Information Science and Technology, 56*(3), 221–234.
33. Sun, H., Xu, M., & Zhao, P., (2021). Modeling malicious hacking data breach risks. *North American Actuarial Journal, 25*(4), 484–502.
34. Thomas, C., (2020). Introductory chapter: Computer security threats. In: *Computer Security Threats* (Vol. 1, No. 1, pp. 1–20). IntechOpen.
35. Thonnard, O., Bilge, L., O'Gorman, G., Kiernan, S., & Lee, M., (2012). Industrial espionage and targeted attacks: Understanding the characteristics of an escalating threat. In: *Research in Attacks, Intrusions, and Defenses: 15th International Symposium, RAID 2012, Amsterdam, The Netherlands Proceedings 15* (pp. 64–85). Springer Berlin Heidelberg.
36. Ziegeldorf, J. H., Morchon, O. G., & Wehrle, K., (2014). Privacy in the internet of things: Threats and challenges. *Security and Communication Networks, 7*(12), 2728–2742.

CHAPTER 3

Computer Viruses

LEARNING OBJECTIVES

After studying this chapter, you will be able to:

- The basic concept of computer viruses, Trojan horses, and worms.
- Taxonomy of viruses.
- Different classes of IBM-PC viruses.
- History and security features of the Macintosh Operating System and Hardware.
- Concept of macro viruses and their reliance on the macro functionalities of software applications.

INTRODUCTORY EXAMPLE

Consider the case of Soft Solutions Corporation, a company renowned for its innovative software solutions. Soft Solutions Corp. prides itself on its state-of-the-art infrastructure, employing both IBM-PCs and Macintosh systems across various departments to fulfill diverse business needs. In recent times, however, the company encountered a severe setback due to a widespread occurrence of computer viruses.

Initially, employees received seemingly harmless emails purportedly containing important updates or attachments related to ongoing projects. Unknown to them, these phishing emails contained malicious attachments, such as Trojan horses, cleverly disguised as legitimate files. Once opened, these Trojans infiltrated the company's network, causing disruptive behavior within the IBM-PC systems.

Simultaneously, the Macintosh systems, long believed to be immune to such threats, faced an unexpected challenge. Despite their robust hardware and operating system defenses, a newly emerged Macintosh-specific virus exploited their vulnerabilities, spreading rapidly across the otherwise secure environment.

This scenario brought to light the critical importance of understanding the taxonomy of viruses, including the distinctions between Trojan horses, worms, and traditional computer viruses. It highlighted the need for comprehensive protection strategies tailored not only for IBM-PCs but also for Macintosh systems, addressing both software and hardware vulnerabilities.

UNIT INTRODUCTION

The discovery of computer viruses was a major factor in bringing network security concerns to the public's attention. All PC users are vulnerable to contracting computer virus intrusions. The widespread distribution of macro viruses, transmitted through document interchange in certain word-processing packages, has greatly increased the number of computer users affected by computer viruses, surpassing previous levels (Cohen, 1987).

3.1. COMPUTER VIRUS

→Learning Objectives

- Understand the concept of computer viruses in detail.
- Comprehend the modifications that viruses can make to computer programs.

Malicious software, or malware, comes in several forms, such as computer worms, viruses, and Trojan horses. According to Cohen, a computer virus is any program that can "infect" other programs by changing them in a way that they contain a potentially altered copy of the virus. To propagate themselves, viruses modify the code of computer programs. Changes can occur in various ways, including:

a) Destroying data – The Brain virus targeted the IBM PC and could overwrite file components while infecting them, leading to the deletion of program files.

b) Stealing CPU time – Let's consider a virus that requires permission before infiltrating an executable file. The creator of the virus may view it as a helpful tool, while those whose work is disrupted by the virus may see it as an inconvenience and a waste of time.

c) Reducing the functionality of the infected program (Balthrop et al., 2004).

d) Integrating additional functionalities into the infected application, which may not necessarily be harmful – Cohen examines a computer virus that applies compression to executable files upon attack and subsequently decompresses them during operation.

Research on identifying and eliminating computer viruses has seen a significant surge. Identifying viruses is challenging due to their tendency to mutate. That is why Cohen incorporated the concept of potential evolution in his definition. The creators of computer viruses deliberately design them to possess the ability to evolve following infiltration, hence increasing the challenge of detecting these infiltrations by antivirus software (Subramanya & Lakshminarasimhan, 2001).

Cohen's description appears to be a good fit for the term "computer virus." However, it is too limited because it excludes programs that can attach themselves to host programs by methods other than changing the host program's code (Adleman, 1988).

Did you know?

The term "computer virus" was coined by computer scientist Fred Cohen in 1983.

3.2. TROJAN HORSES AND WORMS

→Learning Objectives

- Learn about computer worms, including examples.
- Understand the functionality of a Trojan horse.

A computer worm refers to a self-contained and self-replicating program capable of infecting other computers. A worm is self-contained and does not rely on host software like a virus.

Probably the most well-known example is the *Internet Worm*, which was introduced in November 1988. The worm took advantage of multiple known flaws in the UNIX operating system. It consists of two components: the main program and a grappling hook. The grappling hook was a simple C code. Once the foreign device had been successfully installed, the grappling hook was compiled and executed. It connected to the original computer while it was running and uploaded a copy of the main software. The primary objective of the main software was to search the Internet for vulnerable PCs, specifically those that would allow unauthorized remote operation of the grappling hook (Kwon et al., 2016).

A Trojan horse program is a program that deceives computer users by pretending to offer a desirable function, leading them to execute the program. Instead of performing its designated purpose, the Trojan horse carries out an undocumented action, often malicious, as intended by the programmer (Kumar et al., 2016). It is important to note that this definition does not include programs that cause damage due to programming errors. Unlike viruses and worms, Trojan horses do not have the ability to self-replicate. The attacks performed by a Trojan horse can vary from basic tasks like file deletion to more subtle activities such as collecting confidential user information. A Trojan horse is easily detectable as it retrieves private session keys from a user's hard drive and sends them over the Internet to be collected at a remote site (Hughes & DeLone, 2007).

3.3. TAXONOMY OF VIRUSES

→Learning Objectives

- Understand the taxonomy of computer viruses.
- Classify viruses based on their infiltration methods and their impacts on systems.

The hardware platform being used has a significant impact on the risk of infiltration. Let's consider the following three platforms:

a) **IBM PC**: Users of this platform are heavily affected by viruses. As of November 1996, there were reportedly over 10,000 DOS-based computer viruses.

b) **Macintosh**: Macintosh users have been affected by the computer virus problem, but not to the same extent as IBM PC users. Although estimates vary, there are less than 100 viruses specifically designed for the Macintosh operating system.

c) **UNIX:** UNIX users are fortunate as this platform is not usually susceptible to common virus attacks. However, new viruses are being created to target this platform (Fauquet & Fargette, 2005).

Computer platforms that store programs on media susceptible to modification are vulnerable to computer virus attacks. Viruses can generally be categorized into two broad classifications:

a) Platform dependent; and

b) Platform independent.

Viruses that are specific to a certain platform (platform dependent) usually utilize a specific hardware or software configuration feature of that platform. Macro viruses can function on any platform and are a relatively new addition to the area. Widely used programs that work with different operating systems provide interpreted languages that are used to code macro viruses. An instance of such software is Microsoft Word. The software is compatible with both Macintosh machines and IBM PCs. Viruses exclusively target executable files for infection. To activate them, the host program must be executed (Lefkowitz et al., 2018). A virus can be either:

a) **Memory resident:** The virus remains functional long after the host program has ceased to operate.

b) **Non-memory resident**: The virus is only activated when the host program is running.

Writers of computer viruses employ two primary strategies to enhance the complexity of virus detection. The strategies are as follows:

a) **Polymorphism:** A virus undergoes structural changes using a range of mechanisms, including encryption.

b) **Stealth:** A virus attempts to mask its existence while operating within infected components.

The term "virus signature" refers to a specific sequence of bytes indicative of a virus (Ward, 1993). Detecting a virus can be done by scanning the software program for a virus signature. Polymorphism aims to reduce the available byte count for a virus signature. The strategy consists of two steps:

a) The virus employs variable key encryption to protect its primary code throughout infection. Various uncomplicated schemes might be employed to propagate the virus. Before executing the encrypted virus, it is necessary to decrypt it.

b) Furthermore, the virus employs various encryption and decryption methods, allowing the selection of different schemes. Additionally, it employs identical machine instructions, reorganizes instructions if the revised sequence yields identical operations, inserts dummy instructions (such as no operation instructions), generates code during runtime (which subsequently executes the required task), and integrates intermixing operations (Walker et al., 2020).

Did you know?

The first computer virus, called the "Creeper Virus," was developed in the early 1970s as an experimental program.

3.4. IBM-PC VIRUSES

→Learning Objectives

- Comprehend the classes of IBM-PC viruses:
- Learn about the techniques used by IBM-PC viruses for infection, replication, and concealment within the system.

This group of viruses is the most widespread and may be classified into three separate classes:

a) File-infecting viruses;
b) Multipartite viruses (which infect both executable files and boot sectors)
c) Boot-sector-infecting viruses.

3.4.1. File-Infecting Viruses

It is the simplest type of virus that infects files and alters a portion of the host program but discards the initial code that was altered. An illustration of the host program is shown in Figure 3.1 both before and during infection. The virus modifies the first segment of the file, ensuring that it is run whenever the host application is called upon. The host software is likely to be affected severely, making it incapable of functioning properly. The viral code can also be inserted in other parts of the file to be run whenever the host software is called while keeping most of the host program operations unaffected (Morales et al., 2010).

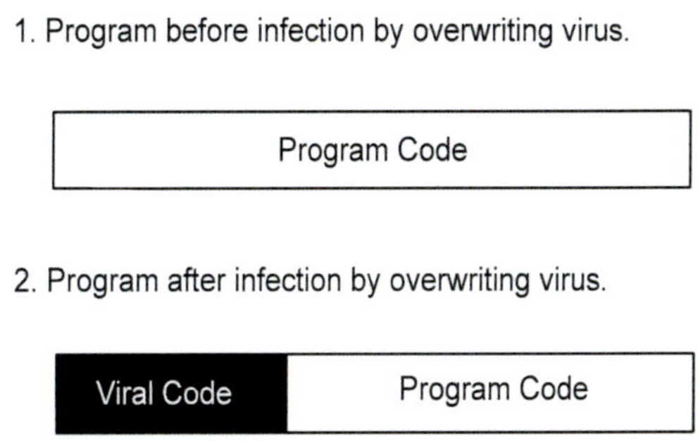

Figure 3.1. An example of the host program both before and after the virus was overwritten (Source: Dr Joeph, Creative Commons License).

Advanced viruses employ a method of attaching themselves to the host program that allows the virus to repair any damage caused to the host software. Attaching the virus code to the end of an executable file is an effective method to infect it and make reversible alterations possible. The first few code bytes are saved for potential restoration and are replaced with a jump instruction that points to the viral code that is inserted. When the host program runs, the viral code gains control first before fixing the host program's code and running it (Figure 3.2). Moreover, the viral code might also be added at the start of the host file (Figure 3.3) (Kephart et al., 1997).

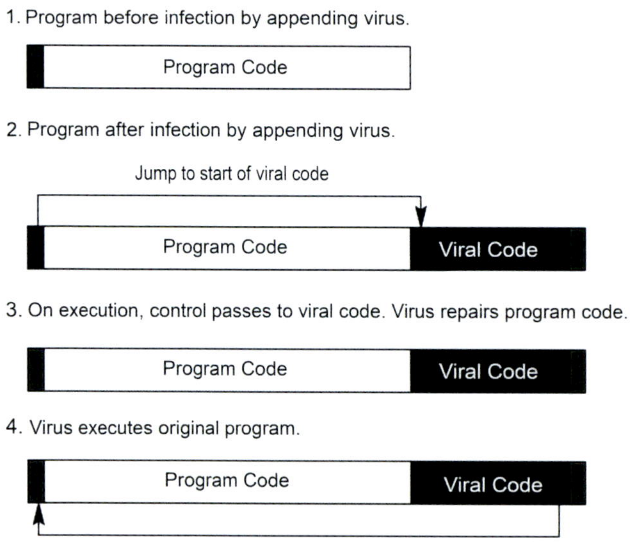

Figure 3.2. Illustration of an appending virus (Source: Dr. Thomas Hardjono, Creative Commons License).

When a virus shows signs of not overwriting itself, it indicates that the host, on which the virus is attached, has increased in size. This fact is observable by both users and programs that monitor executable file sizes. However, a file can become infected without altering its size. In such cases, the virus can restore the host code when the file is executed (Thomas & Jyoti, 2008).

A cavity virus identifies a region of consistent information within the host program that is spacious enough to accommodate its presence. It then records the original value stored in that region and replaces it with its own data. This was the method employed by the Lehigh virus. An executable file may contain unused spaces where a cavity virus could be present due to the file's format. This technique is utilized by the CIH (Chernobyl or spacefiller) virus.

A compression virus employs techniques to compress all or a portion of the host file's contents. This enables the virus to conceal itself within the host software without altering the file's size. During runtime, the compressed component can be decompressed (Horton, 1997).

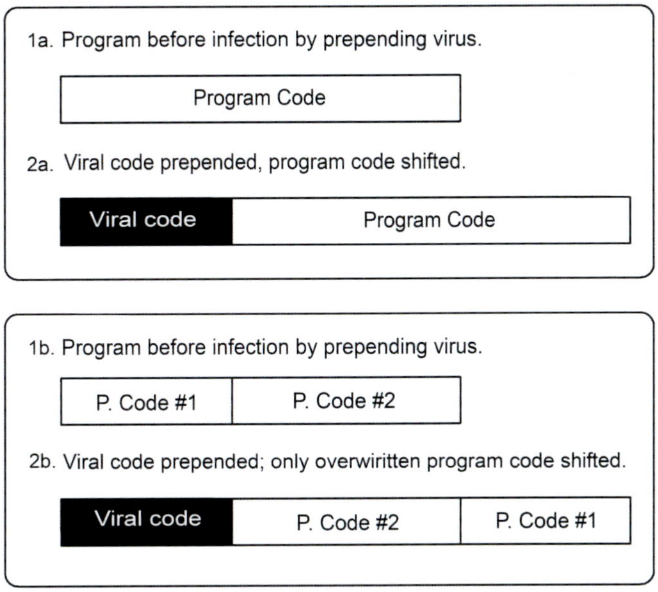

Figure 3.3. Illustration of a prepending virus (Source: Dr. JenefierSebery, Creative Commons License).

3.4.2. Boot-Sector-Infecting Viruses

The operating system is loaded onto a hard drive when a computer is turned on. This particular approach is often known as bootstrapping. There are various stages in the bootstrapping process. The boot sector, often known as the DOS boot sector, is the first sector on a disk where the operating system loads. It contains a brief program that launches the subsequent step. In case of absence of an operating system, a software program notifies the user that an operating system is not present and prompts for loading a different disk (White et al., 1995).

Remember

The "Brain" virus, created in 1986, is considered one of the first IBM-PC viruses, infecting the boot sectors of hard disks.

Hard drives are sometimes divided into numerous smaller logical partitions due to their significant storage capacity. The master boot record (MBR) or master boot sector (MBS) is the name given to the main physical sector of a hard disk. The boot sector includes information on the disk's partitions as well as a small program that locates a bootable partition and launches the boot process from it. The boot sector, which is the first logical sector of a bootable partition, is primarily responsible for loading the operating system (Figure 3.4) (Mukkamala, 2007).

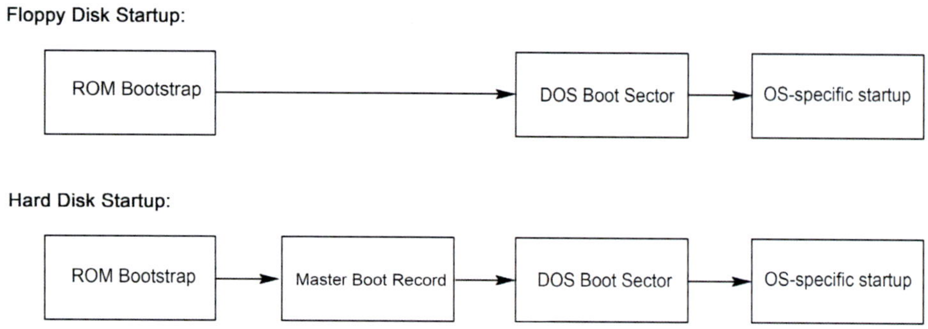

Figure 3.4. Diagram showing how hard drives and floppy media boot up (Source: Dr. JenefierSebery, Creative Commons License).

Boot sector viruses affect the master boot record of hard drives and the boot sector of floppy disks and hard drives used by the operating system. This is the typical infection process pattern. A virus finds the intended sector and shifts it to a new location to complete the boot process (Pieprzyk et al., 2003). It then installs a copy of itself into the area after that.

A few examples of this type of virus are:

a) Brain viruses – Storage disks are the only media that are affected by the virus.
b) AntiCMOS viruses – This family of viruses attempts to execute boot activities independently by deleting the relevant code from the affected sector.
c) Hare virus – This alters the position of the partition tables.
d) Monkey viruses – These viruses reorganize partition tables and invade boot sections, making infected hard drives unusable (Slade & Slade, 1994).

3.4.3. Companion Viruses

The host programs that companion viruses infiltrate are not altered by them. Instead, they generate multiple executable files that are different versions of themselves. In the context of MS-DOS, companion viruses can be classified into three basic types.

a) **Regular Companion**: This type of virus creates a file within the same directory as the host file, but with a filename extension that runs before the host program extension. For example, if two files with the same name exist in the same directory but with different extensions, the .com file will be processed first before the .exe file (Filiol, 2005).
b) **Path Companion**: Prior to checking the directory containing the host program for executable files, this virus creates a file with an executable extension in that directory.
c) **Surrogate Companion**: The virus modifies the name of the host program and replaces it with a replica of itself (Gronenschild et al., 2012).

3.5. MACINTOSH OPERATING SYSTEM

→Learning Objectives

- Understand the basics of the Macintosh operating system.
- Identify different parts of a Macintosh file.

An overview of the history of the Macintosh operating system is necessary before discussing the viruses that affect the Macintosh platform.

Each Macintosh file is made up of two parts:

a) Resource fork (or resource file)
b) Data fork

The fundamental feature of the Macintosh operating system is that every file has a unique property:

i. Type, such as application (appl) or ASCII text (text)
ii. Creator, or the application software that has ownership of the file (Williams, 1984).

Resources are defined in a resource file as follows:

i. An id number (two-byte integer),
ii. A resource type (four-letter code),
iii. A name (string of characters).

To identify a particular resource, it is sufficient to provide its name, ID number, or resource type. An application resource file contains a range of data, including the following:

a) The MENU offers information about the options that can be selected from within a certain application menu.
b) MBAR offers a list of the menus that may be found in an application's menu bar.
c) WIND describes the dimensions and other attributes of a window that a software generates.

d) A control is defined by CNTL, which is a user interface element provided by an application, such as a button or scrollbar (Lam, 2001).

e) CODE contains the main components of an application's executable code.

Numerous resource forks can comprise a loading resource. The desired resources are located by following a search path. The search concludes at the System file, which contains essential resources for the operating system, after commencing with the current resource file.

Consider the graphical user interface (GUI) displayed by an application (Hasnain & Rafi, 2019). A Definition Procedure (DP) is utilized to exhibit the interface components, such as windows, buttons, menus, etc. When the operating system necessitates displaying a user interface element, it retrieves the compiled code of the DP from a resource. The operating system offers a user-modifiable default implementation. A few examples of definition procedures include:

a) **Menu DP:** It is responsible for creating menu items within a menu and is stored in an mdef resource.

b) **Menu bar DP**: It is stored in an mbdf resource and is responsible for tasks related to menu presentation.

c) **Window DP**: The window display process is a component stored within a wdef resource. It is accountable for resizing a window or drawing a frame.

d) **Control DP**: It is stored in a cdef resource and has various tasks, such as drawing the control and identifying user clicks within the control (Mudiraj, 2013).

The INIT is an essential store that houses executable code. These resources consist of code designed to be executed during the initialization of the system. The INIT resources can be found either directly within the System file or in specific formats.

The Finder is an essential component of the Macintosh operating system. It possesses the following characteristics:

a) It manages the user's desktop.

b) It tracks the location of files and folders on the screen and disk directory hierarchy.

c) It ensures that when a user double-clicks on a file, the appropriate program engages with it (Jones, 2002).

The term "Finder" referred to a software version that allowed only one application to run at a time in Macintosh system software versions prior to System 7 (e.g., System 6). Users could run another program or the Finder, but not both simultaneously. MultiFinder was an improved version of the Finder that supported the simultaneous use of multiple applications, including MultiFinder. A software version developed from MultiFinder that allows the running of numerous applications at once, including the Finder itself, will also be referred to as "Finder" (Leopard et al., 2018).

Every file that an application creates or owns can have an icon assigned to it by the application developer. The Finder utilizes these symbols to represent the user documents.

Details about icons can be located in the resources of the application's resource fork. The Finder puts the information in a database for easy access after retrieving this and other data from the application resource fork. The disk location of the application is also maintained.

To display the icon for a particular document, the Finder searches its database for an icon that has the same author code as the file itself and the document type that the application has specified. When a user double-clicks a document in the Finder, it searches its database for an application with the same creator code as the document. The Finder launches the program to process the document if found (Jia et al., 2008).

3.5.1. Macintosh Hardware

→Learning Objectives

- Learn about the history of Macintosh Hardware.
- Comprehend the security measures of Macintosh Hardware.

Motorola 68,000 microprocessors served as the foundation for the first Macintosh models. *68K Macintoshes* are Macintosh computers that were made with microprocessors from the 680x0 series. Likewise, *68K code* describes software applications created especially for these microprocessors. In recently released Macintosh models, the 680x0 microprocessors were replaced by the PowerPC series of microprocessors. Computers that are integrated with the PowerPC microprocessor are widely referred to as *PPC Macintoshes*, and the code specifically designed for these computers is known as *PPC code*. The machine code employed by the 680x0 microprocessors is incompatible with the newer PowerPC microprocessors. Apple resolved this problem by integrating 68LC040 emulation into the operating system of PPC Macintosh systems (Tinnirello et al., 2012).

Three primary strategies can be used to incorporate an application's execution within the application file:

a) The 68K code application can be divided into multiple code fragments. These applications can operate under emulation on a PPC Macintosh.

b) A program created using 68K code can be divided into code fragments, followed by launching the code fragment in situations where the OS version is unable to handle it automatically. These applications are not compatible with emulation on a PPC Macintosh.

c) The PPC-based application can be divided into smaller code segments, specifically targeting and modifying the 68K code, which is susceptible to the present generation of Macintosh viruses (Tittelbach et al., 2010).

However, this makes PPC Macintoshes vulnerable to viruses due to the following reasons:

a) Most PPC programs contain a small segment of 68K code that notifies the user about the program's incompatibility with a 68K Macintosh.

b) Not all viruses attempt to alter the program's code. Certain viruses, like the MDEF resource, can append executable resources to a program. In a PowerPC environment, if a virus incorporates 68K definition procedures into a PPC application, the application will still function as intended (Zhao & Wang, 2008).

c) It is reasonable to assume that viruses of this nature will be developed in the future.

Code fragments can be stored in resources in the resource fork, although they are often stored in the data fork of an application file. The fragments are indexed using a resource called the code fragment resource, or cfrg resource with identity 0. Code fragment-based applications can also import shared libraries. While no such Macintosh viruses are currently known to exist, code fragments in a shared library could be affected by a virus (Westall et al., 1989).

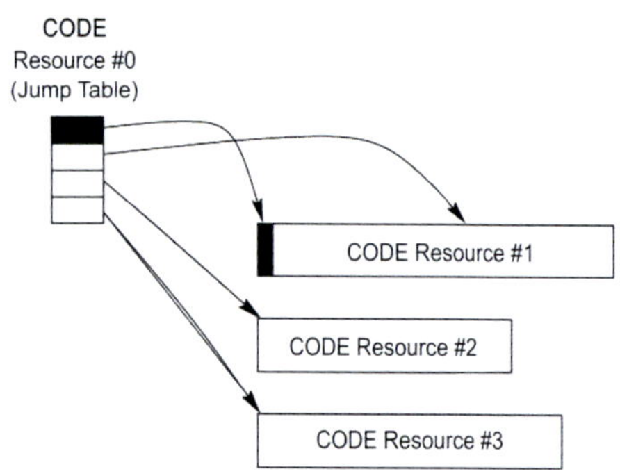

Figure 3.5. Diagram of Code-segment-based 68K application (Source: Dr. Joseph, Creative Commons License).

A program written using code segments has a much simpler structure (Figure 3.5). The executable code of a 68K application is divided into multiple segments, each stored in a CODE resource. These segments may contain one or more routines. In Figure 3.5, the path to the second routine is stored in CODE resource #1 and can be found in the second entry of the Jump Table. As a result, programs can run without needing to utilize the entire RAM at once (Meyer, 1987).

A mechanism must be in place to invoke another routine from within a code segment. A jump table, known as a so-called jump table, is utilized to manage intersegment calls. To call a routine in a different segment, a jump to the jump table, which contains the routine addresses, is performed. The CODE resource stores the jump table with ID 0. The first entry of the table contains the address of the initially executed routine. It is worth noting that not every compiler keeps the complete jump table within the CODE 0 resource up to date. Instead, a jump table is created in memory upon execution (Horton & Seberry, 1999).

3.5.2. Macintosh Viruses

Most Macintosh viruses modify the executable code of application programs, causing the viral code to run during program execution. There are two main methods to achieve this:

a) A virus alters the code segments of the application.

b) A virus adds a definition procedure, which will be implicitly called when the application is executed, into new resources.

Let's consider the standard 68K application shown in Figure 3.5. There are three methods by which a virus can alter the code segments within the program:

a) By introducing an additional CODE resource and changing the initial of the jump table, the virus inserts a code segment into the program.

As a result, once the application is launched, the malicious code takes over. After the program completes its designated task, the virus retains control of the application by keeping the first jump table entry. All of the application's original code remains intact, except for the jump table. Figure 3.6 illustrates the infiltration of this group of viruses, represented by the viruses nVIR and INIT29 (Harley, 1997).

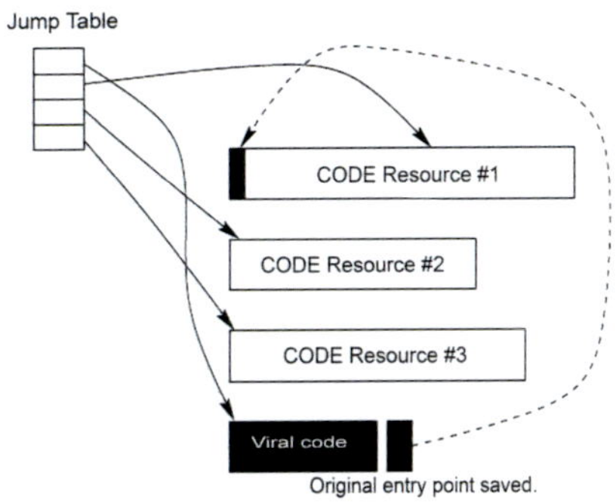

Figure 3.6. Representation of modifications made by virus that add CODE resource to an application (Source: Dr. JenefierSeberry, Creative Commons License).

b) The virus adds its code to the end of an already-existing CODE resource rather than adding a new code segment to the application itself. There is no need for the virus to come into direct contact with the jump table. Rather, it modifies the starting bytes of a routine in the CODE resource so that, upon execution of the routine, the viral code is triggered. After the virus's code is run, the replaced bytes can be preserved and recovered by the virus. The virus's operational mechanism is depicted in Figure 3.7 (Belk & Tumbat, 2005).

Did you know?

In 1987, the nVIR virus became one of the earliest major viruses affecting Macintosh computers.

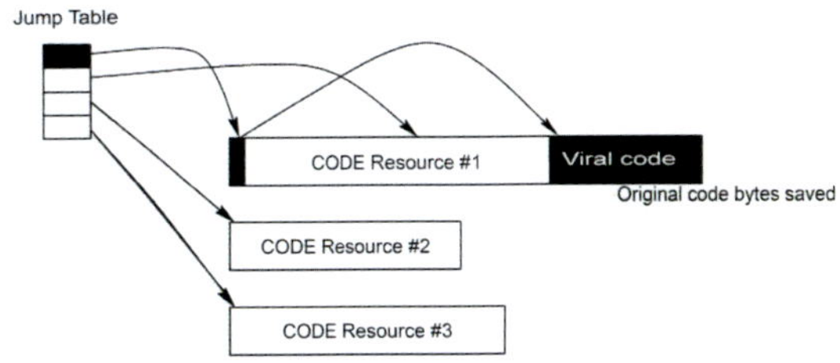

Figure 3.7. Representation of virus modifications that add its code to an existing CODE resource and modify a routine to jump to the viral code (Source: Dr. JenefierSeberry, Creative Commons License).

c) The virus modifies the jump table by attaching itself to an already-existing CODE resource. The infectious code takes over the application at first when it runs. To allow the program to regain control, the first jump table entry is kept safe. Figure 3.8 shows the infiltration process.

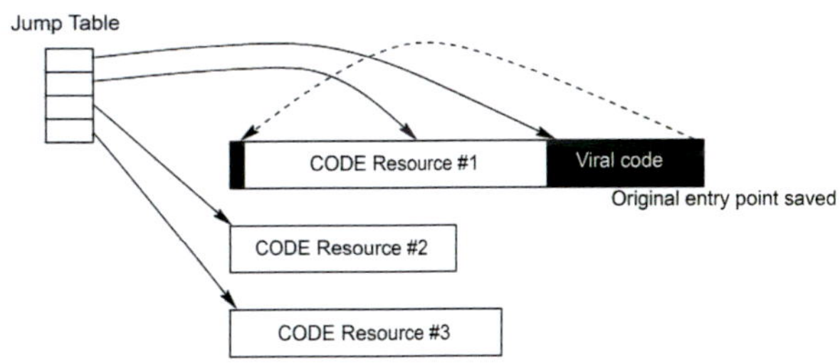

Figure 3.8. Representation of virus modifications that add its code to an existing CODE resource and modify a jump table entry (Source: Dr. Thomas Hardjono, Creative Commons License).

An application can be infiltrated by including a resource containing the code for a definition procedure through many means.

Let's explore the following methods of spreading the virus in this situation:

a) The virus incorporates a viral definition mechanism that mimics the type and identity of a standard DP resource from the System file.

b) The virus incorporates a viral definition procedure while altering its identity (Kaplan et al., 2000).

The WDEF virus deserves particular attention. This malware propagates by exploiting a definition resource. Nevertheless, the definition resource is not included in an executable file. On each disk where the Finder keeps its desktop database, or the Desktop file, the WDEF virus installs a WDEF 0 resource containing the infectious code. This file opens automatically in the Finder when the disk is mounted. To perform a drawing operation, the operating system searches for a WDEF 0 resource when the user opens a window in the Finder. The viral WDEF 0 resource in the Desktop file will be found and executed in place of the original WDEF 0 resources since resource files are searched in the order of their most recent opening (Jaiswal, 2017).

3.6. MACRO VIRUSES

→Learning Objectives

- Interpret the concept of macro viruses
- Understand the emergence of macro viruses.

A macro is a group of statements in a programming language that, when interpreted, carries out a specific action. By creating customized macros, users of various software programs can automate complex and repetitive tasks. Some application packages offer both a general-purpose programming language interpreter and a simple scripting language for managing application usage. Among these applications, Microsoft Word is widely recognized as the most popular. WordBasic, a variation of BASIC, served as the macro language in Microsoft Word 6. The first version of Microsoft Word that was compatible with both Macintosh and IBM PCs was version 6, which was released on multiple platforms (Gaj et al., 1990).

The concept of a macro virus, coded in the macro language, is not uncommon. Highland accurately predicted the potential existence of a macro virus in 1989. The first documented macro virus emerged in 1995. In March 1999, the Virus Test Center at the University of Hamburg documented nearly 600 distinct strains of macro viruses. The majority of these macro viruses specifically targeted Microsoft Word versions.

Typically, macro viruses are embedded as viral macros in document files. These macros can run within their host program on any computer hardware platform where the application package has been translated, as they are interpreted by the application package rather than being compiled into machine-specific executable code. When infected documents are shared via email, macro viruses have the potential to spread more rapidly than other viruses (Gryaznov, 1999).

PRACTICE PROBLEMS

1. Explain why Macintosh systems were historically less susceptible to viruses.
2. How do macro viruses operate and spread?
3 Provide measures to protect against macro viruses.

SOLUTIONS TO PRACTICE PROBLEMS

1. The lower incidence of virus infections on Macs can be attributed to their smaller user base and distinct operating system architecture, which presents difficulties for virus developers.
2. Macro viruses incorporate malicious code into macro languages found in software such as Microsoft Word or Excel. They spread by infecting documents and executing malicious actions when opened.
3. It is necessary to implement strict security protocols that automatically disable macros. Moreover, it is advisable to employ the latest antivirus software and educate users on exercising caution when activating macros in documents from unfamiliar sources.

3.7. PROTECTION AGAINST VIRUSES

→Learning Objectives

- Identify preventive measures and best practices to combatviruses

There are two primary approaches to counteracting viruses:

a) Blocking the establishment of viruses within a computer system,

b) Detecting and eliminating them.

Several non-technical measures can be taken to decrease the likelihood of virus infiltration and minimize the potential impact if it does occur. These include:

a) Carefully designing the sequence in which the operating system searches for a bootable device.

b) Modifying the email system to ensure that received emails are opened securely.

c) Deleting any executable programs received from untrusted sources without running them.

d) Systematically creating backups of the system.

Antivirus techniques can be classified into three primary categories:

a) Scanners

b) Integrity checkers

c) Behavior blockers or activity monitors (Nachenberg, 1997).

3.7.1. Scanners

A virus scanner attempts to identify a virus in a file by searching for the distinctive pattern or characteristics of the infiltration. Due to the tendency of viruses to alter their code, scanners must check a file for specific signatures unique to the virus. Upon detecting a virus, scanners may attempt to eradicate the virus by eliminating it from the affected file. Nevertheless, there are instances where the file's original state cannot be recovered, such as when a virus has caused damage to a portion of the file. An optimal approach would involve substituting the contaminated file with a copy from a previously saved version (Wang et al., 2003). Scanners possess some limitations, such as:

a) They are only capable of identifying viruses that have established signatures.
b) Scanners must be regularly updated to keep pace with the release of new viruses.
c) Polymorphic viruses pose a challenge for scanners in terms of detection.
d) Users should routinely do scans to detect any infections on their drives.
e) The scanner frequently produces false positive results when processing files written in a foreign language.

The initial drawback can be partially mitigated through the implementation of heuristic analysis. Heuristics are predefined principles that can be utilized to evaluate the program's integrity in the event of executable code contamination by a virus. Heuristics can function as follows:

i. Positive – Identifying code that exhibits operations indicative of a virus,
ii. Negative – Identifying code that exhibits operations unlikely to be found in virus code (Kim & Spafford, 1994).

To overcome the challenges associated with detecting polymorphic viruses, it is possible to tailor scanners effectively to target specific groups of polymorphic viruses. An alternative method that appears to be more effective is the utilization of a technique known as generic decryption. This strategy proves effective for viruses that employ encryption to modify their structure. Such viruses must decrypt the primary section of their code before executing their operations. Generic decryption aims to simulate the program being analyzed beyond the stage when the virus code has been deciphered, enabling the identification of the virus based on its unique characteristics.

To prevent users from manually running scanners at set intervals, a scanner component that remains in the computer's memory could be provided. This component automatically analyzes files and drives for viruses upon access (Rohith & Kaur, 2021).

3.7.2. Integrity Checkers

It is reasonable to assume that once a virus enters a file, it will inevitably alter it. Hashing is an effective technique for confirming integrity. The hash value of a file is determined after its creation. Any modifications made to the file will result in a change in the hash value. It is crucial to understand that integrity checkers can detect any changes made to a file, regardless of whether they were caused by a virus. If the hash value has been altered, it is conceivable that the file has been infected (Singh et al., 2021). There are visible limitations to integrity checks, including:

a) A virus that infiltrates a system before an integrity checker determines the initial hash values of its files will go undetected.
b) If a file has been both infected by a virus and modified by the user simultaneously, integrity checkers are unable to identify the infection.
c) Viruses cannot be identified until they have propagated and caused some damage.

Integrity checks offer a significant advantage in their ability to identify unfamiliar viral infiltrations, including well-known polymorphic viruses (Sharma et al., 2021).

3.7.3. Behavior Blockers and Activity Monitors

Antivirus systems constantly observe computer activities and strive to identify the existence of any viruses. Behavior blockers and activity monitors aim to differentiate between abnormal (viral) and normal behavior based on the assumption that such distinction is feasible. However, this strategy has several disadvantages:

a) Most viruses perform legitimate actions instead of taking advantage of vulnerabilities in the operating system.

b) Certain viruses may attempt to evade antivirus programs. For instance, some Macintosh infections possess code that redirects traps produced by the virus to ROM code. If successful, the antivirus application will be bypassed, resulting in the failure to identify the virus (Kose & Samet, 2021).

c) Blocking a suspicious action can lead to unfavorable outcomes. For example, files can be left in incompatible states following a questionable operation.

d) When detecting potentially malicious activity, the antivirus program may defer the decision-making process to the user. This can be frustrating, especially when it happens frequently (Mira, 2021).

SUMMARY

- This chapter provides a comprehensive understanding of computer viruses, which are malicious software that self-replicate and attach to other programs, potentially resulting in data corruption or system dysfunction.
- It has been discussed that worms can independently attach themselves to host software. They undergo self-replication and propagate through networks. Trojan horses, on the other hand, are deceptive programs that appear as normal software but contain harmful code.
- Furthermore, this chapter offers insights into the taxonomy of different viruses. The nature of viruses and their attacks has been examined in relation to various operating systems.
- The chapter also delves into IBM PC viruses and Macintosh viruses. The IBM-PC platform has historically been a popular target for viruses due to its widespread usage, particularly in commercial settings. Conversely, Macintosh infections are less prevalent compared to PC viruses.
- Additionally, the chapter highlights that macro viruses are coded using macro languages integrated into software products such as Microsoft or Excel.
- The final section of the chapter emphasizes the importance of installing reliable antivirus software and regularly updating it to effectively identify and eliminate malware. Frequent system upgrades and patches are essential for addressing identified vulnerabilities commonly exploited by viruses.

MULTIPLE CHOICE QUESTIONS

1. **How do worms differ from viruses?**
   a) Worms require a host program to spread
   b) Viruses spread via email attachments
   c) Worms do not need a host program to propagate.
   d) None of the above
2. **What is the property of a polymorphic virus?**
   a) It embeds itself in memory
   b) It changes its code to avoid detection
   c) It spreads through macros in software applications
   d) None of the above
3. **Why were Macintosh systems historically considered less susceptible to viruses compared to PCs?**
   a) Due to their smaller user base
   b) Due to their operating system architecture
   c) Due to their resistance to malware attacks
   d) None of the above

4. Where do macro viruses embed malicious code?

a) In system boot sectors

b) In email attachments

c) In macro languages within software applications.

d) None of the above

REVIEW QUESTIONS

1. Define viruses, worms, and Trojan horses, highlighting their differences in behavior and infection methods.
2. Explain the characteristics and behaviors of resident and non-resident viruses.
3. Discuss the historical significance of viruses targeting IBM-PC systems.
4. How do macro viruses differ from traditional viruses, worms, and Trojan horses?
5. Outline effective measures individuals or organizations can take to protect systems against virus infections.

Answers to Multiple Questions

1. (c) 2. (b) 3. (b) 4. (c)

REFERENCES

1. Adleman, L. M., (1988). An abstract theory of computer viruses. In: *Conference on the Theory and Application of Cryptography* (Vol. 1, No. 1, pp. 354–374). New York, NY: Springer New York.
2. Baghirov, E., (2021). Techniques of malware detection: Research review. In: *2021 IEEE 15th International Conference on Application of Information and Communication Technologies (AICT)* (Vol. 1, No. 1, pp. 1–6). IEEE.
3. Balthrop, J., Forrest, S., Newman, M. E., & Williamson, M. M., (2004). Technological networks and the spread of computer viruses. *Science, 304*(5670), 527–529.
4. Belk, R., & Tumbat, G., (2005). The cult of macintosh. *Consumption Markets & Culture, 8*(3), 205–217.
5. Cohen, F., (1987). Computer viruses: Theory and experiments. *Computers & Security, 6*(1), 22–35.
6. Dagon, D., Martin, T., & Starner, T., (2004). Mobile phones as computing devices: The viruses are coming! *IEEE Pervasive Computing, 3*(4), 11–15.
7. Fauquet, C. M., & Fargette, D., (2005). International committee on taxonomy of viruses and the 3,142 unassigned species. *Virology Journal, 2*, 1–10.
8. Filiol, E., (2005). Companion viruses. *Computer Viruses: From Theory to Applications, 1*(1), 207–255.
9. Gaj, K., Górski, K., Kossowski, R., & Sobczyk, J., (1990). Methods of protection against computer viruses. *IFAC Proceedings Volumes, 23*(6), 43–48.

10. Gronenschild, E. H., Habets, P., Jacobs, H. I., Mengelers, R., Rozendaal, N., Van Os, J., & Marcelis, M., (2012). The effects of FreeSurfer version, workstation type, and Macintosh operating system version on anatomical volume and cortical thickness measurements. *PloS One, 7*(6), e38234.

11. Gryaznov, D., (1999). Scanners of the year 2000: Heuristics. In: *Proceedings of the 5th International Virus Bulletin* (Vol. 113, pp. 1–20).

12. Harley, D., (1997). Macs and macros: The state of the Macintosh nation. In: *Virus Bulletin 1997 Conference Proceedings: Virus Bulletin* (Vol. 1, No. 1, pp. 1–20).

13. Hasnain, S. G. M., & Rafi, F. A., (2019). Windows, Linux, Mac operating system and decision making. *International Journal of Computer Applications, 975*, 8887.

14. Horton, J., & Seberry, J., (1999). Companion viruses and the Macintosh: Threats and countermeasures. In: *Information Security and Privacy: 4th Australasian Conference, ACISP'99 Wollongong, NSW, Australia, Proceedings 4* (pp. 202–212). Springer Berlin Heidelberg.

15. Horton, J., (1997). Computer viruses. *Virus, 21*, 2.

16. Hughes, L. A., & DeLone, G. J., (2007). Viruses, worms, and trojan horses: Serious crimes, nuisance, or both? *Social Science Computer Review, 25*(1), 78–98.

17. Jaiswal, M., (2017). Computer viruses: Principles of exertion, occurrence, and awareness. *International Journal of Creative Research Thoughts (IJCRT), 1*(1), 648–651.

18. Jia, J., Zhang, Q., & Shen, X. S., (2008). HC-MAC: A hardware-constrained cognitive MAC for efficient spectrum management. *IEEE Journal on Selected Areas in Communications, 26*(1), 106–117.

19. Jones, C. H., (2002). User-driven integrated software lives: "Paleomag" paleomagnetics analysis on the Macintosh. *Computers & Geosciences, 28*(10), 1145–1151.

20. Kaplan, J. E., Hanson, D., Dworkin, M. S., Frederick, T., Bertolli, J., Lindegren, M. L., & Jones, J. L., (2000). Epidemiology of human immunodeficiency virus-associated opportunistic infections in the United States in the era of highly active antiretroviral therapy. *Clinical Infectious Diseases, 30(Supplement_1), 1*(1), S5–S14.

21. Kephart, J. O., Sorkin, G. B., Chess, D. M., & White, S. R., (1997). Fighting computer viruses. *Scientific American, 277*(5), 88–93.

22. Kim, G. H., & Spafford, E. H., (1994). The design and implementation of tripwire: A file system integrity checker. In: *Proceedings of the 2nd ACM Conference on Computer and Communications Security* (Vol. 1, No. 1, pp. 18–29).

23. Köse, Ü., & Samet, R., (2021). Detection of malware with deep learning method. In: *2021 6th International Conference on Computer Science and Engineering (UBMK)* (Vol. 1, No. 1, pp. 665–669). IEEE.

24. Kumar, M., Mishra, B. K., & Panda, T. C., (2016). Predator-prey models on interaction between computer worms, Trojan horse, and antivirus software inside a computer system. *International Journal of Security and Its Applications, 10*(1), 173–190.

25. Kwon, B. J., Srinivas, V., Deshpande, A., & Dumitra⊠, T., (2016). *Catching Worms, Trojan Horses and Pups: Unsupervised Detection of Silent Delivery Campaigns, 1*(1), 1–20.

26. Lam, P. Y., (2001). May the force of the operating system be with you: Macintosh devotion as implicit religion. *Sociology of Religion, 62*(2), 243–262.

27. Lefkowitz, E. J., Dempsey, D. M., Hendrickson, R. C., Orton, R. J., Siddell, S. G., & Smith, D. B., (2018). Virus taxonomy: The database of the international committee on taxonomy of viruses (ICTV). *Nucleic Acids Research, 46*(D1), D708–D717.

28. Leopard, C. B., Rowe, N. C., & McCarrin, M. R., (2018). Memory forensics and the macintosh OS X operating system. In: *Digital Forensics and Cyber Crime: 9th International Conference, ICDF2C 2017, Prague, Czech Republic, Proceedings 9* (pp. 175–180). Springer International Publishing.

29. Mane, T., Nimase, P., Parihar, P., & Chandankhede, P., (2022). Review of malware detection using deep learning. In: *Soft Computing for Security Applications: Proceedings of ICSCS 202* (Vol. 1, No. 1, pp. 255–262). Springer Singapore.

30. Meyer, M., (1987). A shell for modern personal computers. *ACM SIGSMALL/PC Notes, 13*(3), 13–19.

31. Mira, F., (2021). A systematic literature review on malware analysis. In: *2021 IEEE International IOT, Electronics and Mechatronics Conference (IEMTRONICS)* (Vol. 1, No. 1, pp. 1–5). IEEE.

32. Morales, J. A., Clarke, P. J., & Deng, Y., (2010). Identification of file infecting viruses through detection of self-reference replication. *Journal in Computer Virology, 6*, 161–180.

33. Mudiraj, A. R., (2013). Windows Linux and Mac operating system booting process: A comparative study. *International Journal of Research in Computer and Communication Technology, 2*(11), 2278–5841.

34. Mukkamala, S., (2007). Limitations of current anti-virus scanning technologies. In: *Advances in Enterprise Information Technology Security* (Vol. 1, No. 1, pp. 190–209). IGI Global.

35. Nachenberg, C., (1997). Computer virus-antivirus coevolution. *Communications of the ACM, 40*(1), 46–51.

36. Pieprzyk, J., Hardjono, T., Seberry, J., Pieprzyk, J., Hardjono, T., & Seberry, J., (2003). Network security. *Fundamentals of Computer Security, 1*(1), 591–629.

37. Rohith, C., & Kaur, G., (2021). A comprehensive study on malware detection and prevention techniques used by anti-virus. In: *2021 2nd International Conference on Intelligent Engineering and Management (ICIEM)* (Vol. 1, No. 1, pp. 429–434). IEEE.

38. Sharma, A., Mohanty, S., & Islam, M. R., (2021). An experimental analysis on malware detection in executable files using machine learning. In: *2021 8th International Conference on Smart Computing and Communications (ICSCC)* (Vol. 1, No. 1, pp. 178–182). IEEE.

39. Singh, P., Kaur, S., Sharma, S., Sharma, G., Vashisht, S., & Kumar, V., (2021). Malware detection using machine learning. In: *2021 International Conference on Technological Advancements and Innovations (ICTAI)* (Vol. 1, No. 1, pp. 11–14). IEEE.

40. Slade, R., & Slade, R., (1994). Introduction: Definitions, jargon, and myths. *Robert Slade's Guide to Computer Viruses: How to Avoid Them, How to Get Rid of Them, and How to Get Help, 1*(1), 3–28.

41. Subramanya, S. R., & Lakshminarasimhan, N., (2001). Computer viruses. *IEEE Potentials, 20*(4), 16–19.
42. Suciu, G., Istrate, C. I., Răducanu, R. I., Dițu, M. C., Fratu, O., & Vulpe, A., (2019). Mobile devices forensic platform for malware detection. In: *6th International Symposium for ICS & SCADA Cyber Security Research 2019 6* (pp. 59–66).
43. Thomas, V., & Jyoti, N., (2008). Combating file infectors on corporate networks. In: *2008 3rd International Conference on Malicious and Unwanted Software (MALWARE)* (Vol. 1, No. 1, pp. 85–91). IEEE.
44. Tinnirello, I., Bianchi, G., Gallo, P., Garlisi, D., Giuliano, F., & Gringoli, F., (2012). Wireless MAC processors: Programming MAC protocols on commodity hardware. In: *2012 Proceedings IEEE INFOCOM* (Vol. 1, No. 1, pp. 1269–1277). IEEE.
45. Tittelbach-Helmrich, K., Miletić, E., Wcislek, P., & Stamenković, Z., (2010). MAC hardware platform for RF-MIMO WLAN. In: *2010 53rd IEEE International Midwest Symposium on Circuits and Systems* (Vol. 1, No. 1, pp. 339–342). IEEE.
46. Walker, P. J., Siddell, S. G., Lefkowitz, E. J., Mushegian, A. R., Adriaenssens, E. M., Dempsey, D. M., & Davison, A. J., (2020). Changes to virus taxonomy and the statutes ratified by the *International Committee on Taxonomy of Viruses, 1*(1), 1–20.
47. Wang, J. H., Deng, P. S., Fan, Y. S., Jaw, L. J., & Liu, Y. C., (2003). Virus detection using data mining techniques. In: *IEEE 37th Annual 2003 International Carnahan Conference on Security Technology, 2003; Proceedings* (Vol. 1, No. 1, pp. 71–76). IEEE.
48. Ward, C. W., (1993). Progress towards a higher taxonomy of viruses. *Research in Virology, 144*, 419–453.
49. Westall, R. F., Perkey, M. N., & Chute, D. L., (1989). Millisecond timing on the apple MacIntosh: Updating Drexel's millitimer. *Behavior Research Methods, Instruments, & Computers, 21*(5), 540–547.
50. White, S. R., Kephart, J. O., & Chess, D. M., (1995). Computer viruses: A global perspective. In: *Proceedings of the Fifth International Virus Bulletin Conference, Boston* (pp. 185–191).
51. Williams, G., (1984). Apple macintosh computer. *Byte, 9*(2), 30–31.
52. Yadav, N., Kaur, G., Kaur, S., Vashisth, A., & Rohith, C., (2021). A complete study on malware types and detecting ransomware using API calls. In: *2021 9th International Conference on Reliability, Infocom Technologies and Optimization (Trends and Future Directions) (ICRITO)* (Vol. 1, No. 1, pp. 1–5). IEEE.
53. Zhao, D., & Wang, Y., (2008). SD-MAC: Design and synthesis of a hardware-efficient collision-free QoS-aware MAC protocol for wireless network-on-chip. *IEEE Transactions on Computers, 57*(9), 1230–1245.

CHAPTER

4 Physical Security

LEARNING OBJECTIVES

After studying this chapter, you will be able to:

- Physical threats that can compromise computer systems.
- Various physical security measures and controls applicable to computer systems.
- Vulnerabilities specific to laptops.
- Understanding of disaster recovery planning.
- The intersection of physical security and user privacy.

INTRODUCTORY EXAMPLE

Consider a situation in which a multinational firm keeps its private financial information in a centralized data center. The data center contains essential servers, storage devices, and networking equipment that are vital for day-to-day operations. The firm allocates substantial resources towards implementing firewalls, encryption, and cybersecurity technologies to effectively counteract digital attacks. However, despite having strong cybersecurity measures in place, an unpredictable power surge occurs as a result of a nearby lightning strike, leading to a substantial electrical surge that harms the servers and corrupts crucial financial records. This incident not only underscores the system's susceptibility to physical risks but also underscores the significance of comprehensive security measures.

Computer systems are exposed to substantial hazards from physical risks such as power surges, fires, illegal use, theft, spying, and natural disasters. It is crucial to comprehend and deal with these hazards by implementing appropriate physical security measures.

UNIT INTRODUCTION

When computer security is discussed, typical associations include viruses and various network-related security concerns, such as privacy breaches, identity theft, and securing sensitive data transmitted across networks. Computer security covers a range of topics, including protecting computer equipment against physical threats like fire, theft, or flood. Physical protection of sensitive information is also crucial for ensuring its integrity and availability. Understanding and implementing robust physical security measures is essential for reducing the risks of potential threats that may compromise the safety, integrity, and availability of vital information. This chapter provides a concise analysis of diverse topics related to physical security (Weingart, 2000).

4.1. PHYSICAL THREATS

→Learning Objectives

- Identify various physical threats to computer systems.
- Recognize the potential impact of physical threats on data integrity.
- Understand principles of security management.

The following sections illustrate numerous physical hazards that can compromise the security of computer systems.

4.1.1. Surges in Electrical Power

Surges in electrical power may burn out the computer's electronic components and are frequently caused by lightning. To address this issue, an uninterruptible power supply (UPS) is utilized as a solution. This device produces a clean output signal while regulating the incoming voltage. The UPS adjusts the voltage if it exceeds the acceptable level. In the event of a voltage drop, the UPS utilizes its internal battery to provide power to the computer for a short period of time, sufficient to either shut it down (typically for a home computer) or activate a generator (usually for a large installation, such as a hospital or phone exchange) (Heartfield et al., 2018).

4.1.2. Physical Security of Computer Facilities

Even the most effective virus prevention software cannot prevent a personal computer from being stolen. Instead, it can only mitigate the damage caused by computer viruses and other malicious programs. Therefore, safeguarding the locations where computers and computer data are stored is the initial step in computer security. In an industrial environment, this issue is particularly critical. Many businesses can suffer significant losses if their computers are compromised, especially if their vital data is lost or destroyed. Damage can occur accidentally, such as from a fire, power outage, or malfunctioning air conditioner, or intentionally, caused by a criminal or disgruntled employee (Rasmussen et al., 2013).

Protecting computer systems physically is the solution to ward off physical threats. An alarm system and an uninterrupted power supply (UPS) are essential components for homes. For businesses, it is important to have a secure computer room with card-operated locks, strong doors, monitored access, security cameras, and an automatic fire system, preferably using gas instead of water. Unconventional entrance points such as air conditioning ducts and attics also require extra caution. In modern office buildings, each floor typically has a sizable roof above the ceiling, which can be utilized by someone to gain access to a safe room. Therefore, it is necessary to protect these areas. Wide air conditioning ducts can also serve as entry points, so they should be protected by thick screens. Other essentials include emergency lighting, fire-resistant storage bins for documents and drives, and staff training (Goldin et al., 2009).

4.1.3. Fire

Water is traditionally used to extinguish fires. However, when it comes to electronic systems, using water can cause more harm to the equipment and structures than the fire itself. In the past, Halon was utilized to put out fires in delicate areas, but it was later discovered that this contributed to the depletion of the ozone layer in the atmosphere. Nowadays, certain fluids that resemble water but evaporate quickly are being used as modern substitutes for both Halon and water (Cowan & Gaskins, 2006).

One type of damage that can result from a fire is heat. Smoke and soot particles associated with fires can exacerbate the situation by causing damage to removable drives, compromising the delicate mechanics of optical and magnetic disk drives, and contaminating the electrical connections in keyboards. A notable example is the violent eruption of Mount St. Helens in 1980, where volcanic ash destroyed computer equipment located far from the peak (Ahmad et al., 2018).

4.1.4. Theft

Theft deserves special attention because smaller and lightweight computers become easy targets for theft. In law enforcement, a school of thought believes one should think like a thief to catch them. People hear about skilled hackers who create malware and viruses, but even an naive computer thief may do great damage because when a computer is stolen, all of its data is lost. Such data could be sensitive and private; replacing it could be costly and time-consuming. One should remember that computer criminals frequently use a basic brute-force strategy, i.e., just slip inside, collect everything, and leave immediately (Kim et al., 2022).

4.1.5. Electronic Locks or Keys

When implementing physical identification devices or electronic locks and keys to limit access to specific areas, a facility should consider tailgating or piggybacking. A thief might stand at a locked door, waiting for the door to open while pretending to be an employee and possibly clutching disks, paper, or other harmless-looking objects in both hands (Monday et al., 2018).

Such an issue can be avoided with a guard, but this fix is costly. Installing a mantrap or perhaps a turnstile is an alternative. The latter device is a two-door entryway, meaning a person cannot enter or leave a restricted area without passing through both doors. A person must open door B to reach the restricted room after going through door A which leads to the mantrap. The key idea is that door B will not open unless door A is completely shut. A potential layout for a safe and secure computer installation is shown in Figure 4.1 (Bonekeh&Bonekeh, 2016).

The operators' room, located in area 2, has a mantrap-controlled access system that allows entry to the exterior and the other rooms. The network router room facilitates access to the processor room (area 4), making it easier to maintain transparency. Area 5, which houses the disk and tape drives, is maintained at a higher level of security due to its limited access to area 4. This is significant due to the numerous mechanical components in such drives. A rotating platform facilitates simple access to cassettes and disks stored in area 6. Area 7 is a storage space for documents, paperwork, and additional components (Churi et al., 2016).

Additionally, the printers, binders, copiers, and collators are contained within area 8 to isolate their noise and prevent the dispersion of paper particles. The loading dock (area 9) is the only region compromising security due to its additional external entry point. Nevertheless, an exterior door is crucial for emergencies, exemplifying the conciliation between security and convenience (Koprda & Magdin, 2016).

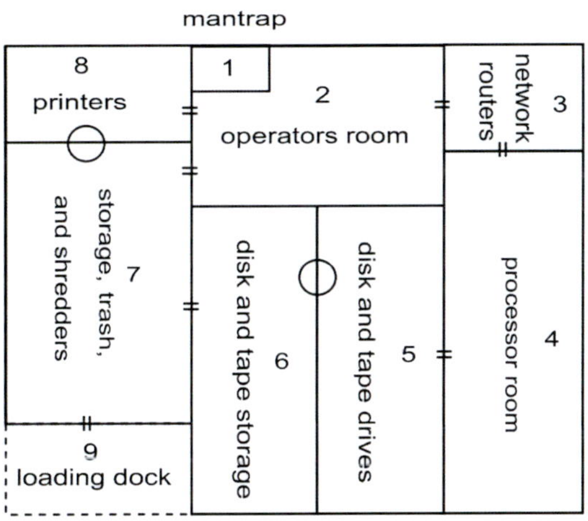

Figure 4.1. Illustration of a design for computer installation (Source: David Salomon, Creative Commons License).

4.1.6. Magnetic Fields

Hard disks utilize magnetic storage technology. The data is stored in tiny magnetic dots on the disk, making it susceptible to magnetic fields. CDs and DVDs, on the other hand, utilize optical storage technology and are resistant to magnetic fields. Empirical evidence demonstrates that carrying a small magnet in one's pocket and entering a computer room is unlikely to cause damage to data storage disks (Guri et al., 2019). However, more powerful magnetic fields can indeed harm magnetic storage. In the 1960s, there was a computer tape storage room where tapes frequently degraded. It took several months before someone noticed that the issue exclusively impacted the tapes stored on the lower shelves. It was discovered that the floor was regularly cleaned with a powerful vacuum cleaner that specifically affected those tapes (Guri, 2021).

4.1.7. User Tracking

Consider a facility equipped with numerous computers and a large workforce, where a user can execute a task on one computer, temporarily retract to attend to other matters, and then transition to the closest computer to carry out another task. An excellent example is a medical facility where physicians and nurses actively attend to patients and consistently update their medical records. Another situation involves a laboratory where workers conduct tests, such as blood or forensic tests, and a worker must input the test findings into a computer. Maintaining a record of the employee, computer, time, and purpose of test usage in such a scenario is crucial. The simplest solution is to assign a password to each user. The user must authenticate themselves on the computer, complete an activity, and log off. However, in the hospital scenario, emergencies frequently arise, and such a technique is time-consuming and impractical (Oberle et al., 2003).

4.1.8. Physical Protection of Data

Typically, data is stored on devices that are susceptible to damage or destruction. Paper, magnetic disks, CDs, and DVDs are vulnerable to fire, magnetic fields, and scratches. Even when stored in optimal conditions, information saved on such devices degrades over time. Therefore, it is necessary to implement physical protection methods to secure data. One effective method is regularly creating backups of critical information to ensure that a recent copy is readily available (Clark, 1988). An ideal setup for a home computer would involve having two external storage devices, such as disks or rewritable CDs or DVDs. One should be stored at home or in the office, while the other should be kept in a separate location. This approach ensures that a recent version of the data, no older than one week, is consistently stored in a distant place (Ahmed et al., 2019).

4.1.9. Spying

Spying is another concern to consider. While spyware is a significant threat, individuals can also engage in classic spying. It is unlikely that a culprit would secretly look into the window of a neighbor's residence at night to observe a computer screen displaying passwords, bank statements, or illicit images. However, such behavior is not uncommon among certain individuals (Wettering, 2001). The existence of corporate hacking and government spying is undeniable. Commercial enterprises often resort to spying on their competitors as a means to remain operational, robust, and competitive. Surveillance of computer users can be accomplished using methods such as hacking, observing someone's activities from close proximity, discreetly observing through a small opening, installing a discreet security camera, implanting spyware into a computer system, and employing other similar techniques (Citron, 2015).

4.1.10. Data Integrity

Bits are the fundamental units of digital data. Text, images, sound, and movies can be scanned and transformed into binary code consisting of zeros and ones. During the process of data storage, whether it is in memory, on a storage device, or when it is being sent over a communication line, there is a possibility that the bits may get corrupted. Maintaining the original value of each bit is known as data integrity, which is a fundamental part of computer security (Sivathanu et al., 2005).

4.1.11. Principles of Security Management

Implementing three fundamental principles may reduce the security risks of staff present in a large computer facility. The separation of duties is arguably the most crucial aspect of the three. This approach, utilized by numerous espionage, counterintelligence, and covert agencies, dictates that employees should only be granted the essential knowledge and data required to execute their responsibilities. If employees are unaware of anything, they cannot reveal or leak that information to others. The second principle involves frequently rotating staff. It is necessary to periodically assign an individual to various shifts, work partners, and jobs (Poore, 1999). Furthermore, those in security-related roles must be obligated to take regular annual vacations (Dhillon & Backhouse, 2000).

The third principle of security management is assigning each security-related work to an employee and verifying its completion by another individual. Adopting this approach means no task is exclusively assigned to a single individual. This idea enables one individual to identify errors (and engage in sabotaging) committed by another. While it may decrease the overall efficiency, it enhances security (Sandhu & Jojodia, 1991).

PRACTICE PROBLEM

1. The corporation encounters regular power surges in its workplace, posing a threat of harm to computer systems. There are 20 computers linked to the main power source. Every computer needs a power source with a capacity of 350 watts. Determine the minimum aggregate power rating required for surge protectors to ensure the protection of these PCs.

SOLUTION TO PRACTICE PROBLEM

1. Total power required = Number of computers × Power supply per computer
   Total power = 20 computers × 350W = 7000W or 7kW

   Therefore, the minimum total power rating needed for surge protectors is 7kW.

4.2. LAPTOP SECURITY

→Learning Objectives

- Understand the physical threats to laptop security
- Identify precautions to secure a laptop

Laptop devices are genuinely portable and have the potential to enhance an individual's efficiency. Unfortunately, they also enhance the appetite of intruders. One may have wondered why such high attention is directed towards their laptop when they carry it in public. It is widely known, often through personal experience, that one prevalent reason is that individuals perceive laptops as desirable objects to steal. Securing a laptop is a matter of physical computer security (Dimkov et al., 2010).

An exceptionally secure approach would be to attach the laptop to the wrist, effectively creating a symbiotic bond. While this technique is highly secure, it is also inconvenient, particularly during meals and restroom breaks, and may be dismissed by most laptop users. An effective measure would be to secure the laptop to a substantial and immovable item, typically a desk, using a robust lock such as a bicycle lock. However, ensuring that the lock is set to a random combination, rather than a predictable number like 123, 666, or any other easily guessed sequence, is crucial (Saarinen, 2004; Sharma et al., 2017). Certain software developers provide theft tracking or tracing software bundled with a service that facilitates tracking stolen computers, regardless of whether they are laptops or not. Users acquire the software, proceed with the installation, and provide an email address for reporting purposes. Upon each computer startup or reset, a secret message containing the computer's current IP address is transmitted to the specified destination. In the event of the computer being stolen, the thief would likely connect to the Internet, transmitting its new IP address to the specified email address. Subsequently, the software manufacturer and law enforcement agencies are alerted and attempt to trace the computer's location based on its IP address (Burnett et al., 2011).

The following safety measures can help ensure the safety and security of your computer:

a) Use an electric engraving pen to write your name and permanent contact information (excluding social security number and address) on the computer case. This can deter thieves from stealing your computer, as it becomes more difficult for them to sell a marked system. While car parts are often stolen for resale, computer parts are typically inexpensive and less attractive to thieves (Mekus, 1993).

b) If you carry your laptop in a distinctive or eye-catching case, it may attract unwanted attention. Consider using a more discreet case when traveling.

c) When driving, place the laptop on the passenger side floor and cover it with a towel or cloth. This location provides a more comfortable temperature inside the car and helps conceal the laptop from potential onlookers. However, it is generally not advisable to leave a computer unattended in a car for an extended period, as even low-temperature environments can cause heat buildup (Chin et al., 2012).

d) When traveling by air, always bring your laptop with you as carry-on luggage. Avoid checking it in with your other belongings. Be aware of airport scams where thieves may attempt to trick passengers at the X-ray checkpoint and steal their bags.

e) The administrator user of the computer can disable the option to boot the computer from a CD or floppy disk in certain versions of the Windows operating system (this can be done through the CMOS setup program). In order for the thief to successfully start the computer after stealing it, the hard drive would need to be replaced (Kepczyk, 1997).

4.3. DISASTER RECOVERY PLANNING

→Learning Objectives

- Understand the significance of disaster recovery plan
- Comprehend the steps of a comprehensive disaster recovery plan

Any organization, whether commercial, non-profit, or government, needs a disaster recovery strategy or plan. It outlines the actions needed to restore services and technological capabilities following an interruption or disaster. This kind of plan aims to lessen the effect that a catastrophic incident will have on the company.

The plan's specifics vary depending on the type of organization and the emergency, but they must address the following organizational components:

a) **Operation:** The strategy should cover the organization's continuous operations. There may be times during some emergencies when the organization cannot function; however, those incidents should be reduced.

b) **Reputation**: The plan should protect the organization's name, trademark, brand, goods, and image.

c) **Confidence:** A carefully considered plan must boost the organization's credibility with its staff, customers, investors, and business partners (Fallara, 2004).

Developing such a plan consists of the following key steps:

i. The fundamental elements of the company, including data, real estate, equipment, and human resources, should be listed and assigned monetary values.

ii. Once the fundamental elements have been determined, they should be prioritized, and qualified staff members should be allocated to each area. These individuals should implement the recovery plan and document plan details for their assigned area.

iii. After implementation, the plan must be shared with every employee and regularly practiced and rehearsed. Management should allocate a day several times a year to simulate a specific incident and execute the recovery plan as accurately as possible.

A thoroughly planned and practiced strategy provides peace of mind and enables a swift and complete recovery from calamities (Hawkins et al., 2000).

4.4. PRIVACY PROTECTION

→Learning Objectives

- Understand how physical security measures contribute to maintaining user privacy in computer systems.

These days, with the advent of a range of computers, massive databases, the Internet, and e-commerce, computer users worry about their privacy being compromised. Experts in networking and communications concur that material uploaded online cannot be removed since several copies are created nearly instantly. Search engines find almost anything on the Internet, whether small or large, beneficial or evil, and they copy, mirror, and preserve it for themselves and other entities (Chen & Zhao, 2012). This section discusses two methods of maintaining privacy: the first relies on deception, and the second modifies a random variable.

Marketers and social media experts frequently offer free materials and resources for collecting personal data of individuals, such as email addresses and Facebook IDs. However, it is unlikely that anyone would disclose their household income for such incentives. Nevertheless, many individuals are willing to provide details about their online purchasing preferences in exchange for a free song or a significant amount of free disk space on a business's computer (Tavani & Moor, 2001).

To avoid sharing personal information, one can create an email address using a false name, address, income bracket, birth year, and profession. This temporary email account can be used for a period of time before deleting the fake personal information, canceling the email account, and repeating the entire process again. It is worth noting that the (fictitious) salary level is an exception, as marketers may use it to send users product offers. Declaring a high income may result in receiving offers for expensive goods, while a low income may lead to receiving numerous inexpensive but often useless products (Bygrave, 2004). Statistics reveal that humans are not very good at lying. One effective method for selecting a fictitious identity and address is to utilize a people search tool such as Intelius, a paid service. Begin by searching for the surname Smith. Then, randomly choose from the numerous first names that appear. Next, search for the first names John or Jane and randomly select from the list of surnames. Finally, search for a street name in a town and choose a non-existent number. This approach to gathering information appears credible and does not pose any risks (Young & Quan, 2013).

Alternatively, when purchasing a product, a registration card is typically included that requests personal information such as name, address, age (or age group), family income, and more. To preserve the product's warranty, individuals often register online or complete and mail the form. However, people frequently provide false personal information due to concerns about privacy (Solove & Hoofnagle, 2006; Bettini & Riboni, 2015). Nevertheless, the product manufacturer is interested in obtaining the statistical distribution of users' ages, including the number of users who are 18 years old, 19 years old, and so on (Feng et al., 2019).

SUMMARY

- This chapter discusses the importance of physical security in computer systems. Physical security plays a crucial role in safeguarding computer systems from potential threats that could compromise data integrity, system availability, and overall security.
- To protect against hardware damage caused by unregulated power fluctuations, it is necessary to have robust fire detection systems and comprehensive disaster recovery plans in place. These measures help safeguard the physical infrastructure and data from fire-related harm.
- To prevent theft and unauthorized access to valuable equipment or sensitive data, it is important to implement security measures such as locks, alarms, biometric systems, and security guards. Additionally, physical security measures like server enclosures, safe cabinets, and data encryption provide protection against theft or unauthorized manipulation.
- Implementing strategies that include encryption, robust password restrictions, disabling remote access, installing tracking software, and taking physical security measures (such as locks) is crucial for ensuring the security of laptops and mobile devices.
- Developing thorough disaster recovery plans that encompass data backup procedures, off-site storage, and frequent testing guarantees uninterrupted corporate operations in the event of physical calamities.

MULTIPLE CHOICE QUESTIONS

1. **What is the primary purpose of physical security in computer systems?**
   a) Enhancing network speed
   b) Protecting against software bugs
   c) Safeguarding against physical threats to hardware and data
   d) Ensuring high-speed internet connections
2. **Which of the following is NOT considered a physical threat to computer systems?**
   a) Fire
   b) Unauthorized access
   c) Encryption protocols
   d) Electrical power surges
3. **What is a critical element in a comprehensive disaster recovery plan for computer systems?**
   a) Avoiding data backups
   b) Regularly testing the recovery plan
   c) Storing all data on a single server
   d) Using outdated hardware for recovery

4. How does compliance with data protection regulations relate to physical security?
   a) It doesn't affect physical security measures
   b) Compliance ensures the physical security of servers only
   c) Compliance helps in maintaining user privacy by requiring physical access controls.
   d) Compliance primarily focuses on network encryption

REVIEW QUESTIONS

1. Discuss the potential physical threats to computer systems and their impact on data integrity and system availability.
2. What are the primary strategies to protect against electrical power surges in computer systems?
3. Outline at least three physical security measures to prevent unauthorized access to sensitive equipment or data centers.
4. What elements should be included in a comprehensive disaster recovery plan for computer systems?

Answers to Multiple Questions

1. (c) 2. (c) 3. (b) 4. (c)

REFERENCES

1. Ahmad, Y. K. M., AlMajali, A., Ghalyon, S. A., Dweik, W., & Mohd, B. J., (2018). Analyzing cyber-physical threats on robotic platforms. *Sensors, 18*(5), 1643.
2. Ahmed, A., Krishnan, V. V., Foroutan, S. A., Touhiduzzaman, M., Rublein, C., Srivastava, A., & Suresh, S., (2019). Cyber physical security analytics for anomalies in transmission protection systems. *IEEE Transactions on Industry Applications, 55*(6), 6313–6323.
3. Bettini, C., & Riboni, D., (2015). Privacy protection in pervasive systems: State of the art and technical challenges. *Pervasive and Mobile Computing, 17*, 159–174.
4. Bonekeh, B., & Bonekeh, B. G., (2016). *The Use of Electronic Code Locks for the SECURITY of Homes and Properties, 1*(1), 1–20.
5. Burnett, R. D., Friedman, M., & Rodriguez, Jr. R. P., (2011). Managing laptop security. *Journal of Corporate Accounting & Finance, 22*(5), 53–61.
6. Bygrave, L. A., (2004). Privacy protection in a global context—A comparative overview. *Scandinavian Studies in Law, 47*(2004), 319–348.
7. Chen, D., & Zhao, H., (2012). Data security and privacy protection issues in cloud computing. In: *2012 International Conference on Computer Science and Electronics Engineering* (Vol. 1, pp. 647–651). IEEE.

8. Chin, E., Felt, A. P., Sekar, V., & Wagner, D., (2012). Measuring user confidence in smartphone security and privacy. In: *Proceedings of the Eighth Symposium on Usable Privacy and Security* (Vol. 1, No. 1, pp. 1–16).
9. Churi, A., Bhat, A., Mohite, R., & Churi, P. P., (2016). E-zip: An electronic lock for secured system. In: *2016 IEEE International Conference on Advances in Electronics, Communication and Computer Technology (ICAECCT)* (Vol. 1, No. 1, pp. 45–49). IEEE.
10. Citron, D. K., (2015). Spying Inc. *Wash. & Lee L. Rev., 72*, 1243.
11. Clark, A. J., (1988). Physical protection of cryptographic devices. In: *Advances in Cryptology—EUROCRYPT'87: Workshop on the Theory and Application of Cryptographic Techniques Amsterdam, The Netherlands, Proceedings 6* (pp. 83–93). Springer Berlin Heidelberg.
12. Cowan, C., & Gaskins, C., (2006). Monitoring physical threats in the data center. *Buildings, 100*(12), 26.
13. Dhillon, G., & Backhouse, J., (2000). Technical opinion: Information system security management in the new millennium. *Communications of the ACM, 43*(7), 125–128.
14. Dimkov, T., Pieters, W., & Hartel, P., (2010). Laptop theft: A case study on the effectiveness of security mechanisms in open organizations. In: *Proceedings of the 17th ACM Conference on Computer and Communications Security* (Vol. 1, No. 1, (pp. 666–668).
15. Duggineni, S., (2023). Impact of controls on data integrity and information systems. *Science and Technology, 13*(2), 29–35.
16. Fallara, P., (2004). Disaster recovery planning. *IEEE Potentials, 23*(5), 42–44.
17. Feng, Q., He, D., Zeadally, S., Khan, M. K., & Kumar, N., (2019). A survey on privacy protection in blockchain system. *Journal of Network and Computer Applications, 126*, 45–58.
18. Goldin, P. R., Manber, T., Hakimi, S., Canli, T., & Gross, J. J., (2009). Neural bases of social anxiety disorder: Emotional reactivity and cognitive regulation during social and physical threat. *Archives of General Psychiatry, 66*(2), 170–180.
19. Guri, M., (2021). Magneto: Covert channel between air-gapped systems and nearby smartphones via CPU-generated magnetic fields. *Future Generation Computer Systems, 115*, 115–125.
20. Guri, M., Zadov, B., & Elovici, Y., (2019). Odini: Escaping sensitive data from faraday-caged, air-gapped computers via magnetic fields. *IEEE Transactions on Information Forensics and Security, 15*, 1190–1203.
21. Hawkins, S. M., Yen, D. C., & Chou, D. C., (2000). Disaster recovery planning: A strategy for data security. *Information Management & Computer Security, 8*(5), 222–230.
22. Heartfield, R., Loukas, G., Budimir, S., Bezemskij, A., Fontaine, J. R., Filippoupolitis, A., & Roesch, E., (2018). A taxonomy of cyber-physical threats and impact in the smart home. *Computers & Security, 78*, 398–428.

23. Horney, J., Nguyen, M., Salvesen, D., Tomasco, O., & Berke, P., (2016). Engaging the public in planning for disaster recovery. *International Journal of Disaster Risk Reduction, 17*, 33–37.
24. Isaak, J., & Hanna, M. J., (2018). User data privacy: Facebook, Cambridge Analytica, and privacy protection. *Computer, 51*(8), 56–59.
25. Kepczyk, R. H., (1997). Laptop security for CPAs. *The CPA Journal, 67*(11), 85.
26. Kim, S., Park, K. J., & Lu, C., (2022). A survey on network security for cyber–physical systems: From threats to resilient design. *IEEE Communications Surveys & Tutorials, 24*(3), 1534–1573.
27. Koprda, Š., & Magdin, M., (2016). Implementation of innovative technologies in the fields of electronic locks. *TELKOMNIKA (Telecommunication Computing Electronics and Control), 14*(4), 1329–1337.
28. Liu, B., Yu, X. L., Chen, S., Xu, X., & Zhu, L., (2017). Blockchain based data integrity service framework for IoT data. In: *2017 IEEE International Conference on Web Services (ICWS),* (Vol. 1, No. 1, pp. 468–475). IEEE.
29. Mekus, B., (1993). Laptop security. *Internal Auditor, 50*(1), 56–58.
30. Monday, H. N., Li, J. P., Nneji, G. U., Ukwuoma, C. C., Dike, I. D., & Nneii, R. I., (2018). Design of an improved cost effective electronic locking system. In: *2018 IEEE 9th Annual Information Technology, Electronics and Mobile Communication Conference (IEMCON)* (Vol. 1, No. 1, pp. 493–499). IEEE.
31. Nepal, S., Chen, S., Yao, J., & Thilakanathan, D., (2011). DIaaS: Data integrity as a service in the cloud. In: *2011 IEEE 4th International Conference on Cloud Computing* (Vol. 1, No. 1, pp. 308–315). IEEE.
32. Oberle, D., Berendt, B., Hotho, A., & Gonzalez, J., (2003). Conceptual user tracking. In: *Advances in Web Intelligence: First International AtlanticWeb Intelligence Conference, AWIC 2003, Madrid, Spain; Proceedings 1* (pp. 155–164). Springer Berlin Heidelberg.
33. Poore, R. S., (1999). Generally accepted system security principles. *Information Systems Security, 8*(3), 27–77.
34. Rasmussen, C. A., Hogh, A., & Andersen, L. P., (2013). Threats and physical violence in the workplace: A comparative study of four areas of human service work. *Journal of Interpersonal Violence, 28*(13), 2749–2769.
35. Rattan, A. K., (2018). Data integrity: History, issues, and remediation of issues. *PDA Journal of Pharmaceutical Science and Technology, 72*(2), 105–116.
36. Saarinen, M. J. O., (2004). Encrypted watermarks and Linux laptop security. In: *International Workshop on Information Security Applications*, (Vol. 1, No. 1, pp. 27–38). Berlin, Heidelberg: Springer Berlin Heidelberg.
37. Sahebjamnia, N., Torabi, S. A., & Mansouri, S. A., (2015). Integrated business continuity and disaster recovery planning: Towards organizational resilience. *European Journal of Operational Research, 242*(1), 261–273.
38. Sandhu, R., & Jajodia, S., (1991). Integrity principles and mechanisms in database management systems. *Computers & Security, 10*(5), 413–427.

39. Sharma, A., Kumar, N., & Sharma, H., (2017). Infrared sensor based laptop security system to avoid theft & misuse: A patented idea. *International Journal of Advanced Research in Science and Engineering, 6*(8), 1–20.

40. Sivathanu, G., Wright, C. P., & Zadok, E., (2005). Ensuring data integrity in storage: Techniques and applications. In: *Proceedings of the 2005 ACM Workshop on Storage Security and Survivability* (Vol. 1, No. 1, pp. 26–36).

41. Solove, D. J., & Hoofnagle, C. J., (2006). A model regime of privacy protection. *U. Ill. L. Rev., 1*(1), 357.

42. Tavani, H. T., & Moor, J. H., (2001). Privacy protection, control of information, and privacy-enhancing technologies. *ACM Sigcas Computers and Society, 31*(1), 6–11.

43. Weingart, S. H., (2000). Physical security devices for computer subsystems: A survey of attacks and defenses. In: *International Workshop on Cryptographic Hardware and Embedded Systems* (Vol. 1, No. 1, pp. 302–317). Berlin, Heidelberg: Springer Berlin Heidelberg.

44. Wettering, F. L., (2001). The Internet and the spy business. *International Journal of Intelligence and Counterintelligence, 14*(3), 342–365.

45. Young, A. L., & Quan-Haase, A., (2013). Privacy protection strategies on Facebook: The Internet privacy paradox revisited. *Information, Communication & Society, 16*(4), 479–500.

CHAPTER

5 Cryptography

LEARNING OBJECTIVES

After studying this chapter, you will be able to:

- Comprehend the basic cryptography technologies.
- Identify the uses of cryptography in computer systems.
- Examine crucial factors that must be taken into account when utilizing cryptography in computer systems.
- Learn interdependencies between cryptography and other security mechanisms.

INTRODUCTORY EXAMPLE

In today's interconnected digital landscape, imagine Alice and Bob, two individuals communicating over the internet, exchanging sensitive information, such as personal identification details or financial data. However, they are aware that malicious entities could intercept and eavesdrop on their conversation, attempting to access and misuse their private information.

To secure their communication from prying eyes, Alice and Bob employ cryptographic techniques. They each possess a cryptographic key—a unique piece of information used to encrypt and decrypt their messages. Alice uses her key to encrypt her message, converting it into an unreadable format, which only Bob, possessing the corresponding decryption key, can decipher back into its original form.

This process of encryption and decryption forms the foundation of modern cryptography, providing confidentiality to the exchanged information. Additionally, they could use digital signatures—a cryptographic mechanism—to ensure the integrity and authenticity of their messages, guaranteeing that the received information is unchanged and originated from the expected source.

Cryptography plays a crucial role in securing their communication by thwarting unauthorized access and manipulation of their sensitive data. Its implementation involves various technologies and methodologies, emphasizing the importance of understanding both its fundamentals and its interdependence with other security mechanisms in computer systems.

UNIT INTRODUCTION

The field of mathematics known as cryptography utilizes the transformation of data as its foundation. It serves as an essential tool for the protection of information and is utilized in a large number of computer security-related issues. Cryptography can assist in the provision of data confidentiality and integrity, as well as electronic signatures and enhanced user authentication technologies. Consumers can obtain the benefits of modern cryptography without having to comprehend its mathematical foundations, despite the fact that modern cryptography is dependent on complex mathematics (Rivest, 1990).

The use of cryptography as a tool to meet various objectives and requirements related to computer security is covered in this chapter. It explains several particular ways in which cryptography can be used to increase security, as well as some basic principles of cryptographic technologies. The chapter also examines some of the most important issues that should be considered while utilizing cryptography in computer systems (Goldwasser & Bellare, 1996).

5.1. BASIC CRYPTOGRAPHIC TECHNOLOGIES

→Learning Objectives

- Understand the principles of symmetric and asymmetric encryption and decryption.
- Comprehend key escrow and its role in managing encryption keys.
- Recognize the advantages of combining symmetric and asymmetric encryption in hybrid cryptographic systems.

The two fundamental elements of cryptography are a key and an algorithm, often referred to as cryptographic methodology. Algorithms are complex mathematical formulas, while keys are bit strings in contemporary cryptography systems. Two parties need to use the same algorithm (or algorithms that are designed to work together) to communicate with each other. They also need to use the same key in certain situations. Many cryptographic keys (and sometimes algorithms) need to be kept private. Public key systems (also known as asymmetric systems) and secret key systems (also known as symmetric systems) are two fundamental forms of cryptography. A comparison of some major differences between public and private key systems can be seen in Table 5.1. Both types of systems have advantages and disadvantages. They are often combined to create a hybrid system that leverages the strengths of each type. To determine which type of cryptography best meets its objectives, a company must first assess its operating environment and security needs (Hellman, 2002).

Table 5.1. Different Characteristics of Public and Secret Key Systems (Source: Barbara Guttman, Creative Commons License)

Distinct Features	Secret Key Cryptography	Public Key Cryptography
Number of keys	One key	Two keys

Types of keys	Secret Key	There is a public key and a private key.
Protection of keys	Disclosure and modification.	Modification and Disclosure. Modification for private keys and public keys.
Relative speeds	Quicker	Slower.

5.1.1. Secret Key Cryptography

In secret key cryptography, data is encrypted and decrypted using a shared key that is known only to two or more individuals. Secret key cryptography, as its name suggests, depends on maintaining the key's secrecy. The security provided by cryptography is significantly diminished or removed if the key is compromised. The fundamental principle of secret key cryptography is that individuals who share a key must depend on each other to maintain its confidentiality and protect it from any modifications (Cook et al., 2005).

The most well-known secret key scheme is the Data Encryption Standard (DES), Federal Information Processing Standard (FIPS 46–2) published by NIST. Even if there have occasionally been doubts about DES's sufficiency, DES is still widely used. Currently, it is the most extensively used cryptographic system that is accessible to the public. The encryption, integrity, access control, and key management requirements are based on DES, which has been approved by the American National Standards Institute (ANSI). A secret key mechanism is also used by the FIPS 185 standard, known as the Escrowed Encryption Standard (Leighton & Micali, 1993).

5.1.2. Public Key Cryptography

Public key cryptography requires a pair of keys for each participant, while secret key cryptography relies on a single key that is shared among multiple parties. There are two keys in the pair: "public" and "private." The private key must be securely maintained and exclusively known by its owner, whereas the public key can be openly shared with third parties. Nevertheless, both keys must be protected against any form of modification.

When parties who want to communicate cannot trust one another nor have a common key, public key cryptography comes into use. Numerous public key cryptography systems exist. RSA was one of the original public key systems and offers a wide range of security services (Garfinkel, 1996).

5.1.3. Hybrid Cryptographic Systems

Both public key cryptography and secret key cryptography have benefits and drawbacks. Despite the fact that neither secret key cryptography nor public key cryptography requires users to share a common key, the former is far faster than the latter. Secret key cryptography solutions can achieve a speed that is 1,000–10,000 times faster than public key cryptography.

Together, public and secret key cryptography can be used by a computer system to maximize their benefits and minimize their drawbacks, with each playing a specific role. Data encryption is the usual use for secret key cryptography due to its speed advantage. Public key cryptography has less resource-intensive applications, such as signing messages or encrypting the keys employed in secret-key cryptography (Premarathne et al., 2016).

5.1.4. Key Escrow

Due to its ability to offer robust encryption, cryptography can hinder the government's efforts to conduct electronic surveillance. For instance, using strong encryption to encrypt a phone conversation makes a court-approved wiretap ineffective. To address this, the US federal government has implemented voluntary key escrow encryption to meet government requirements and ensure privacy. This technology allows strong encryption to be used and allows the government to obtain decryption keys held by escrow agents with proper legal authorization. The FIPS 185 standard, also known as the Escrowed Encryption Standard, was published by NIST. The voluntary key escrow approach of the Federal Government involves segmenting the decryption keys and distributing them among multiple escrow authorities. To decode the data, both keys must be obtained; having only one part of the key is not enough (Denning & Branstad, 1996).

5.2. USES OF CRYPTOGRAPHY

→Learning Objectives

- Identify methods to ensure data confidentiality using encryption techniques.
- Comprehend how encryption protects sensitive information from unauthorized access.
- Understand how cryptographic digital signatures help maintain data integrity.
- Comprehend how cryptographic techniques authenticate users and prevent repudiation of actions.

Data within and outside of computer systems is protected through the use of cryptography. Encryption is often the sole method for securing data that is unrelated to computer systems. Within a computer system, data is commonly safeguarded by implementing logical and physical access controls, which can be further enhanced by employing encryption. However, when data is transmitted through communication networks or stored on another individual's device, the access controls of the originator cannot provide protection. Cryptography offers a solution by ensuring the security of data, even after it has been transmitted by the sender (Bellovin, 1998).

5.2.1. Data Encryption

Encryption is a highly effective method for achieving cost-efficient data secrecy. Encryption is the transformation of comprehensible data, referred to as plaintext, into a form that is incomprehensible, known as ciphertext. Decryption is used to reverse the process. After the information is encrypted, the ciphertext is naturally secure and does not need any extra security to prevent leakage. However, if the ciphertext is changed, it will not be decrypted correctly (Davis, 1978).

Data encryption can be achieved by both public key cryptography and secret key cryptography, even though not all public key methods support data encryption. Data is encrypted with a key to apply a secret key algorithm. To decrypt the data, the same key needs to be used. Any party may encrypt a message using any other party's public key when public key cryptography is employed; however, only the party with the matching private key may decrypt and read the message. Larger amounts of data are usually encrypted using secret key encryption since it is usually faster (Nadeem & Javed, 2005).

5.2.2. Integrity

The human ability to visually analyze data in computer systems for indications of erasure, addition, or alteration is frequently limited. Even if the process of scanning were feasible, the person might lack the means to determine the accurate information. For instance, the word "do" can be altered to "do not," or the amount of $1,000 can be modified to $10,000. Having an automated method to identify both deliberate and accidental alterations of data is highly desirable.

While error-detecting codes are not new to communications protocols—they have been around for a while—they are especially good at spotting and fixing accidental changes. Adversaries can overcome them. Cryptography is capable of accurately identifying both deliberate and accidental alterations; nevertheless, it does not protect against file modifications. To ensure integrity, cryptography using public key and secret key techniques can be used. While the more flexible public key methods of today may be superior to the more traditional secret key method, technology for secret key integrity verification has been successfully integrated into many applications (McFall, 1987).

A message authentication code (MAC) is calculated from the data and added to it when using secret-key cryptography. Anyone with the correct secret key can recalculate the MAC to guarantee the data's integrity in the future. When the verifier compares the new and old Message Authentication Codes (MACs), and they match, it means that no unauthorized party has changed the data. To ensure data integrity, a standardized procedure for generating a Message Authentication Code (MAC) is defined in FIPS 113, Computer Data Authentication.

By using secure hashes and public key signatures, public key cryptography guarantees integrity. A hash function used in cryptography is utilized to produce a message digest. A message digest, also known as a hash, is a truncated copy of the message that is updated anytime the original message is altered. The hash is then verified using a private key. Anyone may recalculate the hash and utilize the corresponding public key to confirm the integrity of the message (Taylor & Gaita, 1981).

5.2.3. Electronic Signatures

Computer systems of today store and handle large amounts of paper-based documents in electronic format. Electronic papers allow for quicker processing and transmission, which increases productivity. Nonetheless, a written signature has historically been used to show approval of a paper document. Therefore, what is required is an electronic signature that has the same legal standing as a written signature and can be recognized as such. As with written signatures, cryptography can offer a way to associate a document with a specific individual in addition to integrity protection. For electronic signatures, public key cryptography is frequently easier to employ than secret key encryption (Parmentier, 2000). Cryptographic signatures provide strong evidence that the message was signed by a particular key and has not been changed. On the other hand, analogous functions are served by systems other than cryptography-based electronic signatures. These systems offer varying degrees of assurance regarding the message's origin, message integrity verification, or both.

a) When a message is transmitted across a network, such as the Internet, the message's physical route and source are documented as components of the message. These can be inspected either manually or digitally to determine the source of a transmission.

b) The network provider can verify the authenticity and integrity of messages sent through a third-party network by confirming their origin and ensuring they have not been tampered with.

c) By returning an acknowledgment statement, the recipient of an electronic message can verify the message's origin and substance.

d) For future reference, audit trails can monitor the transmission of messages and their contents (Wehling et al., 2007).

To guarantee security, simply taking a digital picture of a written signature is insufficient. This kind of digital written signature would be easy to replicate from one electronic document to another without any way to confirm its authenticity. On the other hand, electronic signatures are unique to the message to which they are attached, and copying them to another document will not validate them (McCullagh et al., 1998).

5.2.3.1. Secret Key Electronic Signatures

Secret key-encrypted message authentication codes (MACs) can be utilized for the implementation of an electronic signature. It is possible for one party to assume that the other has signed the document if they both possess a shared secret key and the receiving party verifies the data using the MAC generated with the shared key. However, this assumption relies on the presence of mutual trust between the two parties. Consequently, the use of a MAC not only ensures data integrity but also provides an electronic signature. Even in situations where suspicion exists between the parties, an electronic signature can be achieved by incorporating additional measures such as keynotarization and key characteristics (Rivest et al., 1978).

5.2.3.2. Public Key Electronic Signatures

Digital signatures are another form of electronic signature that is created using public key cryptography. By applying the private key of the originator to the data, it can be electronically signed. The private key is then converted into a "hash" or "message digest" that contains an edited version of the data instead of the complete set, in order to expedite the process. The generated digital signature can be either broadcasted or kept alongside the data. Anyone with access to the signer's public key can verify the signature. This feature is particularly useful when distributing software versions that have been signed and certified as virus-free. Recipients can verify the continued virus-free status of the software. If the signature is verified correctly and the signer is the owner of the public key, the verifier can be confident that the data has not been altered after signing (Boudrez, 2007).

The National Institute of Standards and Technology (NIST) has established guidelines for digital signatures and secure hashes in two publications: FIPS 186, which outlines the Digital Signature Standard, and FIPS 180, which defines the Secure Hash Standard. These standards are intended for use by the federal government.

5.2.4. User Authentication

Integrating crypto can enhance security in user auth ops. Crypto is the foundation for advanced auth techniques. Auth can be achieved by proving familiarity with a crypto key, instead of transmitting passwords over an unsecured network. By using these techniques, a single-use password that is not susceptible to eavesdropping can be used. Auth can employ either a private or a public crypto key. Crypto is the practice of securing communication by converting info into an intricate code that is difficult to read without the correct key (Das, 2009).

PRACTICE PROBLEM

1. A company uses a symmetric encryption algorithm and needs to securely share a key with five different employees. If the key length is 128 bits, each employee will receive 25 bits if the key is divided equally among them?

SOLUTION TO PRACTICE PROBLEM

Total key length = 128 bits

Number of employees = 5

To divide the key equally among employees:

Bits per employee= Total key length/ Number of employee

Bits per employee= 128/5

Each employee will receive approximately 25 bits of the key.

5.3. IMPLEMENTATION ISSUES

→Learning Objectives

- Identify challenges related to key generation, storage, distribution, and revocation.
- Comprehend the security of cryptographic modules.
- Understand how cryptography is implemented in networks.

This section examines many crucial factors that must be taken into account when utilizing (e.g., creating, executing, incorporating) cryptography in a computer system.

5.3.1. Selecting Implementation Standards and Design

Numerous standards have been set by NIST and other organizations to facilitate the development, application, and use of cryptography, as well as its integration with automated systems. By adhering to these established criteria, firms can reduce expenses and safeguard their technology investments. Standards provide approved answers from a large segment of society and have been examined by experts in related subjects. Standards promote compatibility among equipment manufactured by different companies, allowing businesses to choose cost-efficient equipment from a range of options. When managers and users of computer systems decide to adopt cryptography, they must select from a variety of standards. The choice should be based on a cost-effectiveness analysis, considering prevailing trends in standard acceptance and interoperability requirements. Additionally, it is crucial to thoroughly evaluate each standard's relevance to the company and intended use. The Data Encryption Standard and the Escrowed Encryption Standard are suitable for certain applications, such as data transfer using commercial modems. Federal computer systems must comply with standards like DSS (FIPS 181) and DES (FIPS 46–2) (Lambert et al., 1998).

5.3.2. Deciding on Software vs. Hardware Implementations

Managers seeking to acquire various security products that meet a specific standard must assess the trade-offs between security, affordability, simplicity, efficiency, and ease of deployment. Cryptography can be implemented either in hardware or software. Each option has its own costs and benefits.

Typically, software is more cost-effective but slower compared to hardware. However, for extensive applications, hardware may be more cost-efficient. Additionally, software may be less secure due to its vulnerability to modifications or bypassing, unlike hardware components of the same nature. Hardware is often considered to have superior tamper resistance (Harrison & Waldron, 2008). Cryptography is often used in a hardware component, such as an electrical chip or a processor with ROM protection, but its operations are controlled by software. Integrity protection is essential for this program to ensure that the hardware device receives accurate information, including controls and data, and is not bypassed. As a result, a combination of different approaches is typically employed, even if the fundamental cryptographic techniques are implemented using physical components. Effective security requires the precise management of the entire hybrid system.

5.3.3. Managing Keys

Effective utilization of cryptography for security necessitates the proper administration of cryptographic keys. The degree of protection afforded to the encryption keys ultimately determines the security of the data protected by cryptography (Latif et al., 2020).

It is essential to safeguard all keys from being altered, while secret keys and private keys must be shielded from unwanted exposure. Key management encompasses the manual and automated methods and protocols employed during the complete life cycle of the keys. This encompasses the entire process of creating, distributing, storing, inputting, utilizing, erasing, and archiving cryptographic keys.

When using secret-key cryptography, the parties seeking to communicate should have the secret key(s) safely transferred (i.e., protected from unauthorized replacement, modification, and disclosure). This work might not be simple, depending on how many people there are and where they are located. Allocating some resources for this operation is necessary, however, using automated methods for creating and distributing cryptographic keys can reduce the costs associated with key administration. Key Management (FIPS 171) provides key management solutions for different operational scenarios using ANSI X9.17 (Chandramouli & Chokhani, 2013).

Users of public key cryptography must additionally adhere to specific key management specifications. For example, the public key of a private-public key pair must be bound to the user since the key pair is linked to (i.e., generated or held by) a particular user.

Merely sharing public keys (for example, placing them on a CD-ROM or other media) could establish robust associations between public keys and their "owners" within a limited community of users. However, when engaging in electronic business on a larger scale, involving geographically and organizationally dispersed users, a mechanism for electronically acquiring public keys with an enhanced level of confidence in their integrity and connection to individuals becomes necessary. A public key infrastructure is a framework that facilitates the linking of a key with its owner (Alohali et al., 2015).

5.3.4. Security of Cryptographic Modules

Cryptography is generally implemented in hardware, firmware, software, or a combination of these. This module encompasses the cryptographic algorithm(s), control parameters, and a temporary storage place for the key(s) utilized by the algorithm(s). Ensuring the cryptography operations effectively requires the cryptographic module to be developed, executed, and used securely. This involves safeguarding the module from any form of tampering or alteration (Pub, 1994).

5.3.5. Applying Cryptography to Networks

When utilizing cryptography in networking applications, it is crucial to exercise increased caution and attention. The effectiveness of a cryptographic module in various applications may depend on its ability to adequately address the unique requirements imposed by network protocols and software, as well as locally attached communication devices.

Transparent protocols for communication or equipment may be necessary to ensure that encrypted data, MACs, or digital signatures are not mistaken for control information by communication hardware or software. In order to prevent confusion for the communication hardware or software, it may be necessary to format the digital signature, MAC, or encrypted data. It is imperative that cryptography adheres to the specifications established by the communication equipment without impeding the network's ability to function correctly and efficiently (Szczechowiak et al., 2009).

In a network environment, end-to-end or link encryption is employed to safeguard data. Service providers, such as data communications providers, typically handle link encryption. Link encryption is utilized to encrypt any data transmitted through a communication channel, such as a satellite connection, phone circuit, or T1 line. Communications nodes must decipher the data in order to resume routing, as connection encryption also encrypts routing data. End-to-end encryption is often managed by the end-user organization. Routing information remains accessible as data is transmitted over the network, albeit still encrypted. It is feasible to combine these two encryption schemes (Chen & Wu, 2010).

5.3.6. Complying with Export Rules

The exportation of cryptographic implementations is regulated by the United States government. Due to the consideration of multiple variables, export regulations can be quite intricate. Additionally, the field of cryptography is ever-evolving, and regulations are subject to periodic revision. Any inquiries regarding the export of a specific implementation should be directed to the appropriate legal advisor (Diffie & Landau, 2007).

5.4. INTERDEPENDENCIES

→Learning Objectives

- Understand the interplay between cryptography and access control mechanisms.
- Identify how cryptography enhances access control for securing data and resources.

This section highlights the numerous interdependencies between cryptography and other security mechanisms. Cryptography is both dependent upon and contributes to other security measures.

To prevent or detect the physical substitution or modification of the cryptographic system and its keys, it is necessary to provide physical protection for the cryptographic module. In numerous cases, such as open offices and portable laptops, the cryptography module must offer the appropriate degrees of physical protection. In alternative settings (such as steel-encased cash-issuing terminals or closed communications facilities), a cryptography module can be used safely inside a secured facility (Phillips, 1998).

Passwords that are transmitted between computers and those that are stored in computer systems can both be secured with cryptography. Moreover, to enable more robust user authentication, cryptography-based authentication methods can be employed instead of or in addition to password-based methods.

Since cryptographic software is frequently integrated into host systems, it may not always be feasible to provide strong physical protection to the host system. In such situations, logical access control can offer a means to separate the cryptographic software from other components of the host system, prevent tampering with it, and safeguard the keys from being altered or exposed. When employing these measures, it is important to ensure an equivalent level of protection as that provided by physical means (Karamkar et al., 2017).

The application of cryptography can be beneficial for audit trails. For instance, requiring signatures on audit records can help prevent their disclosure or alteration. Cryptography can also be employed to safeguard audit records stored on computer systems. Additionally, audit trails are utilized to support electronic signatures.

To effectively utilize cryptography, it is crucial to ensure the safe and correct implementation of a module. NIST maintains up-to-date validation programs for several cryptographic standards. Vendors can have their products' compliance with the standard validated through a rigorous set of tests. This type of testing increases confidence among system integrators, designers, and users that verified products adhere to recognized standards and meet specified requirements (Arner et al., 2023).

To ensure that a cryptographic system is meeting its security goals, it should be regularly monitored and audited. All parameters related to the proper functioning of the cryptographic system should be examined, and the system's functionality should be routinely checked with audited findings. It is not recommended to conduct audits on certain types of data, such as private keys or secret keys used in public key systems. However, public keys may be used in a simulated audit procedure (Todorovska et al., 2023).

SUMMARY

- This chapter provides an overview of the basic cryptographic technologies used in computer systems. Symmetric cryptography involves the use of the same secret key for both encryption and decryption. Algorithms such as AES (Advanced Encryption Standard) and DES (Data Encryption Standard) fall into this category. On the other hand, asymmetric cryptography utilizes a pair of keys: a public key for encryption and a private key for decryption. RSA, Diffie-Hellman, and Elliptic Curve Cryptography (ECC) are well-known examples.
- Furthermore, this chapter explores the various applications of cryptography. Cryptography serves to protect sensitive information from unauthorized access, ensuring the integrity of data during transmission or storage. It also verifies the identity of users or systems and prevents individuals from denying their actions in communication.
- Additionally, the chapter delves into key management, which encompasses the generation, storage, exchange, and revocation of cryptographic keys. Different cryptographic algorithms may have varying performance impacts, with some being computationally intensive. Given the constantly evolving threat landscape, it is crucial to conduct rigorous analysis and regularly update cryptographic systems to maintain security.

MULTIPLE CHOICE QUESTIONS

1. **Which encryption algorithm is commonly used for secure communication over the internet in protocols like HTTPS?**
   a) RSA
   b) DES
   c) AES
   d) None of the above
2. **What purpose does key escrow serve in cryptographic systems?**
   a) It allows for secure storage of encryption keys.
   b) It provides a method to recover lost encryption keys.
   c) It generates random cryptographic keys.
   d) It allows authorized entities to access encrypted data if needed.
3. **What does SSL/TLS primarily use to establish a secure connection between a client and a server?**
   a) Symmetric encryption
   b) Asymmetric encryption
   c) Key escrow
   d) None of the above

4. Which of the following is NOT a use of cryptography in computer systems?

a) Data Confidentiality

b) Performance Enhancement

c) Data Integrity

d) Authentication

REVIEW QUESTIONS

1. Define symmetric and asymmetric cryptography. What are the primary differences between these two encryption methods?
2. How does hybrid cryptography combine the strengths of symmetric and asymmetric encryption? Provide examples of its practical applications.
3. Explain how cryptography ensures data confidentiality, integrity, authentication, and non-repudiation in computer systems.
4. What are the performance considerations when implementing cryptographic algorithms in computer systems?

Answers to Multiple Questions

1. (c) 2. (d) 3. (a) 4. (b)

REFERENCES

1. Alohali, B. A., Kifayat, K., Shi, Q., & Hurst, W., (2015). A survey on cryptography key management schemes for smart grid. *Journal of Computer Sciences and Applications, Science and Education, 3*(3A), 27–39.
2. Arner, D. W., Ratna, T., Animashaun, S., & Bedi, J., (2023). Interdependencies in crypto ecosystems: Drivers, implications, and policy responses. *Implications and Policy Responses, 1*(1), 1–20.
3. Bellovin, S. M., (1998). Cryptography and the Internet. In: *Annual International Cryptology Conference* (Vol. 1, No. 1, pp. 46–55). Berlin, Heidelberg: Springer Berlin Heidelberg.
4. Boudrez, F., (2007). Digital signatures and electronic records. *Archival Science, 7*(2), 179–193.
5. Chandramouli, R., Iorga, M., & Chokhani, S., (2013). Cryptographic key management issues and challenges in cloud services. *Secure Cloud Computing, 1*(1), 1–30.
6. Chen, J., & Wu, J., (2010). A survey on applied cryptography in secure mobile ad hoc networks and wireless sensor networks. In: *Handbook of Research on Developments and Trends in Wireless Sensor Networks: From Principle to Practice* (Vol. 1, No. 1, pp. 262–289). IGI Global.

7. Cook, D. L., Ioannidis, J., Keromytis, A. D., & Luck, J., (2005). CryptoGraphics: Secret key cryptography using graphics cards. In: *Topics in Cryptology–CT-RSA 2005: The Cryptographers' Track at the RSA Conference 2005, San Francisco, CA, USA, Proceedings* (Vol. 1, No. 1, pp. 334–350). Springer Berlin Heidelberg.
8. Das, M. L., (2009). Two-factor user authentication in wireless sensor networks. *IEEE Transactions on Wireless Communications, 8*(3), 1086–1090.
9. Davis, R., (1978). The data encryption standard in perspective. *IEEE Communications Society Magazine, 16*(6), 5–9.
10. Denning, D. E., & Branstad, D. K., (1996). A taxonomy for key escrow encryption systems. *Communications of the ACM, 39*(3), 34–40.
11. Devi, T. R., (2013). Importance of cryptography in network security. In: *2013 International Conference on Communication Systems and Network Technologies*, (Vol. 1, No. 1, pp. 462–467). IEEE.
12. Diffie, W., & Landau, S., (2007). The export of cryptography in the 20th and the 21st centuries. In: *The History of Information Security* (Vol. 1, No. 1, pp. 725–736). Elsevier Science BV.
13. Garfinkel, S. L., (1996). Public key cryptography. *Computer, 29*(6), 101–104.
14. Goldwasser, S., & Bellare, M., (1996). Lecture notes on cryptography. *Summer Course "Cryptography and Computer Security" at MIT, 1999.*
15. Harrison, O., & Waldron, J., (2008). Practical symmetric key cryptography on modern graphics hardware. In: *USENIX Security Symposium* (Vol. 195, pp. 1–20).
16. Hellman, M. E., (2002). An overview of public key cryptography. *IEEE Communications Magazine, 40*(5), 42–49.
17. Hussain, I., Ahmed, F., Khokhar, U. M., & Anees, A., (2018). Applied cryptography and noise resistant data security. *Security and Communication Networks, 2018*, 1, 2.
18. Karmakar, R., Prasad, N., Chattopadhyay, S., Kapur, R., & Sengupta, I., (2017). A new logic encryption strategy ensuring key interdependency. In: *2017 30th International Conference on VLSI Design and 2017 16th International Conference on Embedded Systems (VLSID)* (Vol. 1, No. 1, pp. 429–434). IEEE.
19. Lalith, T., Umarani, R., & Kadharnawaz, G. M., (2010). Key management techniques for controlling the distribution and update of cryptographic keys. *International Journal of Advanced Computer Science and Applications, 1*(6), 1–20.
20. Lambert, D. M., Cooper, M. C., & Pagh, J. D., (1998). Supply chain management: Implementation issues and research opportunities. *The International Journal of Logistics Management, 9*(2), 1–20.
21. Latif, M. A., Ahmad, M. B., & Khan, M. K., (2020). A review on key management and lightweight cryptography for IoT. In: *2020 Global Conference on Wireless and Optical Technologies (GCWOT)* (Vol. 1, No. 1, pp. 1–7). IEEE.
22. Leighton, T., & Micali, S., (1993). Secret-key agreement without public-key cryptography. In: *Annual International Cryptology Conference* (Vol. 1, No. 1, pp. 456–479). Berlin, Heidelberg: Springer Berlin Heidelberg.

23. McCullagh, A., Little, P., & Caelli, W., (1998). Electronic signatures: Understand the past to develop the future. *UNSWLJ, 21*, 452.
24. McFall, L., (1987). Integrity. *Ethics, 98*(1), 5–20.
25. Nadeem, A., & Javed, M. Y., (2005). A performance comparison of data encryption algorithms. In: *2005 International Conference on Information and Communication Technologies* (Vol. 1, No. 1, pp. 84–89). IEEE.
26. Parmentier, M. A., (2000). Electronic signatures. *Colum. J. Eur. L., 6*, 251.
27. Phillips, D. J., (1998). Cryptography, secrets, and structuring of trust. *Technology and Privacy: The New Landscape* (Vol. 1, No. 1, pp. 243–276). The MIT Press, Cambridge, MA.
28. Premarathne, U., Abuadbba, A., Alabdulatif, A., Khalil, I., Tari, Z., Zomaya, A., & Buyya, R., (2016). Hybrid cryptographic access control for cloud-based EHR systems. *IEEE Cloud Computing, 3*(4), 58–64.
29. Pub, F. I. P. S., (1994). Security requirements for cryptographic modules. *FIPS PUB, 140,* 140–142.
30. Qureshi, S., Aftab, M., Bouri, E., & Saeed, T., (2020). Dynamic interdependence of cryptocurrency markets: An analysis across time and frequency. *Physica A: Statistical Mechanics and its Applications, 559*, 125077.
31. Rivest, R. L., (1990). Cryptography. In: *Algorithms and Complexity* (Vol. 1, No. 1, pp. 717–755). Elsevier.
32. Rivest, R. L., Shamir, A., & Adleman, L., (1978). A method for obtaining digital signatures and public-key cryptosystems. C*ommunications of the ACM, 21*(2), 120–126.
33. Sarkar, A., Chatterjee, S. R., & Chakraborty, M., (2021). Role of cryptography in network security. *The" Essence" of Network Security: An End-to-End Panorama, 1*(1), 103–143.
34. Szczechowiak, P., Kargl, A., Scott, M., & Collier, M., (2009). On the application of pairing based cryptography to wireless sensor networks. In: *Proceedings of the Second ACM Conference on Wireless Network Security* (Vol. 1, No. 1, pp. 1–12).
35. Taylor, G., & Gaita, R., (1981). Integrity. *Proceedings of the Aristotelian Society, Supplementary Volumes, 55*, 143–176.
36. Todorovska, A., Peshov, H., Rusevski, I., Vodenska, I., Chitkushev, L. T., & Trajanov, D., (2023). Using ML and explainable AI to understand the interdependency networks between classical economic indicators and crypto-markets. *Physica A: Statistical Mechanics and its Applications, 624*, 128900.
37. Vaz De, M. M. B., & Fluminense, C. A., (2020). A comprehensive statistical analysis of the six major crypto-currencies from August 2015 through June 2020. *Journal of Risk and Financial Management, 13*(9), 192.
38. Wehling, T. O., Balatsky, A. V., Katsnelson, M. I., Lichtenstein, A. I., Scharnberg, K., & Wiesendanger, R., (2007). Local electronic signatures of impurity states in graphene. *Physical Review B, 75*(12), 125425.

CHAPTER 6

Operating System Security

LEARNING OBJECTIVES

After studying this chapter, you will be able to:

- Understand the basic concept of operating systems.
- Learn how to protect a computer system during its operation.
- Comprehend the security of file and memory systems.
- Learn about access control systems within the file system.

INTRODUCTORY EXAMPLE

Operating systems form the foundational layer of computing systems, responsible for managing hardware resources and providing an interface for user applications. However, their critical role also makes them a prime target for security threats and vulnerabilities. Understanding operating system security is essential for safeguarding against unauthorized access, data breaches, and system compromises.

Consider a scenario where a company relies on a multi-user operating system to manage its daily operations. Within this system, different users have varying levels of access to resources and files based on their roles and permissions. For instance, the finance department accesses sensitive financial data, while the human resources team deals with employee records.

The concept of process security within the operating system ensures that these different tasks running concurrently remain isolated and protected from each other. Unauthorized access to a process could lead to potential data leaks or system instability. Memory security plays a pivotal role in preventing unauthorized access or modification to critical system memory areas. File security, on the other hand, ensures that files are protected against unauthorized reads, writes, or deletions, thereby maintaining the integrity and confidentiality of data stored within the system.

Understanding the fundamentals of operating system security involves delving into these core concepts: managing processes to prevent interference, securing memory to protect critical system areas, and implementing robust mechanisms to safeguard files and data.

UNIT INTRODUCTION

Operating systems are the foundation of computing environments because they bridge software and hardware, manage resources, and facilitate user interaction. An operating system's security is crucial for protecting data, guaranteeing system integrity, and preventing unauthorized access or malicious activities. This chapter explores operating system security fundamentals, including important elements such as memory protection, file system integrity, process management, kernel functions, and their implications for strengthening system defenses (Gramp & Morris, 1984). It also examines the dynamic entities' processes in an operating system, explaining the mechanisms of their creation, management, and isolation (Stallings, 2012).

The chapter then examines process security, exploring process isolation, privilege escalation, and access control techniques. It examines how strong process security controls reduce risks, stop unauthorized access, and uphold the principle of least privilege.

This chapter acts as a thorough introduction to the security of operating systems, explaining the critical components and mechanisms essential for enhancing the resilience of modern computing systems. By grasping the intricate interplay between operating system components and security protocols, readers will be well-prepared to navigate the complexities of securing these foundational elements in the realm of computer security.

6.1. OPERATING SYSTEMS CONCEPT

→Learning Objectives

- Understand the role of the kernel within an operating system.
- Comprehend the fundamental functions of processes.
- Learn about the file system architecture.
- Gain insights into memory management techniques.

The interface between a computer's hardware and users of a computer is provided by the operating system (OS). An operating system has the specialized function of managing the access of applications to various computer resources such as hard drives, CPU, main memory, input and output devices, or network interfaces. It serves as the intermediary that facilitates the connection between applications and users with a computer's hardware. Operating systems relieve application developers from the burden of managing many hardware devices, including a wide range of printers that users may connect to their computers. Thus, operating systems enable users to run applications simply and consistently (Walder & Platzner, 2003).

Operating systems perform many intricate functions directly connected to basic security issues. For example, operating systems must accommodate numerous users on the same computer, each with varying access levels. In a university lab, several people can use computer resources simultaneously, including administrators, faculty members, and students. The operating system is responsible for ensuring that the rights and requirements of different user types for computing resources are fulfilled, while also preventing malicious activities (Yokote, 1992).

Operating systems support numerous users and allow many different programs to run simultaneously; this is called multitasking. This method is helpful, not just because users can simultaneously enjoy email reading, web browsing, and music listening on the same computer. However, this feature means that every operating application must be protected from outside intervention by potentially malicious applications. Also, applications running on the same computer may have access to common resources like the file system, even if they are not running concurrently. Therefore, the operating system should have measures to prevent applications from maliciously or unintentionally harming resources required by other applications (Tanenbaum & Van, 1985).

6.1.1. The Kernel and Input/ output

The kernel serves as the central component of the operating system. The operating system oversees the low-level hardware components such as processors, memory, and input/output (I/O) devices such as keyboards, mice, and video displays. The kernel in most operating systems is conceptualized using a layered metaphor, with users and applications being at the top and hardware components such as the central processing unit (CPU), memory, and input/output devices being at the bottom (Brouard et al., 2016).

The operating system lies in the middle, with its kernel sitting just above the hardware of the computer and its non-essential OS services (such as the software that prints the contents of a folder as attractive icons) interacting with the kernel. Operating systems differ in how the kernel is implemented in specific aspects, and experts have disagreed greatly on how much responsibility the kernel should have over other operating system layers. Regardless, the kernel provides the framework that allows userland applications—ordinary programs—to run (See Figure 6.1) (Massalin & Pu, 1989).

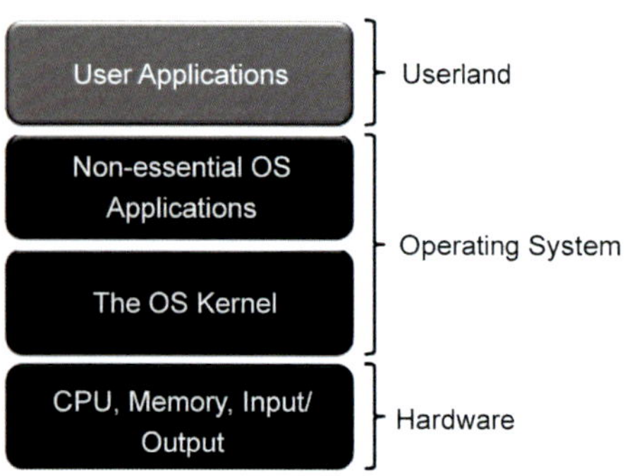

Figure 6.1. Illustration of the layers of a computer system (Source: Micheal Goodrich, Creative Commons License).

6.1.1.1. Input/output Devices

Input/output devices of a computer include its mouse, keyboard, display, network card, and additional optional devices such as a scanner, Wi-Fi user interface video camera, USB ports, and other input/output ports. In an operating system, every device is portrayed through a device driver, serving to encapsulate the specifics of how interactions with that device are to be executed. The Application Programmer Interface (API) provided by these device drivers to application programs enables a relatively high-level interaction with the devices. Meanwhile, the operating system takes on the task of carrying out the low-level interactions essential for the proper functioning of these devices. This discussion will specifically concentrate on the operating system calls necessary to facilitate input/ output and other hardware interactions (Psaltis, 1984).

6.1.1.2. System Calls

There needs to be a way for user applications to request the kernel to perform actions on their behalf because they do not directly interact with low-level hardware components; instead, they delegate these responsibilities to the kernel. There are several mechanisms for this purpose, but one of the most widely used is the system call, or simply syscall. System calls are commonly found in libraries, such as the C library (libc), which are collections of programs that provide an interface through which applications can utilize a predefined set of APIs that define the functions for interacting with the kernel (Tchakounte & Dayang, 2013).

System calls are responsible for executing application programs (exec) and performing file input/output operations (open, close, read, and write). The implementation details of system calls vary depending on the specific processor architecture. However, many systems handle these calls by treating them as software interrupts, which are program requests to the processor to pause the ongoing execution flow and transfer it to a specialized handler. Transitioning to kernel mode in response to an interrupt is referred to as a trap. In simple terms, system calls establish a secure bridge that enables processes to communicate between kernel space and user space. An operating system restricts how and when applications communicate with its kernel to maintain security and accuracy, as accessing kernel space requires direct hardware interaction (Hofmeyr et al., 1998).

6.1.2. Processes

The kernel establishes the concept of a process, which represents an active instance of a program. While the program's original contents reside in persistent storage, such as a hard drive, execution requires loading it into random-access memory (RAM) and assigning a unique identification as a process. As a result, multiple instances of the same program can run concurrently, with various processes initiated using identical program code. For example, it is feasible to run four distinct instances of a word processing program simultaneously, each within a separate window (Agne et al., 2013).

The kernel manages the execution of all running processes, ensuring equitable allocation of the computer's CPU(s) to facilitate the execution of instructions for all running applications. The ability to slice time is what enables multitasking. The operating system allocates a small time interval to each running process for execution before transitioning to the next process. Due to the brief duration of each time slice and the rapid context switching between operating processes, the active processes appear to be executing simultaneously from a human perspective, as the user's processing rate is much slower than that of computers (Carlson & McKenzie, 1984).

6.1.2.1. Users and Process Tree

As mentioned previously, most modern computers are designed to allow multiple users, each with potentially different levels of access, to utilize the same computer and initiate operations. When a user creates a new process, such as by requesting the execution of a program, the kernel interprets this as an existing process attempting to generate a new process. The process of duplicating an already-running process to create a new process is known as "forking." In this operation, the existing process is referred to as the parent process, while the process being forked is referred to as the child process (Jouck & Depaire, 2019).

Typically, on most systems, the new child process assumes the same permissions as its parent, unless the parent intentionally forks a new child process with reduced permissions. The process tree is a rooted tree structure that organizes processes based on the parent-child relationships defined by the forking mechanism for process creation. In Linux, the root of this tree is represented by the process called "init." This process begins execution immediately after the kernel has been loaded and is operational, usually during the boot process. Process "init" spawns new processes for operating system functions and user login sessions. Additionally, for any "orphaned" process, the "init" process assumes the role of the parent process (Pourbafrani et al., 2021).

6.1.2.2. Process IDs

Each process running on a particular computer is identified by a unique non-negative integer known as the process ID (PID). The process "init," which has a unique process identifier (PID) of 0, represents the root of the Linux process tree.

6.1.2.3. Process Privileges

An operating system associates each process with a user's information to grant the appropriate rights to the processes. Unix-based systems utilize an ID system where each process is assigned a group ID (gid) to identify a group of users for that process, and a user ID (uid) to identify the user associated with it. The uid is a numeric integer that uniquely identifies each user and ranges from 0 to 32,767 (0x7fff in hexadecimal notation). Typically, only the root (administrator) account is assigned the user identification (uid) 0. The group that the user is linked with is identified by the gid, a numerical value that falls within a predetermined range. Every group has a distinct identification, and an administrator can assign individuals to groups to provide them with different access levels. These identifiers are used to determine the resources that each process can access. Furthermore, processes inherently inherit the permissions of their parent processes (Weaver & Jones, 1989).

In Unix-based systems, processes also have an effective user ID (euid) in addition to uid and gid. The euid represents the user's identification within the process and is typically equivalent to the uid. However, certain designated processes operate with their effective user ID (euid) configured to the ID of the application's owner, who may have elevated privileges compared to the user initiating the process. In such cases, the effective user ID typically takes precedence in determining a process's privileges (Igure & Williams, 2008).

6.1.2.4. Inter-Process Communication

In order to efficiently manage shared resources, inter-process communication (IPC) is necessary. As a result, operating systems often provide tools to facilitate IPC. Processes can communicate by reading and writing files, which serves as a basic means of communication. Multiple processes can access files as part of a shared resource, the file system, making communication simple. However, this approach can be inefficient. What if a process needs to establish confidential communication with another process without leaving any traceable data on a disk that other processes could potentially access? Additionally, writing to or reading from an external hard drive is a common step in file management, but it typically results in slower performance compared to using RAM (Venkataraman & Jagadeesha, 2015).

Another method to enable communication between processes is by sharing the same physical memory space. By sharing RAM, processes can communicate with each other using this technique. With proper management of shared and private memory areas by the kernel, this strategy can facilitate fast and effective process communication. Pipes and sockets are two additional options for process communication. These mechanisms essentially act as pipes, connecting one process to another. When using pipes or sockets for communication, the pipe or socket is shared as an in-memory object between the sending and receiving processes. This sharing allows for fast message exchange, where messages are generated at one end of the pipe and consumed at the other end while still being stored in RAM (Gaspar et al., 2001).

6.1.3. The File System

The file system is another essential part of an operating system. It is a representation of the computer's external and non-volatile memory structure. Typically, operating systems hierarchically arrange files into folders, also known as directories.

Files and subfolders may be found inside each folder. As a result, a drive or volume comprises several nested folders arranged in a tree structure. This tree's root, also known as the root folder, is the topmost folder. A file system is shown as a tree in Figure 6.2.

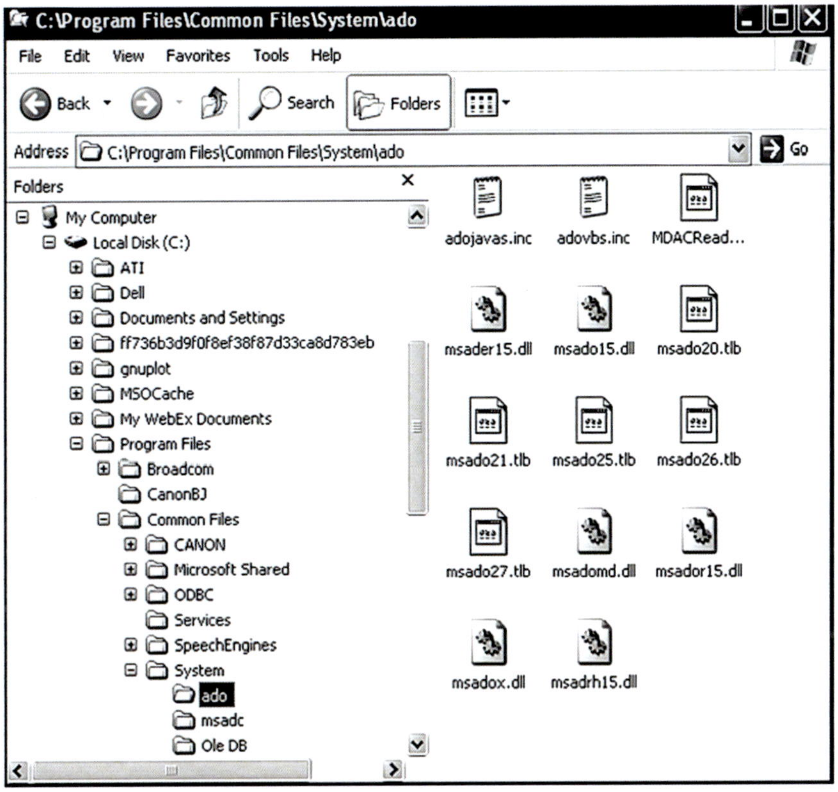

Figure 6.2. Representation of a file system as a tree, displayed by Windows Explorer (Source: Roberto Tamassia, Creative Commons License).

6.1.3.1. File Access Control

A key challenge in operating system security lies in describing which users can access which resources, including file reading, data writing, and program execution. This idea is most often captured in the notion of file permissions, which vary depending on the operating system. To be more precise, permissions are connected to all resources on disk, such as applications and data files (Mochel, 2005).

6.1.3.2. File Permissions

The operating system examines file permissions to establish whether a user or a group can read, write, or execute a file. Together with other attributes like the file type, this permission data is usually kept in the file's metadata. When a program requests to access a file, the operating system evaluates whether to allow access by considering the file's permissions after verifying the process's identification.

A file permission matrix is a simple file permission scheme seen in several operating systems resembling UNIX. This matrix, which shows the permissions for three classes, each with a combination of bits, represents who can do what to the file. Files have an owner, corresponding to a user's UID, and a group, corresponding to a group ID (Parkinson et al., 2016).

First, the permissions provided for the file creator are managed by the owner class. Next, the group class determines the permissions for users belonging to the same group as the file. Finally, the others class controls the permissions of users who are not members of the same group as the file and also are not the owner of the file.

A set of bits is present in each of these classes to identify which permissions are applicable. Users can read the file using the read bit, which is the first bit. The second is the write bit, which lets users edit the contents of the file. The execute bit, which is the last one, allows users to run the file as a program or script or, in the case of a directory, to change their current working directory to that one. Figure 6.3 shows an example of a file permission matrix for a group of files in a directory (Parkinson & Crampton, 2016).

```
rodan: ~/java % ls  -l
total 24
-rwxrwxrwx   1 goodrich faculty      2496 Jul 27  08:43 Floats. class
-rw-r--r--   1 goodrich faculty      2723 Jul 12   2006 Floats. java
-rw-------   1 goodrich faculty       460 Feb 25  2007 Test. Java
rodan:~/Java % █
```

Figure 6.3. Example of permission matrices for multiple files on a Unix system, using the ls -l command. The Floats.class file grants read, write, and execute access to both its owner, Goodrich, and non-owners. The Floats.java file is viewable by all users, writable only by its owner, and does not have execute permissions for any user. The Test.java file has exclusive read and write permissions granted solely to its owner, while all others have no access privileges. (Source: Doeppner, Creative Commons License).

6.1.3.4. Unix File Permissions

While the read, write, and execute bits are stored in binary data, they are commonly expressed in decimal form. The read bit has a weight of 4, the write bit has a weight of 2, and the execute bit has a weight of 1. Consequently, every possible combination of the three bits results in a distinct integer between 0 and 7, representing the class's permissions. For instance, a value of 3 signifies that both the write and execute permissions are enabled, while a value of 7 indicates that the permissions for reading, writing, and executing are all enabled (Hitz et al., 1998).

Using this notation, the complete file permission matrix can be expressed as three decimal numbers. Let's consider a file with a 644 permission matrix. This means that users in the same group have read-only access (group class set to 4), and other users are similarly restricted to read-only access (other users' classes set to 4). On the other hand, the owner of the file has the privilege to both read and write the file (with the owner class set to 6). The chown command can modify the owner or group of a file, while the chmod command can edit the permission matrix of a file. To modify the permissions of a file, a user must have ownership of the file (Berman et al., 1995). Permissions also apply to folders. A user who has write access to a folder can add new files to it, and a user who has read permissions can list the contents of that folder. Unix-based systems use path-based file access control. The operating system monitors the current working directory of the user. When requesting access to a file or directory, one must specify its path, which begins at the current working directory or the root directory, indicated by the / symbol. To gain access, the user must have execute permissions for each directory in the path. Specifically, the path is accessed one directory at a time, beginning with the start directory, and the execute permission is verified for each accessed directory (Landwehr, 2001).

As an example, let's say Bob has execute permission to access the home directory of Alice, his employer, at directory /home/Alice, and he wants to read a file.

/home/alice/administration/memos/raises.txt.

When Bob gives the Unix command

cat administration/memos/raises.txt

To view the file, the operating system first confirms that Bob possesses the necessary permissions to execute the first folder in the path, namely "administration." Subsequently, the operating system assesses whether Bob possesses the necessary permissions to execute actions on the memos folder, which follows in sequence. If so, the operating system verifies that Bob has read permission for the raises.txt file. Access is refused if Bob is not authorized to read raises.txt or execute permissions for administration or memos (Wang et al., 2017).

6.1.4. Memory Management

Memory management, the organization and allocation of memory within a computer, is another function of an operating system. The address space of a process is the area of memory allotted to it during execution. The address space is where the program code, data, and storage required for a process to operate are stored. The Unix memory architecture, which is utilized by the majority of PCs, is partitioned into five segments. These segments are organized in ascending order, from low address to high address (See Figure 6.4).

a) **Text**: This segment includes the program's actual machine code generated from the source code before it was run.
b) **Data**: This segment includes static variables for the program set in the source program before execution.
c) **BSS:** This segment, which is named for an antiquated acronym for block started by symbol, comprises uninitialized static variables (or variables initialized to zero).
d) **Heap:** The dynamic segment is accountable for keeping data that is generated during the execution of a procedure, such as objects created dynamically in an

object-oriented program written in Java or C++.

e) **Stack:** A downward-expanding stack data structure is present in this segment. It is used to keep track of the call structure of subroutines, including functions in C and methods in Java (Tofte & Talpin, 1997).

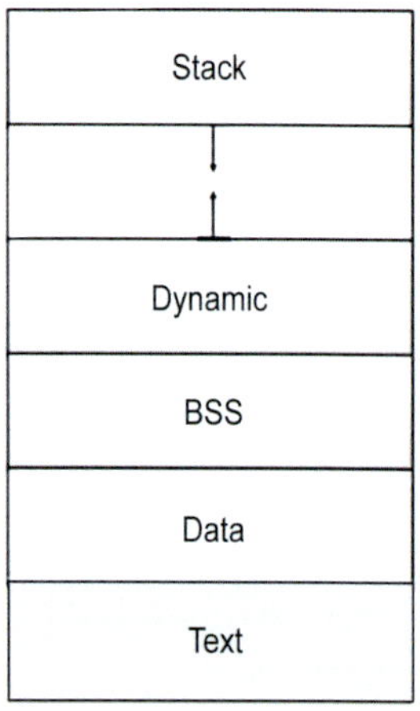

Figure 6.4. Illustration of the Unix memory model (Source: Fetzer, Creative Commons License).

6.1.4.1. Memory Access Permissions

The operating system imposes access permissions for each of the five memory segments, each with its own set of permissions for reading, writing, and executing. The text region is typically designated as read-only to prevent program code alterations while running. Except for this one, every region is writable, as the contents within them can be changed while the application is running.

A core principle in the security of operating systems is that processes are strictly forbidden from accessing the address space of other processes unless they have explicitly requested to share a part of that address space. If this rule is not executed, processes would be able to alter the execution and data of other processes, unless a process-based access control system is created. By establishing and enforcing address space boundaries, a multitude of critical security concerns can be addressed. This ensures that processes are protected from unauthorized modifications by other processes (Witchel et al., 2002).

Furthermore, operating systems partition the address space into two distinct regions: user space and kernel space. User space is designated for executing user-level applications, while kernel space is exclusively reserved for core operating system operations. Usually, the operating system allocates a fixed amount of space (such as one GB) at the bottom of each process's address space for the kernel, which normally has the most limited access privileges compared to the rest of the memory.

6.1.4.2. Contiguous Address Spaces

Every process has an address space that is a continuous block of memory, as previously mentioned. Since arrays are designed as contiguous memory blocks, programs that extensively use arrays require a continuous address space to store their data. It is preferable for the text part of the address space, which stores computer code, to be contiguous. This enables programs to incorporate instructions such as "jump forward 10 instructions," which is a frequently used instruction in machine code (Chase et al., 1992).

However, assigning a contiguous slab of real memory to every executing process would be highly inefficient and, in some cases, impractical. For example, let's assume that the total amount of continuous address space exceeds the computer's memory capacity; under such circumstances, it becomes impossible for all running processes to acquire a continuous memory region that matches the size of their address space.

6.1.4.3. Virtual Memory

Despite the adequacy of memory to accommodate the address spaces of all processes, issues may still arise. In such a situation, idle processes would retain their allocated memory. Consequently, if there were a sufficient number of operating processes, a memory shortage would occur (Denning, 1970).

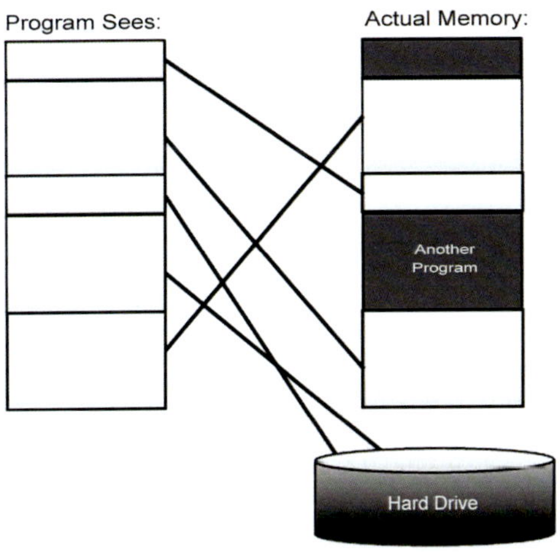

Figure 6.5. Diagram of Mapping virtual addresses to real addresses (Source: Roberto Tamassia, Creative Commons License).

To address these issues, most computer architectures employ a virtual memory system. This system assigns virtual address space to each process and maps each virtual address to a corresponding address in real memory. When a virtual address is accessed, the memory management unit, a hardware component, performs a lookup to determine the corresponding real address and enables access. In simple terms, processes are allowed to operate as if their memory is contiguous, even if it is fragmented and distributed throughout RAM, as depicted in Figure 6.5. Undoubtedly, this feature is valuable as it simplifies various aspects, such as facilitating the implementation of applications that require access to large arrays as contiguous blocks of memory (Li & Hudak, 1989).

Virtual memory systems offer the advantage of enabling the total size of executing processes' address spaces to exceed the physical memory capacity of the computer. The virtual memory system can utilize a section of the external drive to store blocks of memory not currently used by running processes, thereby expanding the available memory capacity. This is a significant advantage as it enables a computer to do a series of tasks that could not multitask if each process had to hold their complete address spaces in main memory constantly (Daley & Dennis, 1968).

6.2. PROCESS SECURITY

→Learning Objectives

- Understand the importance of process isolation and privilege separation in mitigating security risks,
- Comprehend various process security measures and techniques

To protect a computer during its operation, it is crucial to oversee and secure its processes that are running on the computer.

6.2.1. Inductive Trust from Start to Finish

The trust that individuals place in the operations executed on a computer is an instinctive conviction based on the reliability of the processes initiated upon powering up the computer. This trust remains unaffected even when the computer is powered off or put into hibernation.

6.2.1.1. The Boot Sequence

When a device is turned off, the process of loading an operating system (OS) into memory is referred to as booting, formerly known as bootstrapping. This operation may seem challenging because the entire code of the operating system is stored in persistent storage, often the hard disk. However, the operating system needs to be stored in memory in order to function. Upon turning on, a computer executes instructions found in a firmware component called the BIOS (basic input/output system). In modern computers, the Basic Input/Output System (BIOS) loads the second stage bootloader into the computer's memory. The boot loader is responsible for loading the remaining components of the operating system into memory and then handing over control of execution to the operating system (See Figure 6.6) (Frazelle, 2020).

Someone with bad intentions can take control of a computer's functioning at various points during the booting process. To stop an attacker from starting the initial booting process, many computers have a BIOS password that prevents the execution of a second-stage bootloader without proper authentication.

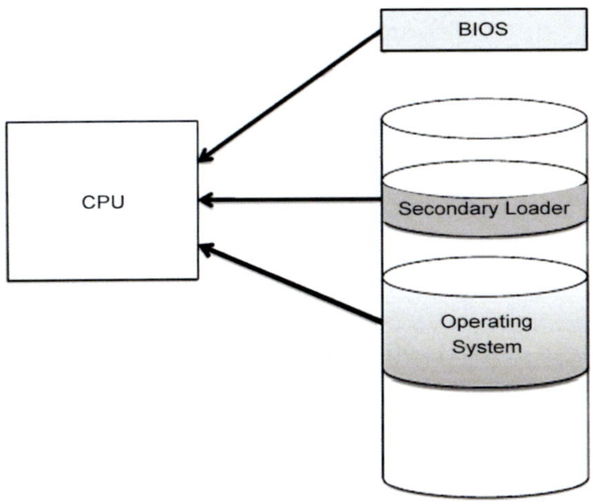

Figure 6.6. Representation of the operation of BIOS (Source: Chapin, Creative Commons License).

6.2.1.2. The Boot Device Hierarchy

There are other security issues related to the boot stage. The majority of second-stage boot loaders allow the user to specify which specific device will be used to load the remaining components of the operating system. Typically, when a user selects this option, the hard disk is automatically chosen for booting. However, if a user is performing a fresh installation, it may automatically select external media such as a DVD drive. Therefore, it is crucial to ensure that the operating system is always booted from trusted media (Mathews et al., 2008).

A customizable hierarchy is implemented to establish the order of precedence for booting devices, with the first available device in the list being used for the booting process. While this adaptability proves beneficial for installations and troubleshooting, it also introduces a potential security vulnerability. An attacker with physical access could exploit this by booting another operating system from external media, thus bypassing the inherent security mechanisms of the intended operating system. To mitigate such attacks, many computers employ second-stage boot loaders equipped with password protections, ensuring that only authorized users can initiate the booting process from external storage media (Yim, 2005).

6.2.1.3. Hibernation

Modern devices have the capability to enter a powered-off state known as hibernation. During hibernation, the operating system saves all the data in the computer's memory into a hibernation file on the disk. This allows for a quick restoration of the computer to its previous state when powered on again. However, it is important to note that hibernation leaves a computer vulnerable to potential forensic examination without additional security measures in place.

Since the hibernation file contains all the data from the computer's memory, any passwords or sensitive information present during hibernation are retained. An attacker can exploit this by using a live CD to gain unauthorized access to the hibernation file. In the case of Windows, hibernation files are stored in the C:\hiberfil.sys directory. Researchers have demonstrated the ability to reverse the compression algorithm used in this file, allowing for the extraction of a visible snapshot of the RAM during hibernation. This discovery introduces the potential for the attack depicted in Figure 6.7 (Ho et al., 2015).

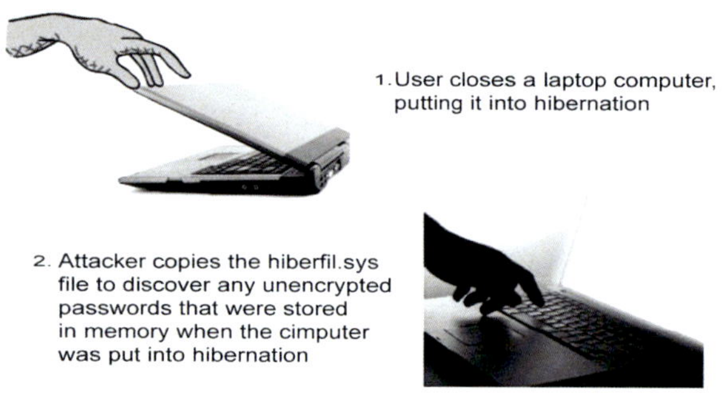

Figure 6.7. Illustration of the hibernation attack (Source: Micheal Goodrich, Creative Commons License).

There have been demonstrations of attacks that edit the hiberfil.sys file, altering program execution on the machine when powered on. Unexpectedly, even after several computer restarts, Windows does not delete the hibernation file when it resumes operation. Hard disk encryption should be used to protect swap files and hibernation files from these attacks.

6.2.2. Monitoring, Management, and Logging

An essential element of ensuring security in operating systems is what military personnel call "situational awareness." Monitoring the system's running processes, what other machines have interacted with the system via the Internet, and any unusual or suspicious behavior experienced by the OS can provide valuable insights for resolving common issues and identifying the source of a security breach. For example, the observation of multiple unsuccessful login attempts in log entries can indicate a brute-force assault, prompting a system administrator to modify passwords to assure security (Rochim et al., 2019).

6.2.2.1. Event Logging

Operating systems incorporate integrated mechanisms for handling event logging. The Windows operating system, for instance, includes a system for logging events known as the Windows Event Log.

Windows logs are categorized into three main categories: "System," "Application," and "Security." While ordinary applications can write to the Application log, only the operating system has the privilege to write to the System log. The Security log, on the other hand, can only be written by a specialized Windows service called the Local Security Authority Subsystem Service, which can be identified in Process Explorer as lsass.exe (Zeng et al., 2016).

This service is responsible for implementing security policies, including access control and user authentication. Additionally, users have the ability to designate their own log sources in addition to the three pre-established sources. Each individual log entry is referred to as an event. Every event on a Windows system is assigned a unique identifier that corresponds to any possible occurrence that could trigger logging. Examples of such occurrences include applications unexpectedly exiting, users failing to properly authenticate, and network connections being established (De et al., 2013).

Unix-based systems, such as Linux, employ various logging mechanisms that differ depending on the distribution. Log files are typically stored in the directory /var/log or a similar location. These log files are simple text files with descriptive names. For instance, the kern.log file reports any unusual kernel behavior, while the auth.log file contains information on user authentication. Entries in these log files include timestamps and descriptions of the events, similar to Windows logs. Usually, only a specific syslog server has the capability to write to these log files.

Unix logs have a straightforward text format with one event per line, making them easy to navigate. However, Windows log files may be more manageable when using Microsoft's event logging tools (Kasmi et al., 2014).

6.2.2.2. Process Monitoring

There are various situations where it's necessary to determine the specific processes currently active on our computer. For instance, sluggish performance may prompt us to identify apps consuming excessive CPU cycles or memory. Alternatively, suspicions of a virus compromise may lead us to check for any suspicious processes. Identifying and terminating the execution of such misbehaving or malicious processes is crucial, but it requires initial identification. Operating systems offer tools for users to monitor and manage currently running processes. Examples include the task manager app in Windows and commands like ps, top, pstree, and kill in Linux. (Ge et al., 2013).

6.2.2.3. Process Explorer

Process monitoring tools may appear to target expert users or administrators because they provide a comprehensive display of running processes and related execution statistics. However, these tools are also valuable for ordinary users. Process Explorer demonstrates the range of features that a proficient process monitoring tool can offer. The toolbar of Process Explorer includes various buttons, including a button specifically designed to terminate processes. The miniature graphs display the utilization patterns of CPU time, main memory, and I/O to identify malevolent or malfunctioning processes. The processes tree pane presents a tabular format of the currently executing processes (Mannhardt et al., 2015). The significant utilization of CPU time and address space often indicates the presence of problematic processes that should be stopped. Different colors are used to highlight different types of processes: those that have just started, those that are about to end, user processes (started by the same user who is also using Process Explorer), and system processes (like services). These capabilities provide a valuable graphical user interface for detecting and identifying malicious and misbehaving processes, as well as a simple method to terminate them once they have been detected (Seeliger et al., 2019).

Apart from performance monitoring, collecting comprehensive data regarding the process image is crucial, which refers to the executable program linked to the process. Process Explorer shows the file location on the disk (Path) for the program image along with the developer's name (Company). The image's location could make it easier to detect a virus that has the same file name as a legitimate application but is located in a nonstandard directory (Aslan & Samet, 2017).

The attacker might even try to replace the image of an authentic program with a modified one that carries out malicious actions. The software developer can use a digital signature for the image to stop this attack. The identity of the entity that signed the picture (Verified Signer) can then be shown and the signature can be verified using the Process Explorer (Kao & Hsiao, 2018).

6.3. MEMORY AND FILE SYSTEM SECURITY

→Learning Objectives

- Comprehend the significance of virtual memory security in preventing memory-based attacks.
- Learn about access control mechanisms within the file system.
- authentication methods, such as password-based authentication.

The contents of a computer are captured in its memory and filesystem. Hence, securing the data stored in a computer necessitates prioritizing the security of its memory and filesystem.

6.3.1. Virtual Memory Security

Virtual memory is a great resource for operating systems. It allows for efficient execution of multiple processes with a combined address space that exceeds the RAM capacity. Plus, it lets each process see their address spaces as contiguous. However, these functionalities come with some security concerns (Amirsoufi et al., 2009).

6.3.1.1. Windows and Linux Swap Files

In Windows, the page file is stored at C:\pagefile.sys, which stores virtual memory pages written to the hard disk. Linux often requires users to establish a dedicated partition on their hard disk, known as the swap partition, to accommodate these memory pages. Linux also supports a swap file and swap disk, which function similarly to the page file in Windows. Regardless of the situation, every operating system has regulations that prohibit users from accessing virtual memory files while the OS is running, and these files can be set up to be deleted upon machine shutdown (Horowitz, 2005).

6.3.1.2. Attacks on Virtual Memory

Suppose the attacker suddenly shuts down the device without following the correct shutdown process and continues to boot up an alternative operating system utilizing external media. Under these circumstances, it is possible for these files to be accessed and parts of memory to be reassembled, potentially exposing personal data (Govindavajhala & Appel, 2003). To decrease these risks, it is recommended to utilize hard disk encryption when personnel who may not be reliable have physical access to a computer. However, it is crucial to recognize that this encryption technique does not prevent an attacker who has physical access to the device from being able to read a swap file. Nonetheless, it effectively blocks an attacker from acquiring valuable data from the files' contents, provided that they are unable to obtain the decryption keys (Xu et al., 2017).

6.3.2. Password-Based Authentication

The question of who is allowed access to the resources in a computer system begins with a central question of operating systems security:

How will the operating system securely verify user identity?

The answer to this question is inside the concept of authentication, which relates to verifying an individual's identity or function, particularly in connection with the resources governed by the operating system. The main authentication method utilized by the majority of operating systems includes users supplying a username and password to log in. If the password that the user provides matches the password stored for the entered username, the system will verify the user's identity and allow access to the system (Conklin et al., 2004).

Operating systems typically utilize cryptographic one-way hashes to store passwords, rather than storing them as plain text in a password file or database. Due to the one-way property of cryptographic hash functions, it becomes challenging for an attacker to derive the actual passwords from the password file, even if they gain access to it. Instead, they are forced to rely on a guessing attack. The primary method of extracting passwords from the password file is through a dictionary attack (Gennaro & Lindell, 2003). This process involves taking each word from a dictionary, converting them into a hashed numerical representation, and then comparing this representation with the passwords stored in the password file. If system users choose weak passwords, such as commonly used English names and terms, a dictionary attack can easily succeed with a dictionary containing only 500,000 words. This highlights the significant disparity between the vast search space of over 5 quadrillion words that can be generated using the eight characters found on a typical keyboard (Ruoti et al., 2016).

6.3.2.1. Password Salt

Using salt is a good method for improving security against dictionary attacks. Salt is a cryptographic technique that involves incorporating random bits into the input of a hash function or encryption process. This technique is employed to enhance the level of randomness in the resulting output. In the case of password authentication, the inclusion of salt entails associating a random integer with each user ID. The system verifies the entered password by comparing the hash of the password and the salt (a randomly generated number) associated with the user ID, rather than directly comparing it with a pre-recorded hash of the password. Let U represent the user identification and P represent the corresponding password. When salt is used, the password file retains the triplet (U, S, h(SjjP)). Here, S represents the salt for U, while h denotes a cryptographic hash function (See Figure 6.8) (Gauravaram, 2012).

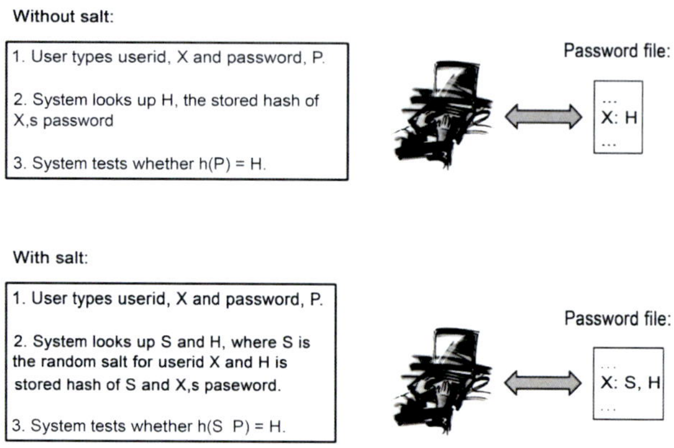

Figure 6.8. Illustration of the password salt (Source: Tom Doeppner, Creative Commons License).

6.3.2.2. Password Authentication in Windows and Unix-based Systems

In Microsoft Windows systems, password hashes are stored in the Security Accounts Manager (SAM) file, which is inaccessible to regular users during system runtime. Older versions of Windows used the LAN Manager hash (LM hash), which was based on the DES algorithm and had notable security weaknesses. This algorithm pads the user's password to 14 characters, converts lowercase letters to uppercase, and generates two DES keys from each 7-byte half to encrypt a predefined string ("KGS!@#$%"). The resulting two 8-byte ciphertexts are concatenated to form the final LM hash. This approach makes dictionary attacks easier due to the separate treatment of each half and the reduction in the search space by converting letters to uppercase. Additionally, the LM hash lacks a salt, making precomputed information tables highly effective (Viega & Voas, 2000).

Windows addressed these issues by introducing the NTLM algorithm, which is a challenge-response protocol for authentication. In NTLM, the operating system sends an 8-byte random challenge to the client. The client then computes two 24-byte responses using the LM hash and the MD4 hash of the password. These responses are generated by DES encrypting segments of the padded hashes. While NTLM has not been completely compromised, vulnerabilities do exist, particularly in the unsalted MD4 and LM hashes that are susceptible to precomputation attacks (Cisneros et al., 2006).

Unix-based systems employ a similar password mechanism, where authentication data is stored in /etc/passwd, often supplemented by /etc/shadow. Unix variants typically use salt and offer flexibility in hash algorithm selection, allowing administrators to choose their preferences. As of the current writing, many systems use a salted MD5 algorithm or a DES variant, with the ability to utilize alternative hash algorithms like Blowfish (Zhang et al., 2015).

6.3.3. Access Control and Advanced File Permissions

After a user has been verified in a system, the subsequent issue that needs to be considered is access control: How will the operating system detect the permissions granted to users? To thoroughly discuss this subject in relation to files, it is necessary to establish specific terminology. A principle refers to an individual user or a collective group of users. A principal refers to a defined group of users, such as a specific group of friends consisting of users Peter and Paul, or it can be one of the pre-established principals recognized by the operating system. Each file (or folder) is associated with specific users and groups in Unix-based systems. The term "user owner" denotes the individual who owns the file. The default group associated with the file is referred to as the owning group. Furthermore, the "group all" category encompasses all users within the system, whereas the "group other" category includes all users except for the file owner (Lovyagin et al., 2020).

Permission refers to a specific activity that can be performed on a file or folder. File permissions encompass the ability to read and write, whereas program files may also be capable of executing. Furthermore, a folder may also have the list permission, which allows one to inspect (list) the contents of the folder, and the execute permission, which allows one to set up the current directory as the folder. In Unix-based systems, the path-based control of access techniques is based on the capacity to execute folders (Heitzmann et al., 2008).

6.3.3.1. Access Control Entries and Lists

The access control entry (ACE) for a file or folder consists of a triplet (principal, type, permission), in which the type may be allowed or denied. A set of access control entries (ACEs) arranged sequentially is called an access control list (ACL) (Gladney, 1997).

Several crucial implementation details must be addressed when designing an operating system permissions scheme. One key consideration is how permissions interact with the file organization of the system. Specifically, the existence of a hierarchy of inheritance needs clarification. Does a file inherit permissions from its parent folder, or does it have the capability to override them with its own permissions? If a user is granted permission to write to a file but lacks permission for the directory housing the file, how does the system handle this scenario? While the meaning of read, write, and execute permissions may be intuitive for files, their impact on folders requires clarification.

Furthermore, when permissions are not explicitly granted or denied, are they implied by default? Interestingly, even between two widely used operating systems like Linux and Windows, there can be substantial variations in the answers to these questions. The intricacies of permission management play a pivotal role in shaping the security and functionality of an operating system (Karjoth, 2003).

6.3.3.2. Linux Permissions

Linux inherits a significant portion of its access control systems from early Unix systems, as discussed previously. Linux employs file permission matrices to dictate the privileges that various users hold concerning a file. Notably, permissions that are not expressly granted are automatically denied, eliminating the necessity for an explicit denial mechanism. Adhering to the path-based access control principle, access to a file necessitates that each ancestor folder in the filesystem tree has execute permission, and the file itself must possess read permission. Furthermore, file owners are endowed with the authority to alter the permissions on those files, a concept referred to as discretionary access control (DAC) (Zhang et al., 2019).

Linux allows users to assign extended attributes to files in addition to the three fundamental permissions (read, write, and execute). These extended attributes are enforced for all users who seek to access the files.

Extended attributes encompass several functionalities, such as enabling the append-only mode for a file, restricting users to only write at the end of the file. Additionally, they allow identifying a file as "immutable," thereby preventing even the root user from deleting or modifying the file unless the attribute is removed first. The chattr and lsattr commands can be used to set and inspect these attributes, respectively (Yaswinski et al., 2019).

In recent times, Linux has started to provide support for an optional permissions mechanism based on ACLs. The getfacl command can be used to verify ACLs on Linux, while the setfacl command is used to configure them. Under this framework, every file has basic Access Control Entries (ACEs) for the specific users or groups called named users and named groups. Additionally, a mask ACE defines the maximum number of permissions that can be granted to the owning group, as well as any specified users and groups. Let U represent the effective user ID (euid) of the process trying to access the file or folder with certain desired permissions.

To determine whether access should be granted, the operating system evaluates the following conditions and selects the Access Control Entry (ACE) associated with the first matching condition:

a) If U is the userid of the file owner, the ACE for the owner is selected.
b) If U is one of the named users, the ACE for U is selected.
c) If one of the groups of U is the owning group and the ACE for the group contains the requested permissions, the ACE for the group is selected.
d) If one of the groups of U is a named group G, and its ACE contains the requested permissions, the ACE for G is selected.
e) For each group G of U that is the owning group or a named group, and the ACE for G does not contain the requested permissions, the empty ACE is selected.
f) Otherwise, the ACE for other is selected.

If the Access Control Entry for the owner, other, or the empty ACE has been chosen, then the access is determined by its permissions. Alternatively, the chosen ACE is "ANDed" with the mask ACE and the resulting ACE's permissions dictate the level of access granted. It is important to understand that while numerous ACEs can be chosen in the fourth condition, the access decision is not influenced by the selected ACE. Linux's ACL scheme has not been extensively adopted despite its capability to provide greater flexibility in access control (Jayaprakash & Meeran, 2018).

Access control systems in certain Linux variants are even more advanced. The United States National Security Agency is the primary developer of Security-Enhanced Linux (SELinux), a set of security improvements intended for use with Unix-like systems. Strictly enforced required access control (SELinux) defines almost every operation permitted on a machine. Every rule comprises an object representing the resource being accessed, a subject that refers to the process trying to access it, and many permissions that the operating system suitably verifies. The concept of least privilege is embodied by SELinux, which greatly reduces the impact of a security violation by granting each process only the minimal amount of permissions required to operate (Felt et al., 2011).

Furthermore, users are not granted the authority to select the security attributes of their files, in contrast to DAC. Rather, a central security policy administrator has been charged with this. With these improvements, SELinux can establish a far more stringent security environment.

6.3.3.3. Windows Permissions

Windows employs the ACL model, in which users can establish rule sets specifically for users or groups. These regulations grant or withhold different permissions for the relevant principal. In the case where no applicable rule is relevant, access is prohibited by default. The terms "basic permissions" and "standard permissions" refer to the following: modify, read and execute, read, write, and full control, which allows all permissions on a file (Zavarsky & Lindskog, 2016).

Advanced permissions are composed of the standard permissions and are used to fine-tune permissions. Read data, read attributes, read extended attributes, and read permissions are just a few of the advanced permissions included in the standard read permission. All these advanced permissions are automatically enabled when read is set to allow for a specific principle; however, it is also possible to set only the advanced permissions one desires (Tamizi et al., 2005).

Similar to Linux, folders can also have permissions. Write permission allows a user to add new files to a folder, while read permission is equivalent to being able to list a folder's contents. However, Windows uses a different approach. In Linux, access is granted only after verifying that every folder in the path to a file exists. On the other hand, in Windows, the path of a file is just an identifier and is unrelated to permissions. Access to the file is granted only after inspecting its ACL (Access Control List). This difference allows administrators in Windows to grant access to a file inside a folder but refuse access to the folder itself, which is not possible in Linux (Derochers & Soumis, 1988).

In Windows, any ACEs (Access Control Entries) given to a folder can be configured to apply to files and subfolders inside the folder as well. These automatically generated ACEs are referred to as inherited ACEs, while explicitly defined ACEs are those specifically established. Administrators also have the ability to prevent inheritance from spreading to a specific folder, thus preventing ACEs from parent folders from being inherited by the children of that folder (Sarma et al., 2012).

This inheritance structure raises the issue of how ACEs should take precedence. In reality, the operating system bases its decisions about access control on a simple hierarchy. Deny ACEs take precedence over Allow ACEs at any level in the hierarchy. Additionally, explicit Access Control Entries (ACEs) hold precedence over inherited ACEs, and the priority of inherited ACEs is determined by the distance between the ancestor and the object in question. In this hierarchy, the ACEs of the parent take precedence over those of the grandparent and so forth. With this algorithm, resolving permissions involves enumerating the entries of the Access Control List (ACL) in the appropriate order until a relevant rule is identified. While this hierarchical structure, coupled with the nuanced control of Windows permissions, offers administrators considerable flexibility, it also introduces the potential for security vulnerabilities due to its complexity. If rules are not meticulously applied, there is a risk of exposing sensitive resources (Hanner & Hormanseder, 1999).

SUMMARY

- This chapter provides a brief introduction to operating system security. Operating systems serve as the foundational component of computing devices, overseeing resources and serving as an intermediary between hardware and software. The protection of confidential information, preservation of system integrity, and defense against threats rely on a comprehensive understanding of operating system security features.
- The kernel of an operating system serves as its central component, managing system resources, executing operations, and enforcing security regulations.
- The operating system handles processes, which are units of execution that possess their own memory, resources, and permissions.
- The File System is a hierarchical system that utilizes access control methods to safeguard data while organizing files, directories, and data storage.
- Memory management effectively allocates and controls memory resources, preventing unauthorized access to private information stored in memory.
- Access controls, privileges, and process separation are employed to ensure process isolation and protect against unauthorized access or interference.
- Enforcing memory protection, executing code from non-executable memory areas, and overflowing buffers are examples of memory-based attacks that can be prevented by adopting virtual memory security measures.
- Password-based authentication protects against unwanted access to the system by using strong authentication processes to confirm user identities.
- Access control and advanced file permissions involve implementing access control lists (ACLs), file permissions, and role-based access control (RBAC) to govern access to the file system. This ensures that only authorized users can change files and directories.

MULTIPLE CHOICE QUESTIONS

1. **What is the primary role of the kernel in an operating system?**
   a) Managing user interfaces
   b) Handling system resources and processes
   c) Storing application data
   d) Providing network connectivity
2. **Which of the following is responsible for organizing and managing files in an operating system?**
   a) Kernel
   b) Processes
   c) File System
   d) Memory Management

3. What is the purpose of sandboxing in the context of process security?

a) Isolating processes to prevent interactions with other processes

b) Allowing multiple processes to share the same memory space

c) Enhancing process speed and performance

d) Providing unrestricted access to system resources

4. Which principle restricts a process's access rights to only those necessary to perform its function?

a) Least Privilege

b) Admin Privilege

c) Superuser Access

d) Unlimited Access

5. How does virtual memory enhance security in an operating system?

a) It provides additional memory space for every process.

b) It enforces memory protection and prevents unauthorized access.

c) It reduces memory allocation for better performance.

REVIEW QUESTIONS

1. Define the role of the kernel in an operating system. How does it manage system resources and processes effectively?
2. Explain the significance of the file system in an operating system. How does it organize and manage data?
3. What are the key objectives of process isolation in enhancing system security?
4. Explain the potential risks associated with inadequate process security. How can these risks impact the overall system integrity?
5. How does access control play a crucial role in file system security?

Answers to Multiple Questions

1. (b) 2. (c) 3. (b) 4. (a) 5. (c)

REFERENCES

1. Abadi, M., Burrows, M., Lampson, B., & Plotkin, G., (1993). A calculus for access control in distributed systems. *ACM Transactions on Programming Languages and Systems (TOPLAS), 15*(4), 706–734.
2. Agne, A., Happe, M., Keller, A., Lübbers, E., Plattner, B., Platzner, M., & Plessl, C., (2013). ReconOS: An operating system approach for reconfigurable computing. *IEEE Micro, 34*(1), 60–71.
3. Amirsoufi, R., Taghiloo, M., & Ahmadi, A., (2009). Efficient security-aware virtual

memory management. In: *2009 International Conference of Soft Computing and Pattern Recognition* (Vol. 1, No. 1, pp. 208–211). IEEE.

4. Aslan, Ö., & Samet, R., (2017). Investigation of possibilities to detect malware using existing tools. In: *2017 IEEE/ACS 14th International Conference on Computer Systems and Applications (AICCSA)* (Vol. 1, No. 1, pp. 1277–1284). IEEE.
5. Berman, A., Bourassa, V., & Selberg, E., (1995). TRON: Process-specific file protection for the UNIX operating system. In: *USENIX* (Vol. 1, No. 1, pp. 165–175).
6. Brouard, C., Shen, H., Dührkop, K., D'Alché-Buc, F., Böcker, S., & Rousu, J., (2016). Fast metabolite identification with input output kernel regression. *Bioinformatics, 32*(12), i28–i36.
7. Carlson, B. R., & McKenzie, T. L., (1984). Computer technology for recording, storing, and analyzing temporal data in physical activity settings. *Journal of Teaching in Physical Education, 4*(1), 24–29.
8. Chase, J., Levy, H., Baker-Harvey, M., & Lazowska, E., (1992). Opal: A single address space system for 64-bit architecture address space. In: *[1992] Proceedings Third Workshop on Workstation Operating Systems* (Vol. 1, No. 1, pp. 80–85). IEEE.
9. Cisneros, R., Bliss, D., & Garcia, M., (2006). Password auditing applications. *Journal of Computing Sciences in Colleges, 21*(4), 196–202.
10. Conklin, A., Dietrich, G., & Walz, D., (2004). Password-based authentication: A system perspective. In: *37th Annual Hawaii International Conference on System Sciences, 2004. Proceedings of The* (Vol. 1, No. 1, p. 10). IEEE.
11. Daley, R. C., & Dennis, J. B., (1968). Virtual memory, processes, and sharing in multics. *Communications of the ACM, 11*(5), 306–312.
12. De La Piedra, A., Braeken, A., Touhafi, A., & Wouters, K., (2013). Secure event logging in sensor networks. *Computers & Mathematics with Applications, 65*(5), 762–773.
13. Denning, P. J., (1970). Virtual memory. *ACM Computing Surveys (CSUR), 2*(3), 153–189.
14. Desrochers, M., & Soumis, F., (1988). A generalized permanent labelling algorithm for the shortest path problem with time windows. *INFOR: Information Systems and Operational Research, 26*(3), 191–212.
15. Felt, A. P., Chin, E., Hanna, S., Song, D., & Wagner, D., (2011). Android permissions demystified. In: *Proceedings of the 18th ACM Conference on Computer and Communications Security* (Vol. 1, No. 1, pp. 627–638).
16. Felt, A. P., Greenwood, K., & Wagner, D., (2011). The effectiveness of application permissions. In: *2nd USENIX Conference on Web Application Development (WebApps 11)* (Vol. 1, No. 1, pp. 1–20.
17. Frazelle, J., (2020). Securing the boot process. *Communications of the ACM, 63*(3), 38–42.
18. Futagawa, J., (2004). Integrating network services of Windows and UNIX for single sign-on. In: *2004 International Conference on Cyberworlds* (Vol. 1, No. 1, pp. 323–328). IEEE.

19. Garcia, M., (2006). Password auditing tools. In: *2006 Annual Conference & Exposition* (Vol. 1, No. 1, pp. 11–985).
20. Gaspar, C., Dönszelmann, M., & Charpentier, P., (2001). DIM, a portable, light weight package for information publishing, data transfer and inter-process communication. *Computer Physics Communications, 140*(1, 2), 102–109.
21. Gauravaram, P., (2012). Security analysis of salt|| password hashes. In: *2012 International Conference on Advanced Computer Science Applications and Technologies (ACSAT)* (Vol. 1, No. 1, pp. 25–30). IEEE.
22. Ge, Z., Song, Z., & Gao, F., (2013). Review of recent research on data-based process monitoring. *Industrial & Engineering Chemistry Research, 52*(10), 3543–3562.
23. Gennaro, R., & Lindell, Y., (2003). A framework for password-based authenticated key exchange. In: *International Conference on the Theory and Applications of Cryptographic Techniques* (Vol. 1, No. 1, pp. 524–543). Berlin, Heidelberg: Springer Berlin Heidelberg.
24. Gladney, H. M., (1997). Access control for large collections. *ACM Transactions on Information Systems (TOIS), 15*(2), 154–194.
25. Govindavajhala, S., & Appel, A. W., (2003). Using memory errors to attack a virtual machine. In: *2003 Symposium on Security and Privacy, 2003* (Vol. 1, No. 1, pp. 154–165). IEEE.
26. Grampp, F. T., & Morris, R. H., (1984). The UNIX system: UNIX operating system security. *AT&T Bell Laboratories Technical Journal, 63*(8), 1649–1672.
27. Hanner, K., & Hörmanseder, R., (1999). Managing Windows NT® file system permissions—A security tool to master the complexity of Microsoft Windows NT® file system permissions. *Journal of Network and Computer Applications, 22*(2), 119–131.
28. Harada, T., Horie, T., & Tanaka, K., (2005). Towards a manageable Linux security. In: *Linux Conference* (Vol. 2005, pp. 1–20).
29. Heitzmann, A., Palazzi, B., Papamanthou, C., & Tamassia, R., (2008). Effective visualization of file system access-control. In: *International Workshop on Visualization for Computer Security* (Vol. 1, No. 1, pp. 18–25). Berlin, Heidelberg: Springer Berlin Heidelberg.
30. Hintea, D., Bird, R., & Green, M., (2017). An investigation into the forensic implications of the Windows 10 operating system: Recoverable artefacts and significant changes from Windows 8.1. *International Journal of Electronic Security and Digital Forensics, 9*(4), 326–345.
31. Hitz, D., Allison, B., Borr, A., Hawley, R., & Muhlestein, M., (1998). Merging NT and UNIX filesystem permissions. In: *Proceedings of the 2nd Conference on USENIX Windows NT Symposium* (Vol. 2, pp. 10–10).
32. Ho, C. C., Cheng, S. W., Chang, Y. H., Chang, Y. M., Hong, S. Y., & Chang, C. W., (2015). Efficient hibernation resuming with classification-based prefetching scheme for embedded computing systems. *ACM SIGAPP Applied Computing Review, 15*(1), 33–43.

33. Hofmeyr, S. A., Forrest, S., & Somayaji, A., (1998). Intrusion detection using sequences of system calls. *Journal of Computer Security, 6*(3), 151–180.

34. Horowitz, M., (2005). *Linux vs. Windows: A Comparison of Linux and Windows.* (Vol. 1, pp. 1-2)

35. Igure, V. M., & Williams, R. D., (2008). Taxonomies of attacks and vulnerabilities in computer systems. *IEEE Communications Surveys & Tutorials, 10*(1), 6–19.

36. Jayaprakash, D., & Meeran, N., (2018). Next generation system security measures based on the process behavior and permissions in Linux. In: *IOP Conference Series: Materials Science and Engineering* (Vol. 402, No. 1, p. 012062). IOP Publishing.

37. Joe, Q. S., (2003). Statistical process monitoring: Basics and beyond. *Journal of Chemometrics: A Journal of the Chemometrics Society, 17*(8, 9), 480–502.

38. Jouck, T., & Depaire, B., (2019). Generating artificial data for empirical analysis of control-flow discovery algorithms: A process tree and log generator. *Business & Information Systems Engineering, 61*, 695–712.

39. Kao, D. Y., & Hsiao, S. C., (2018). The dynamic analysis of WannaCry ransomware. In: *2018 20th International Conference on Advanced Communication Technology (ICACT)* (Vol. 1, No. 1, pp. 159–166). IEEE.

40. Karjoth, G., (2003). Access control with IBM Tivoli access manager. *ACM Transactions on Information and System Security (TISSEC), 6*(2), 232–257.

41. Kasmi, C., Lopes-Esteves, J., Picard, N., Renard, M., Beillard, B., Martinod, E., & Lalande, M., (2014). Event logs generated by an operating system running on a cots computer during IEMI exposure. *IEEE Transactions on Electromagnetic Compatibility, 56*(6), 1723–1726.

42. Klieme, E., Wilke, J., Van, D. N., & Meinel, C., (2020). FIDOnuous: A FIDO2/WebAuthn extension to support continuous web authentication. In: *2020 IEEE 19th International Conference on Trust, Security and Privacy in Computing and Communications (TrustCom)* (Vol. 1, No. 1, pp. 1857–1867). IEEE.

43. Landwehr, C. E., (2001). Computer security. *International Journal of Information Security, 1*(1), 3–13.

44. Li, K., & Hudak, P., (1989). Memory coherence in shared virtual memory systems. *ACM Transactions on Computer Systems (TOCS), 7*(4), 321–359.

45. Lovyagin, N. Y., Chernishev, G. A., Smirnov, K. K., & Dayneko, R. Y., (2020). FGACFS: A fine-grained access control for* nix userspace file system. *Computers & Security, 88*, 101632.

46. Mannhardt, F., De Leoni, M., & Reijers, H. A., (2015). The multi-perspective process explorer. In: *13th International Workshops on Business Process Management Workshops (BPM 2015)* (Vol. 1, No. 1, pp. 130–134).

47. Massalin, H., & Pu, C., (1989). Threads and input/output in the synthesis Kernal. In: *Proceedings of the Twelfth ACM Symposium on Operating Systems Principles* (Vol. 1, No. 1, pp. 191–201).

48. Matthews, J., Trika, S., Hensgen, D., Coulson, R., & Grimsrud, K., (2008). Intel® turbo memory: Nonvolatile disk caches in the storage hierarchy of mainstream computer systems. *ACM Transactions on Storage (TOS), 4*(2), 1–24.

49. Mochel, P., (2005). The sysfs filesystem. In: *Linux Symposium* (Vol. 1, pp. 313–326).

50. Moller, R., (1998). Distributed operating systems: Concepts and design. *IEEE Concurrency, 6*(2), 93–94.

51. Parkinson, S., & Crampton, A., (2016). Identification of irregularities and allocation suggestion of relative file system permissions. *Journal of Information Security and Applications, 30*, 27–39.

52. Parkinson, S., Somaraki, V., & Ward, R., (2016). Auditing file system permissions using association rule mining. *Expert Systems with Applications, 55*, 274–283.

53. Pourbafrani, M., Jiao, S., & Van, D. A. W. M., (2021). SIMPT: Process improvement using interactive simulation of time-aware process trees. In: *International Conference on Research Challenges in Information Science* (Vol. 1, No. 1, pp. 588–594). Cham: Springer International Publishing.

54. Psaltis, D., (1984). Input/output devices. In: *Optical Computing* (Vol. 456, pp. 66–71). SPIE.

55. Rochim, A. F., Aziz, M. A., & Fauzi, A., (2019). Design log management system of computer network devices infrastructures based on ELK stack. In: *2019 International Conference on Electrical Engineering and Computer Science (ICECOS)* (Vol. 1, No. 1, pp. 338–342). IEEE.

56. Röpke, C., & Holz, T., (2016). On network operating system security. *International Journal of Network Management, 26*(1), 6–24.

57. Ruoti, S., Andersen, J., & Seamons, K., (2016). Strengthening password-based authentication. In: *Twelfth Symposium on Usable Privacy and Security (SOUPS 2016)* (Vol. 1, No. 1, pp. 1–20.

58. Sandhu, R. S., & Samarati, P., (1994). Access control: Principle and practice. *IEEE Communications Magazine, 32*(9), 40–48.

59. Sarma, B. P., Li, N., Gates, C., Potharaju, R., Nita-Rotaru, C., & Molloy, I., (2012). Android permissions: A perspective combining risks and benefits. In: *Proceedings of the 17th ACM Symposium on Access Control Models and Technologies* (Vol. 1, No. 1, pp. 13–22).

60. Seeliger, A., Ratzke, M., Nolle, T., & Mühlhäuser, M., (2019). Process explorer: Interactive visual exploration of event logs with analysis guidance. In: *Proceedings of the 1st International Conference on Process Mining, Aachen, Germany* (Vol. 1, No. 1, pp. 24–26).

61. Singh, R., (2014). An overview of android operating system and its security. *Int. Journal of Engineering Research and Applications, 4*(2), 519–521.

62. Stallings, W., (2012). Operating system security. *Computer Security Handbook, 1*(1), 24–1.

63. Tamizi, M., Weinstein, M., & Cukier, M., (2005). Automated checking for Windows

host vulnerabilities. In: *16th IEEE International Symposium on Software Reliability Engineering (ISSRE'05)* (Vol. 1, No. 1, pp. 10). IEEE.

64. Tanenbaum, A. S., & Van, R. R., (1985). Distributed operating systems. *ACM Computing Surveys (CSUR), 17*(4), 419–470.
65. Tchakounté, F., & Dayang, P., (2013). System calls analysis of malwares on android. *International Journal of Science and Technology, 2*(9), 669–674.
66. Tofte, M., & Talpin, J. P., (1997). Region-based memory management. *Information and Computation, 132*(2), 109–176.
67. Tsvetkov, K. S., & Georgiev, T., (2012). An alternative approach and attempt to come up with a standard for biometric user authentication in a network based environment. *Procedia-Social and Behavioral Sciences, 47*, 74–78.
68. Venkataraman, A., & Jagadeesha, K. K., (2015). Evaluation of inter-process communication mechanisms. *Architecture, 86*, 64.
69. Viega, J., & Voas, J., (2000). The pros and cons of UNIX and Windows security policies. *IT Professional, 2*(5), 40–47.
70. Walder, H., & Platzner, M., (2003). Reconfigurable hardware operating systems: From design concepts to realizations. In: *Engineering of Reconfigurable Systems and Algorithms* (Vol. 1, No. 1, pp. 284–287).
71. Wang, M., Mayo, J., Shene, C. K., Carr, S., & Wang, C., (2017). UNIXvisual: A visualization tool for teaching UNIX permissions. In: *Proceedings of the 2017 ACM Conference on Innovation and Technology in Computer Science Education* (Vol. 1, No. 1, pp. 194–199).
72. Weaver, R. L., & Jones, J. T., (1989). The deliberative process privilege. *Mo. L. Rev., 54*, 279.
73. Witchel, E., Cates, J., & Asanovi⊠, K., (2002). Mondrian memory protection. In: *Proceedings of the 10th International Conference on Architectural Support for Programming Languages and Operating Systems* (Vol. 1, No. 1, pp. 304–316).
74. Xu, Z., Ray, S., Subramanyan, P., & Malik, S., (2017). Malware detection using machine learning based analysis of virtual memory access patterns. In: *Design, Automation & Test in Europe Conference & Exhibition (DATE), 2017* (pp. 169–174). IEEE.
75. Yaswinski, M. R., Chowdhury, M. M., & Jochen, M., (2019). Linux security: A survey. In: *2019 IEEE International Conference on Electro Information Technology (EIT)* (Vol. 1, No. 1, pp. 357–362). IEEE.
76. Yim, K. S., (2005). A novel memory hierarchy for flash memory based storage systems. *JSTS: Journal of Semiconductor Technology and Science, 5*(4), 262–269.
77. Yokote, Y., (1992). The Apertos reflective operating system: The concept and its implementation. *ACM SIGPLAN Notices, 27*(10), 414–434.
78. Yu, S., Wang, C., Ren, K., & Lou, W., (2010). Achieving secure, scalable, and fine-grained data access control in cloud computing. In: *2010 Proceedings IEEE INFOCOM* (Vol. 1, No. 1, pp. 1–9). IEEE.

79. Zavarsky, P., & Lindskog, D., (2016). Experimental analysis of ransomware on windows and android platforms: Evolution and characterization. *Procedia Computer Science, 94*, 465–472.

80. Zeng, L., Xiao, Y., Chen, H., Sun, B., & Han, W., (2016). Computer operating system logging and security issues: A survey. *Security and Communication Networks, 9*(17), 4804–4821.

81. Zhang, F., Leach, K., Wang, H., & Stavrou, A., (2015). Trustlogin: Securing password-login on commodity operating systems. In: *Proceedings of the 10th ACM Symposium on Information, Computer and Communications Security* (Vol. 1, No. 1, pp. 333–344).

82. Zhang, T., Shen, W., Lee, D., Jung, C., Azab, A. M., & Wang, R., (2019). {PeX}: A permission check analysis framework for Linux kernel. In: *28th USENIX Security Symposium (USENIX Security 19)* (pp. 1205–1220).

83. Zhou, J., Zhang, T., Shen, W., Lee, D., Jung, C., Azab, A., & Ren, K., (2022). Automatic permission check analysis for Linux kernel. *IEEE Transactions on Dependable and Secure Computing, 1*(1), 1–20.

84. Zhu, H., & Cao, G., (2006). rDCF: A relay-enabled medium access control protocol for wireless ad hoc networks. *IEEE Transactions on Mobile Computing, 5*(9), 1201–1214.

CHAPTER

7

Network Security

LEARNING OBJECTIVES

After studying this chapter, you will be able to:

- Identify common internet vulnerabilities affecting network security.
- Comprehend the purpose and methodology behind port scanning.
- Understand the concept of spoofing attacks on network integrity and confidentiality.
- Identify different forms of spam and their effects on network resources.
- Familiarize with effective strategies to mitigate the impact of spam and DoS attacks on network infrastructure.
- Comprehend the role and significance of firewalls in network security.

INTRODUCTORY EXAMPLE

The widespread use of networked devices and the easy sharing of information in today's digital world have greatly improved productivity and connectivity in various sectors. Nevertheless, this enhanced interconnectivity also brings up numerous security issues and risks. Consider a situation in which a vast corporate network, which holds important business data and services, becomes vulnerable to external dangers because of unprotected ports. This vulnerability has the potential to expose the network to unauthorized access, enabling hostile individuals to exploit holes via port scanning techniques. In addition, the increasing number of unauthorized messages flooding employees' inboxes presents a risk to the network's reliability, perhaps enabling phishing endeavors and jeopardizing confidential data. In this setting, the significance of strong firewall setups becomes apparent, serving as a barrier to prevent unwanted entry and safeguarding the network from different forms of harmful activity like spoofing attacks and denial-of-service (DoS) efforts. Comprehending and applying efficient network security measures are crucial for protecting sensitive data, guaranteeing uninterrupted operations, and reducing the dangers presented by advancing cyber threats.

UNIT INTRODUCTION

During the Cold War, the Internet was initially designed to establish a communication network capable of withstanding military attacks. As a result, the Internet evolved to transmit messages through data packets instead of relying on switched lines. This advancement enabled communication to be facilitated by the Internet. A data packet consists of two parts: the payload, which contains the actual information, and the header, which indicates the packet's destination and includes various overhead and accounting details (Marin, 2005).

Therefore, in order for both parties to communicate over the Internet, their messages need to be divided into packets, each packet needs to be assigned a header, and then the packets are allowed to travel through the Internet to reach their respective destinations. This chapter explores the underlying technologies that enable the Internet, including the potential security risks and specific countermeasures (Shiravi et al., 2011).

7.1. INTERNET VULNERABILITIES

→Learning Objectives

- Identify common internet vulnerabilities.
- Understand the impact of vulnerabilities on network security

Network vulnerability is an inherent flaw in the design, implementation, or use of a software function or hardware component. Vulnerability increases the likelihood of attacks and makes the network more susceptible to threats (De Vivo et al., 1999).

A threat refers to any element that has the potential to disrupt the functioning of the network. While a threat can occasionally be unintentional or caused by natural events, most threats are deliberate. A threat can impair the network, hinder its performance, or render it inaccessible. All forms of unauthorized software pose a threat (Butun et al., 2019).

An attack is a planned approach to exploit a recognized vulnerability. A passive attack aims to observe and document network activity to gather knowledge for future use in an active attack. Passive attacks encompass activities such as packet sniffing and traffic analysis. Detecting passive attacks might be challenging (Andrea et al., 2015).

An active attack is a deliberate attempt to disrupt or impair the functioning of a network. These attacks are more easily detectable, although they also cause greater damage. The major threats and attacks that have occurred on the Internet are listed in the following sections. This list excludes malicious software, such as Trojan horses and viruses (Abomhara & Koien, 2015).

7.2. PORT SCANNING

→Learning Objectives

- Concept of port scanning and its significance in network security.
- Identify different types of port scans and their implications.

During data interchange between two programs on different computers, the data packets transmitted between the programs are assigned the same port number (among other specifications). When accessing a network, a port is opened, which is analogous to opening a door. Ports play a crucial role in network security. Upon arrival at a computer, data packets from various sources are assigned a port number for each stream of packets. A port is identified by a 16-bit integer, and there can be a maximum of 65,535 ports (De Vivo et al., 1999).

The ports are divided into three categories: well-known ports (0 through 1023), registered ports (1024 through 49151), and dynamic/private ports (49152 through 65535). Operating system processes usually use the well-known ports assigned by the IANA port registry. SMTP (port 25), HTTP (port 80), TELNET (port 23), and FTP (port 21) are a few examples of protocols and the port numbers that correspond to them. Instead of operating system processes, user applications often use registered ports to communicate with servers. These ports, however, can also be used to identify particular services that other parties have registered. User applications rarely use dynamic/private ports but are used periodically. These ports do not mean anything other than a particular TCP connection (Bhuyan et al., 2011).

A port scanner is a program that monitors the incoming and outgoing data on specific computer ports. Port scanning serves useful purposes in network administration, although hackers also employ it extensively to collect information that reveals vulnerable access points to the computer. Port scanners gather information that allows them to access computers without authorization to identify the operating system utilities present on a computer and take advantage of any known vulnerabilities. Skilled hackers use port scanners and share them online (Ananin et al., 2017).

Identifying a port scanner's activities is frequently possible by keeping an eye on the log files, which the operating system updates regularly. When a port scanner is identified, its transmissions can be found and occasionally shut down. However, port scanning activity is not regarded as illegal. Current port scanners exploit a vulnerability linked with SYN packets half-open connections. Those are much harder to detect because half-open connections are logged by the operating system (Gadge & Patil, 2008).

There exist multiple categories of port scanners, which are as follows:

a) Vanilla: The scanner attempts to establish connections with every input/output port.

b) Strobe: A targeted scan specifically searching for certain services to exploit.

c) Fragmented packets: The scanner transmits fragmented packets. These fragments have the potential to bypass specific packet filters in a firewall.

d) UDP: The scanner searches for open UDP ports.

e) Sweep: The scanner establishes connections to multiple computers (even a large number) over the same port.

f) FTP bounce: The scanner traverses an FTP server to create the impression of legitimacy.

g) Stealth scan: During the stealth scan, the operating system's log service is partially disabled to prevent it from logging the scanner's activity (Nixon et al., 2008).

Remember

SYN Flood: A DDoS assault, known as a "SYN flood," overloads a target system with a large number of SYN packets, rendering it incapable of processing new requests or responding to existing ones.

7.3. SPOOFS

→Learning Objectives

- Identify different types of spoofing attacks.
- Comprehend the risks posed by spoofing attacks.

Spoofing refers to assuming a false identity or hiding one's true intentions to deceive others or conceal one's actions. Unsurprisingly, hackers employ several spoofing techniques to gain unauthorized access or obtain information. This section describes numerous techniques for network spoofing (Ehrenkranz & Li, 2009).

7.3.1. IP Spoofing

To protect a computer from potential attacks, one might implement a security measure by limiting the IP addresses allowed to transmit data. A router maintains a safe list of IP addresses, permitting only data originating from these addresses to be received by the computer. A hacker with access to this list can spoof the router by transmitting data that mimics the characteristics of a genuine IP address. An individual without access to the list can ascertain a permissible IP address by systematically sending computer data packets with sequential IP numbers until one of the packets successfully enters the computer (Ali, 2007).

Protecting against spoofing is inherently poor due to fundamental vulnerabilities in the TCP protocol. Nevertheless, acquiring a complete comprehension of the issue and a handful of simple precautions may reduce this potential threat. The defense encompasses two primary methodologies as outlined below:

a) **Filtering:** The PC is part of a local area network that utilizes multiple IP addresses. When data is uploaded or transferred within the local network, the filter software of the router should block any source IP addresses from outside the network. This measure ensures that sending spoofed data outside the local network is impossible. Similarly, when data is received (downloaded), the filter should block any packets with sender IP addresses within the range of the local network.

b) **Encryption and Authentication:** The details of data encryption and message authentication are described by Internet protocols. These methods could help stop simple IP spoofing attacks, even though they are not ideal (Guo & Chiueh, 2006).

7.3.2. Sequence Number Spoofing

Data packet sequence numbers are used in accordance with the specifications of the TCP protocol. Each data byte is assigned a number, and the receiver must acknowledge the numerical sequence of the last contiguous byte it has received. Once the client and server establish a TCP connection, the server selects an initial sequence number (ISN) and transmits it to the client in three stages (Figure 7.1). The initial sequence number (ISN) of the first packet corresponds to its first byte. The sequence number ISN + N + 1 is found in the last byte of a packet that contains N data bytes. Consequently, the first data byte of the next packet has the sequence number ISN + N. This number is included by the server in the TCP header of the packet. Upon receiving each packet, the client responds with an acknowledgment that includes various pieces of information, one of which is the sequence number indicating the last contiguous byte received. This specific detail informs the server about the extent to which the client has received the data as a single, unbroken block (Baitha & Vinod, 2018).

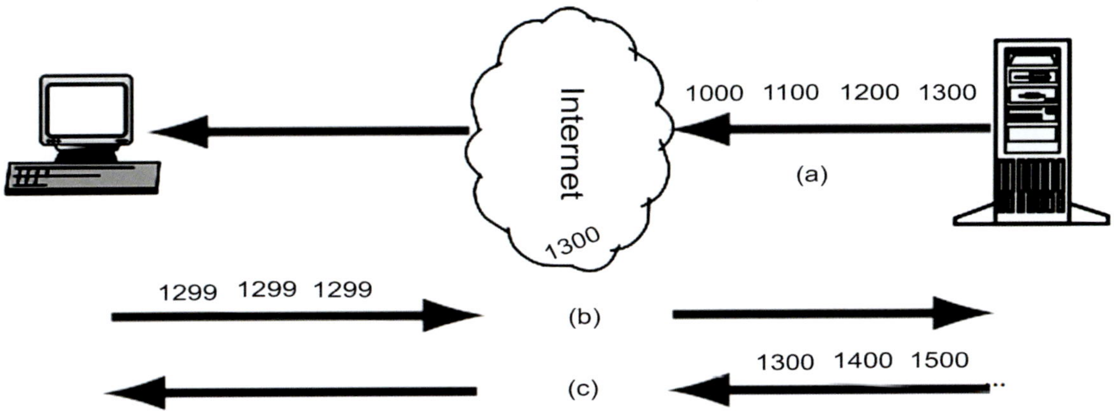

Figure 7.1. Illustration of ISNs and acknowledgments (Source: David Salomon, Creative Commons License).

7.3.3. Session Hijacking

This type of attack occurs when a hacker gains unauthorized access to network hardware, such as a router that serves as a gateway between a client and a server. In this scenario, the hacker can transmit any data, malicious software, or corrupted data to the client's computer, utilizing IP spoofing to take control of the entire data transmission session.

Authentication in the TCP/IP protocol typically takes place during the establishment of a connection, presenting an opportunity for exploitation by hackers. For example, source-routed IP packets can be manipulated to enable a hacker at node A on the network to insert themselves into a data exchange between B and C. This involves the hacker intercepting and redirecting IP packets through their own machine, positioning themselves in the middle of the communication (Jung et al., 2001).

An alternative approach is "blind" hijacking, where the hacker attempts to guess the responses of the computers at B and C. In this scenario, the hacker can send commands without being able to see the responses, but they can make educated guesses about the expected responses to various commands. A common objective is to execute commands such as setting a password that allows unauthorized access to B and C from another location on the network. This emphasizes the significance of robust security measures to counteract potential exploits in TCP/IP-based communication (Nikiforakis et al., 2011).

7.3.4. DNS

One type of computer used exclusively for networking is a domain name server (DNS). It contains a dictionary that includes IP addresses and their corresponding Uniform Resource Locators (URLs). In order to transmit data, a computer must generate packets that include the IP address of the intended recipient. The transmitting program must first establish a connection to the DNS, send the URL, and then obtain the associated IP address. This is because the human user typically knows the URL, which is a meaningful string. At that point, the application will be able to send data with the correct IP and TCP headers. Occasionally, when attempting to access a specific URL, the browser may display the message "looking for..." for a period of time.

One of the DNS-related threats is known as Man-in-the-middle (MIM) (Zhauniarovich et al., 2018). A hacker may register a domain name that is identical to an already-existing, well-known URL, such as "aple.com." If a user mistakenly inputs the word "aple" instead of "apple," the browser will establish a connection with the website controlled by the hacker once it has obtained the IP address from the DNS server (Shaikh et al., 2001). Once the hacker has gained control, their website can send its own malicious software and display content that appears identical to that of the official website. The hacker can obtain desired web pages from apple.com and send them to the user, potentially with modifications (Figure 7.2). Another method employed by the hacker is to use a sniffing application to position themselves "inline" between a user and a website, intercepting the data being exchanged between them (Bilge et al., 2011).

A typical MIM attack involves sending numerous messages to a network node, causing it to become unresponsive to visitors and legitimate users. This technique is known as a denial-of-service (DoS) attack. This attack can target a network connection, resulting in significant packet loss or a server computer crash (Pan et al., 2003).

DNS poisoning is another threat associated with DNS. The Berkeley Internet name daemon (BIND) was once the most widely used DNS software. Due to bugs in earlier program versions, it was relatively simple for a hacker to change the IP addresses linked to any URLs. Once the IP connected to, for example, apple.com, is altered by a hacker, anyone attempting to access that URL will be redirected to the hacker's website, which could have catastrophic consequences (Cranor & LaMacchia, 1998).

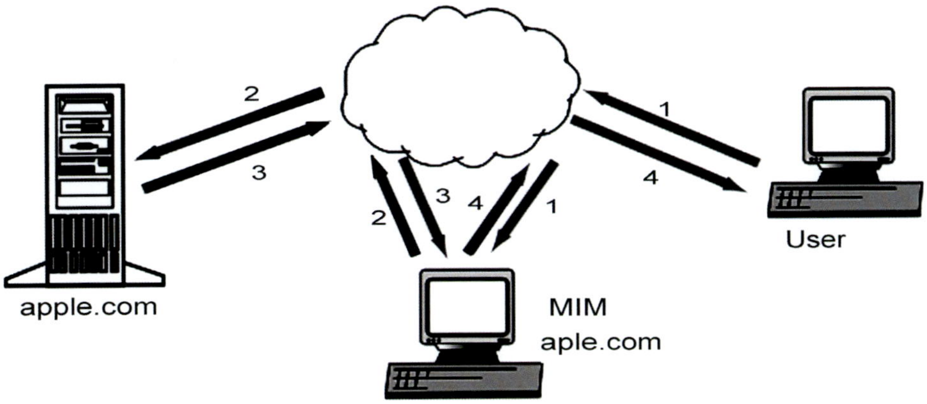

Figure 7.2. Representation of MIM model (Source: Douglas Adams, Creative Commons License).

PRACTICE PROBLEMS

1. A network administrator suspects that their network is being scanned. They notice a large number of SYN packets being sent to various ports. Explain what type of activity this likely represents and suggest measures to mitigate this issue.
2. Explain the difference between IP and MAC spoofing in network security. Also, provide measures to detect and prevent these attacks.

SOLUTIONS TO PRACTICE PROBLEMS

1. This activity likely represents a SYN flood attack, a type of denial-of-service attack where an attacker sends a large number of SYN requests, overwhelming the system's resources and making it unable to respond to legitimate requests. To mitigate this issue, the administrator can implement SYN cookies or rate-limiting techniques on the network devices to reduce the impact of SYN floods.
2. **IP Spoofing:** Involves altering the source IP address in a packet to hide the sender's identity or impersonate another entity. Detection and prevention can be achieved by implementing ingress filtering, where routers verify that the source IP address is from a legitimate range.
3. **MAC Spoofing:** Involves changing the Media Access Control (MAC) address to impersonate another device on a network. Organizations can prevent MAC spoofing by enabling port security on switches and employing MAC address filtering.

7.4. SPAM

→Learning Objectives

- Identify various forms of spam and their impact on networks.
- Recognize methods to avoid spams

Everybody has heard of spam. Spam is an uninvited email delivered in large quantities to many unresponsive recipients. Most of it is promotional advertising for dubious goods, get-rich-quick schemes, or quasi-legal or medical services. It is believed that 75% of all emails are spam, and the percentage is still rising.

The 12-ounce cans of spicy ham produced by the Hormel Corporation since 1937 are the origin of the term "Spam." While Spam itself is not a security risk, it can be utilized as a weapon in a denial-of-service attack. By sending massive volumes of similar emails to multiple users of a central computer for email communication within a major organization, an attack can be launched. This can result in the email server freezing or crashing due to overflowing data structures, consuming valuable network bandwidth, overloading the CPU, and consuming disk space (Jindal & Liu, 2008).

It is important to note that the majority of spam messages are generated from infected computers, particularly personal desktop PCs connected to DSL or high-speed cable networks. These computers have been compromised by specific strains of viruses. These viruses take control of vulnerable computers and transform them into spam proxies. Individuals with significant influence in the field of spamming can oversee vast networks of spam proxies, numbering in the thousands, at any given time. These proxies obediently distribute millions of spam messages without being detected or traced back to their source (Figure 7.3). The Sobig virus, a worm identified in 2003, was the first example of spyware designed to produce spam proxies. However, similar viruses, primarily derived from the original Sobig, are constantly being generated and spread, capable of infecting tens of thousands of computers globally on a weekly basis. The virus installs a specific type of software called spamware, which effectively hijacks the computer and initiates the distribution of spam (Dada et al., 2019).

After releasing such a virus and acquiring a new legion of spam proxies, a hacker would endeavor to resell them to spammers through private online forums. Websites like Specialham.com and Spamforum.biz, predominantly based in Florida but with servers in Russia and China, may not appear particularly captivating or advantageous to a casual visitor, let alone individuals who prioritize security. However, they are widely recognized and highly beneficial to spammers. These websites also facilitate spammers in exchanging news and information, as well as displaying advertisements for bullet-proof hosting (primarily Chinese ISPs that allow spam) (Karim et al., 2019). Currently, much of the news revolves around the actions taken by ISPs, legislators, and law enforcement agencies in various countries to make it more challenging for spammers to sustain their operations. A wealth of information is available on ISPs and networks that turn a blind eye to spam in exchange for the substantial profits generated by spammers. Additionally, experts and security personnel frequently visit these websites, providing specific data to the public to underscore the gravity of the spam problem (Yaseen, 2021).

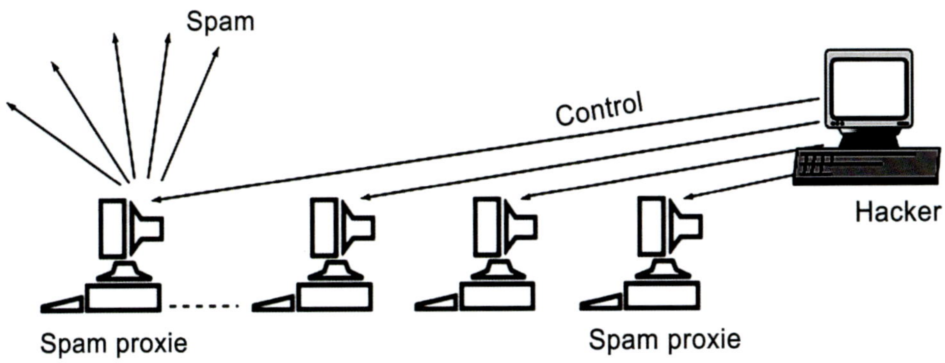

Figure 7.3. Diagram of an army of spam proxies (Source: Douglas Adams, Creative Commons License).

Here are the top four reasons why spam is so harmful:

a) Sending it is very simple: A quick Internet connection and spam software are all that a spammer needs. For only roughly $100 per day, a link of this kind could deliver millions of similar messages daily. However, if even one of the millions of recipients takes ten seconds to delete a spam message, that may amount to thousands of hours lost per day by the recipients. Furthermore, spam delivered by email to mobile phones might cost the recipient money and time (Gomes et al., 2004).

b) Many spam emails request that the recipient click on a link to be removed from the mailing list. As many individuals have found out, clicking to be taken off of such a list, at best, verifies to the spammer that the email address is legitimate and, at worst, might infect one with a virus. The ethical dilemma of why one should be required to unsubscribe from a mailing list they never requested to be added to also exists (Delany et al., 2012).

c) Spammers frequently make unauthorized use of computer resources or even outright theft. A spammer could use an online attack to take control of a computer, after which the computer would be used to distribute spam. When the recipients notice messages arriving from the PC, they complain to the owner, who is frequently an ignorant person unaware of the numerous security flaws found on the Internet.

d) Spam is trash: All of us have seen advertisements of useless merchandise and misleading or fraudulent services (Kruger et al., 2010).

7.4.1. Avoiding Spam

The following measures can be adopted to avoid spam:

a) Utilize anti-spam software, make frequent updates, and operate it regularly. This program can greatly minimize unsolicited email, particularly if it is designed to gather user or reader feedback and utilize it to identify (via the sender's address or subject line) which emails are spam.

b) Never purchase anything advertised in a promotional email, as this will fuel more spam in the future. One will receive even more unsolicited emails once the seller knows his/her email address. This is because his/her email address will be included in the massive mailing lists sold to other spammers. Even worse, answering spam exposes one as an unsuspecting person and invites more fraud and identity theft efforts (Fonseca et al., 2016).

c) Without hesitation, delete the email if the sender's name sounds unfamiliar.

d) While most spam is a nuisance, it frequently contains viruses and other malicious malware.

e) Never reply to spam emails or open any of the links therein. Responding to spam, or even removing oneself from it, lets the sender know that his/her email address is real, which encourages them to send more junk.

f) Never accept any additional information or appealing, free offers. When completing online forms, uncheck any items that provide more details or offers (Goodman & Rounthwaite, 2004).

g) Use of preview mode in an email viewer is not advised. Spammers can verify the preview of an email, even if it has not been fully opened, as the preview itself triggers the opening of the email. The spammers feel satisfied by the fact that the recipient has read their messages.

h) Limit how one utilizes their email address online. It should not be posted on websites, newsgroups, or other publicly accessible internet platforms. Spammers use software to search the internet for addresses in these types of locations, harvest them, and add them to mailing lists.

i) Only share a primary address with people one can rely on, and even then, be prepared for spammers to find and misuse it (Needham, 1993).

7.5. DENIAL OF SERVICE

→Learning Objectives

- Understand the mechanisms of DoS attacks.
- Identify strategies to mitigate the effects of DoS attacks

Numerous cyber-attacks aim to steal personal information or corrupt data. On the other hand, a denial-of-service attack seeks to bring down a specific website, a single server, or the entire network. The goal of the assault is to prevent authorized users from utilizing a service. There are several ways to accomplish this:

a) Overload a network with users. This makes data transmission and reception difficult or impossible for authorized users.

b) Break the linkage between two computers. This stops the machines from being accessed remotely.

c) Make an effort to prevent a certain user from using a service.

d) Interrupt or stop a certain computer or network from being accessed over a network. At an FTP site, a hacker might create an account, store data, and then download it frequently, using up disk space and controlling the site's network capabilities (Wood & Stankovic, 2002).

Denial-of-service attacks take down a valuable resource, such as a computer or network, but they can also be a component of larger attacks. The owner of the resource may not feel comfortable if it is private. Users of the resource may experience service interruptions if it is public. The owner of the resource faces financial losses if it is commercial. A denial-of-service attack is considered a relatively simple type of attack. Faster servers or even entire networks can be shut down (or at least slowed down) by a lone hacker using an outdated, slow PC and a slow modem (Borisov et al., 2007).

Denial-of-service attacks come in three types:

1. Depleting scarce or nonrenewable resources;
2. Erasing or altering network information;
3. Physically destroying or changing network components.

The first type of attack involves the consumption of scarce resources, leveraging the fact that computers and networks require various resources such as electrical power, CPU time, memory space, disk space, and network connections. One tactic employed by hackers is the deliberate consumption of network connectivity, achieved through a SYN flood attack. This type of attack exploits the nature of TCP connections used in client/server networks (Lau et al., 2000).

In a standard client/server network, when a client attempts to connect to a server, both parties engage in a connection protocol involving the exchange of specific messages to establish the connection. This holds true for various TCP connections, including email, telnet, and HTTP. In a SYN flood attack, the hacker initiates the connection protocol by sending a SYN message to the server. If the server is prepared to establish a connection, it responds with a SYN-ACK message, expecting to receive an ACK message from the client to complete the connection. However, in a SYN flood attack, the client deliberately withholds the ACK message, leaving the server waiting and creating a half-open connection (Needham, 1994).

This half-open connection, maintained by the server's memory data structure, can lead to memory overflows, potentially causing damage to other data in memory. To address this, the OS may detect overflow and ignore additional SYN messages. However, the attacker can persist by sending SYN requests, keeping the data structure full for extended periods, hindering legit connection attempts. The SYN flood attack can quickly overwhelm even large servers, illustrating the vulnerability of network resources to such exploitation (Pelechrinis et al., 2010) (Figure 7.4).

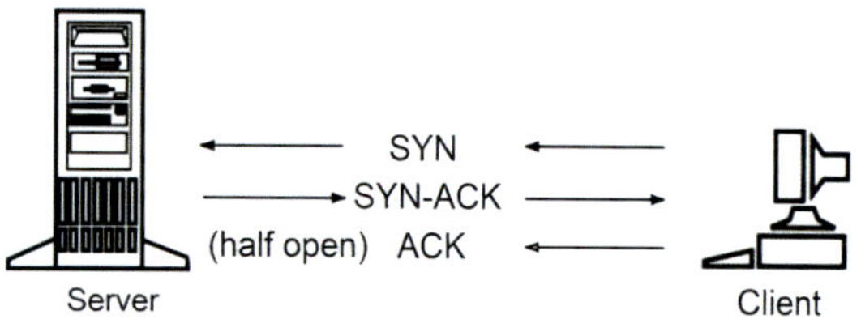

Figure 7.4. Diagram of an SYN flood attack (Source: William Strunk, Creative Commons License).

A DoS attack is executed by a hacker utilizing IP spoofing. The attacking computers send SYN messages to the targeted server, appearing to be from legitimate clients. However, the hacker selects a client that is unable to respond to the server's SYN-ACK, causing the server to hang up and drawing attention to the client.

The existing connections established prior to the attack will continue to function. Additionally, the server can still transmit data while this type of attack is ongoing. However, the attack solely impacts new clients attempting to connect to the service (Long & Thomas, 2001).

The consumption of limited resources can also occur when a hacker turns the victim's resources against them. One example of this is the misuse of the Chargen and Echo services associated with UDP data packets. While providing an in-depth explanation of these services is beyond the scope of this book, the key details are provided in the following paragraphs (Schuba et al., 1997).

Computer networks consistently send and receive data packets, some of which may be dropped or lost. The Chargen service, a character generator, was developed to identify the cause of dropped packets. This service generates random characters within a TCP session or a single UDP packet. The UDP chargen server listens for a UDP packet on port 19 and responds with a packet containing random characters.

When utilizing a TCP chargen, the server transmits a continuous stream of TCP packets until the connection is terminated. This occurs once a connection has been established. Since the data is random, it is disregarded.

Echo (defined in [RFC-862 04]) employs UDP and TCP port 7 and serves as a debugging tool. It sends any received data packets back to their source (Hussain et al., 2003).

A hacker could initiate a denial-of-service attack by spoofing an IP address and causing two computers to exchange packets containing randomly generated data. Specifically, a large number of packets are generated and exchanged when a host's charge service is connected to the echo service on the same or different computer. This can effectively overwhelm all affected computers. Furthermore, if multiple computers are connected in this manner, the network that connects them may become congested and unable to support other computers that require traffic transmission.

An attacker could potentially create and send a significant amount of data packets to a target computer. This represents an attack on bandwidth consumption that multiple intruders could carry out (Householder et al., 2001).

Resources unrelated to network services can be depleted. A program (such as a virus or Trojan horse) crafted by a hacker may simply replicate itself and initiate its execution. Consequently, the CPU will soon be burdened with hundreds, and eventually millions, of copies to process. This can lead to an overflow of the operating system's resources and a slowdown of the CPU. The operating system allocates time slots for each program and switches the CPU between them. Consequently, a comprehensive database listing all currently running programs (or processes) must be present. The table quickly fills up as the virus generates new processes, and the operating system must take appropriate measures to handle the continuous creation of new processes. These processes must be organized in a queue; if this queue becomes overwhelmed, memory data may become corrupted (Tupakula & Varadharajan, 2003).

Attackers can exploit vulnerabilities by consuming substantial amounts of disk space through various methods. For example, they may generate numerous email messages, intentionally provoke errors that require logging, and read large files from anonymous FTP servers, subsequently writing them to the disk. In this type of attack, the malicious activity persists until the disk reaches its maximum capacity, at which point the attack ceases. However, when the user later needs additional disk space, the operating system will issue an error message indicating that the disk is full.

Another method of attack involves causing an operating system to crash or become unstable by sending unexpected data over the network. A well-known example of such an attack is the "ping of death," in which an intruder sends malformed or excessively large ping packets to a target system, exploiting vulnerabilities in the way the system handles such packets. This can result in system instability or a complete crash, compromising the system's availability

Keyword

DDoS (Distributed Denial-of-Service) Attack: It is a coordinated denial-of-service attack from several sources, which makes response more difficult.

and functionality. These attacks demonstrate the various strategies attackers employ to exploit weaknesses in system resources and network protocols (Mirkovic et al., 2004).

The TCP/IP protocol allows data packets to have a maximum size of 65,536 bytes or a minimum of 20 bytes (a short header and no data bytes). The protocol does not provide instructions on how to handle larger packets because no one anticipated an assault based on massive data packets. Consequently, an operating system may exhibit abnormal behavior when it receives a packet larger than 65,536 bytes. The operating system may crash, restart, or freeze (Chandler, 2003).

As part of the Internet Control Message Protocol (ICMP), hackers have discovered that sending large data packets makes their attacks particularly "successful." Between computers, the ICMP module of the TCP/IP protocol transmits control and error signals. The ICMP specifies two distinct data packets: ECHO_REQUEST and ECHO_RESPONSE (Shields, 2002). These messages, often referred to as "ping," are frequently transmitted by a computer to ascertain the accessibility of a remote computer across the network. This technique is usually known as the "smurf attack," but other names occasionally refer to it. Mike Muuss developed the initial ping software as a component of UNIX, which garnered significant attention and subsequently became integrated into the Internet protocol.

An effective defense against the "ping of death" involves patching the low-level routines responsible for sending and receiving data packets. These patches should ensure that large packets are never sent, and the routine receiving packets should be configured to ignore packets that exceed a certain size. Typically, these patches are issued as security updates by the operating system manufacturers, providing users with protection against this specific type of Denial of Service (DoS) attack (Kessler, 2000).

The second type of DoS threat pertains to the destruction or alteration of network information. Attackers may attempt to manipulate the IP number of a victim's personal computer, alter the operating system registration, or modify prerecorded telephone numbers used by modems to connect to external servers (Zaroo, 2002).

The third type involves the physical destruction or alteration of network components, where intruders may physically appear in a computer center to disable, break, or disconnect cables and hardware devices. Additionally, hackers might climb utility poles to disconnect telephone lines or television cables, disrupting service to users in the surrounding area (Weber, 1999).

Mitigating the impact of DoS attacks requires specific actions by security experts, often involving modifications to the operating system. For instance, automatically closing half-open ports after a short duration can be implemented, although this may affect legitimate users with slow communication lines. The operating system can also ignore new processes when the number of active processes in memory reaches a certain limit, but this may hinder legitimate administrative tasks. Another approach involves limiting the size of disk files, but this could potentially inconvenience users with a legitimate need for large files, such as those containing movies. Striking the right balance in implementing these measures is crucial for effective defense against DoS attacks (Kabachinski, 2004).

7.6. FIREWALL BASICS

→Learning Objectives

- Understand the purpose and functions of firewalls in network security.
- Learn about configuring and managing firewall rules to enhance network security.

A firewall is a combination of software and hardware that regulates the flow of requests and specific data packets into and out of a computer or local network. Figure 7.5 shows a conventional hardware firewall that protects an entire local-area network. A personal computer commonly depends on software to effectively deploy a firewall. However, a modest home network, typically consisting of 2–3 computers and a printer, might incorporate a hardware firewall within the router of the network (Curtin & Ranum, 2000).

The primary function of a firewall is to restrict specific data transfer requests by implementing rules to make decisions. Initially, a firewall contains predefined rules, which can be added, removed, and altered by its user/owner. A firewall implements an access policy by utilizing rules that specify the characteristics of a data packet to inspect and determine whether to permit or deny its passage (Hazari, 2000).

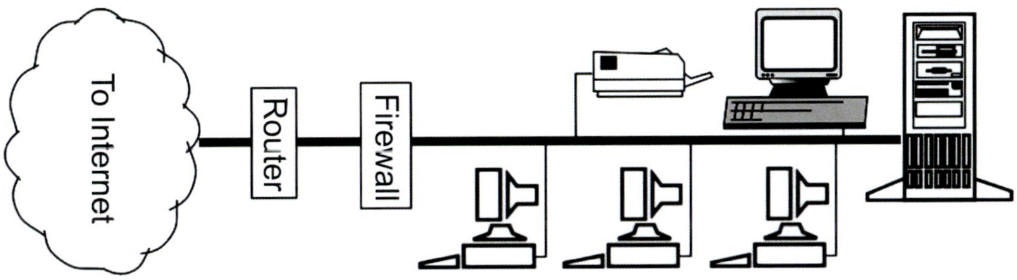

Figure 7.5. Representation of a firewall in LAN (Source: David Salomon, Creative Commons License).

An efficient firewall should readily conform to any user's requirements. An effective firewall must be able to examine every characteristic of a data packet, make appropriate decisions based on its findings, and perform these tasks rapidly to maintain the smooth transmission of data to and from the host computer or network.

A conventional firewall performs the following functions:

1. Restricts incoming data by blocking data from specific senders or with specific attributes.
2. Restricts outgoing data to prevent programs from transmitting data without the owner's awareness.
3. Generates and stores a record of its operations, particularly on blocked data packets.

4. Performs all these tasks rapidly while remaining transparent to the user.

Data packets possess several attributes, including distinct fields in the packet's header. These fields encompass information such as the device, direction, source, destination addresses, and the source and destination ports. A rule can be defined to prevent all packets coming at port 5500 or always to allow packets arriving from IP address 192.168.1.50 (Robertson et al., 2004).

A firewall rule defines a collection of criteria and the corresponding action to be taken when a criterion is met. A complicated rule can evaluate several conditions, whereas a simple rule is restricted to assessing only one condition. Hierarchical structures can also govern rules. Under such circumstances, each rule is uncomplicated and verifies a single condition, although a rule may contain multiple subordinate rules, each evaluating a distinct condition. Thus, while each rule is uncomplicated, the collective performance might be complex (McDermott, 2000).

Typically, a rule consists of a condition and an associated action. The condition refers to a property, a connection, and a value. For example, a condition could be that the destination port equals 5500. When the condition is met, the corresponding action is executed. If not, the firewall proceeds to the next rule. In a hierarchical firewall, each condition is defined with its parent and any associated children. In this firewall, when a rule's condition is satisfied, the subsequent rules are evaluated individually. If the condition is not satisfied, the subsequent rule at the same level, known as the sibling rule, is evaluated. If none of the conditions specified by the sibling rules are satisfied, the subsequent rule at the preceding level is examined. Figure 7.6 illustrates a hierarchical tree of rules and the systematic manner in which they are verified (Abie, 2000).

Some advantageous circumstances may not be related to the content of data packets. The attributes included in this list include the date, day of the week, time, parent idle time, and parent byte count. Network administrators have discovered that restricting access to specific websites or services during peak times can improve the overall performance of the network. Similarly, various limitations on network utilization may be relaxed or removed on weekends (Lynch, 2000).

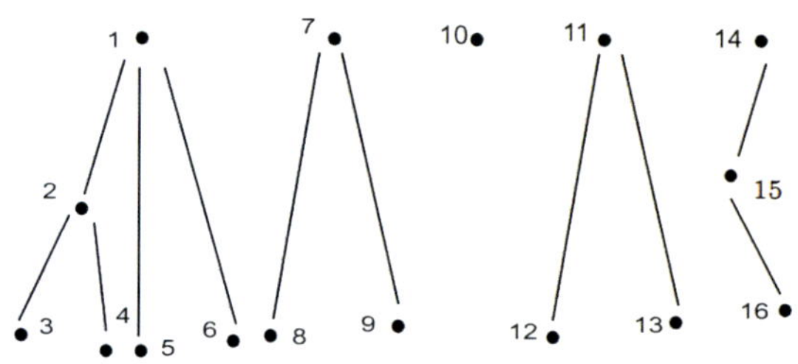

Figure 7.6. Illustration of hierarchical firewall rules (Source: William Strunk, Creative Commons License).

An effective firewall can gather fundamental information about the data packets that satisfy each rule. Upon encountering a rule, a packet's idle time is immediately reset to zero, its match count increases by 1, and the byte count is increased by the size of the packet. These statistics can be advantageous for both the computer owner and the network administrator and can be utilized in the application of rules. For example, consider a scenario where a rule is unable to identify any information from a specific sender for a specified time of inactivity. Under some circumstances, the action specified by the rule is activated, regardless of whether any data packets have been received.

This action may involve sending a probe to the sender or informing the user that the sender's response time is insufficient (Nacht, 1998).

Actions in computer systems encompass various operations. For example, the action of "delete" eradicates a data packet, while "pass" permits its passage, either into or out of the computer. On the other hand, the action of "drop" terminates the connection, particularly in response to a DoS attack that aims to disrupt the connection. Lastly, the action of "log" involves recording the data packet and subsequently applying the next rule to it. During the process of receiving data packets, if an error occurs, the "drop" action is initiated, which involves sending a TCP RESET command to the sender. On the other hand, when a packet is being sent, the identical action causes the transmission of a brief TCP FIN message (Ranum, 1993).

A firewall consists of two primary elements: the gate and the choke. A large firewall may have multiple pairs of gates and chokes. The gate serves the purpose of either allowing the data to pass through or blocking it, whereas the choke acts as a filter that decides which data to block. Experts in firewalls often make an analogy between the gate, which serves as a security checkpoint, and the choke, which functions as a security guard (Tomar & Bhile, 2021).

A modern firewall can perform advanced operations in addition to verifying conditions and implementing actions, as explained below.

a) Modern firewalls may have rules for inspecting the contents of a data packet, not just the header fields. This useful function is known as Content Filtering. When the user instructs the firewall to do so, incoming data packets (and possibly all outgoing packets) containing specific character strings can be blocked. This can effectively prevent the transmission of well-known viruses and worms that have already been identified and analyzed. In order for an advanced firewall to differentiate between external and internal traffic, it must be capable of recognizing Ethernet hardware or MAC addresses (Wilson, 2005).

b) Another complex task involves limiting the amount of data (bandwidth) allocated to specific users or applications. A firewall can assist in managing bandwidth in this way. Let's consider an Internet Service Provider (ISP) that offers cable-based Internet connectivity to individual subscribers. A typical private user usually has one or two computers and generates minimal data traffic, such as web browsing, email communication, and file transfers. Moreover, the majority of this traffic should be inbound. If every user adheres to this usage pattern, the ISP can accommodate a large number of users.

c) Bandwidth management is a critical task for Internet Service Providers (ISPs) to ensure fair usage among users sharing the same network. In a scenario where one user is excessively consuming bandwidth, causing slow speeds and complaints from other users, the ISP may implement limitations on the amount of data each user can send. This bandwidth management task is ideally performed by the ISP's firewall to regulate and distribute network resources equitably.

d) Modern firewalls also play a vital

role in bandwidth accounting, providing the owner/operator of a local network with insights into network usage patterns over time. This includes variations in network activity during different hours, days, and months. By offering information about the traffic flow to and from each computer on the network, firewalls assist network managers in understanding usage trends. Graphical representations of this data can reveal important patterns, such as specific computers being active on weekends or network bandwidth insufficiencies at particular times (Schultz, 1995).

e) A proficient firewall has the capability to generate an elaborate connection log, documenting every connection established between a computer within the network and an external address. This log encompasses details such as the date, time, and the volume of data transferred in each direction. This connection logging serves as an audit trail and can be invaluable when investigating unusual occurrences, such as potential attacks. By providing a comprehensive overview of the network's usage, connection logging assists in identifying areas for enhancement and improving the overall behavior of the local network (Audin, 2004).

SUMMARY

- This chapter discusses network security, which involves the implementation of various techniques, technologies, and practices to protect network infrastructure, data, and communication from unauthorized access, attacks, and vulnerabilities. Effective network security relies on several essential components and principles.
- Internet vulnerabilities are inherent weaknesses or defects in network systems that attackers can exploit maliciously. Prevention involves implementing frequent updates, patches, and strong security measures.
- Port scanning is used to detect active network devices and open ports, which attackers commonly use to gather information about possible weaknesses. Defenses include the utilization of port filtering, intrusion detection systems, and firewalls.
- There are various types of spoofing attacks, such as IP spoofing and MAC spoofing. Attackers manipulate the source IP or MAC addresses to deceive systems in these attacks. Preventive measures include input filtering, MAC address filtering, and robust authentication techniques.
- This chapter also discusses the concept of spam, which refers to unwanted and frequently harmful emails that are sent without prior consent. Mitigation strategies include the implementation of spam filters and blacklisting mechanisms. Denial of Service (DoS) assaults, including Distributed Denial of Service (DDoS) attacks, overload networks or systems with excessive traffic. Defenses against these attacks include the implementation of traffic filtering, rate limitation, and the utilization of content delivery networks.
- Firewalls play a crucial role in regulating the movement of data between networks by establishing rules that authorize or prohibit specific categories of data. Various categories of firewalls include packet filtering, stateful inspection, and application-layer firewalls.

MULTIPLE CHOICE QUESTIONS

1. **Which of the following best describes internet vulnerability?**
   a) A secure and impenetrable network.
   b) Weaknesses or flaws in network systems that can be exploited.
   c) High-speed internet connections
   d) Encrypted data transmissions
2. **What is the main objective of performing port scanning in the context of network security?**
   a) To identify active network devices
   b) To establish secure connections
   c) To prevent unauthorized access
   d) To hide network vulnerabilities

3. Which of the following is an example of a spoofing attack?

a) DDoS attack

b) Phishing attack

c) Brute force attack

d) Social engineering attack

4. What is a common method to mitigate the impact of spam in network communications?

a) Using strong encryption

b) Implementing firewall rules

c) Deploying antivirus software

d) Utilizing spam filters and blacklisting techniques

5. Which type of attack floods a network or system with an overwhelming volume of traffic, rendering it unavailable to users?

a) Spoofing attack

b) Phishing attack

c) Denial-of-Service (DoS) attack

d) Port scanning attack

6. What is the primary purpose of a firewall in network security?

a) To encrypt data transmissions

b) To prevent unauthorized access and control traffic flow

c) To detect phishing attempts

d) To secure physical network devices

REVIEW QUESTIONS

1. Define internet vulnerabilities and provide examples of common vulnerabilities that affect network security.
2. Explain the concept of port scanning in the context of network security. Describe different types of port scans and their implications.
3 What are spoofing attacks in the realm of network security?
4. Describe the various forms of spam and their risks to network security. What strategies can be employed to minimize the impact of spam on both individual users and organizations?
5. Discuss the different types of denial-of-service (DoS) attacks and their mechanisms.

Answers to Multiple Questions

1. (b) 2. (a) 3. (b) 4. (d) 5. (c) 6. (b)

REFERENCES

1. Abie, H., (2000). An overview of firewall technologies. *Telektronikk, 96*(3), 47–52.
2. Abomhara, M., & Køien, G. M., (2015). Cyber security and the internet of things: Vulnerabilities, threats, intruders, and attacks. *Journal of Cyber Security and Mobility, 1*(1), 65–88.
3. Abu, B. R., & Kijsirikul, B., (2023). Enhancing network visibility and security with advanced port scanning techniques. *Sensors, 23*(17), 7541.
4. Ali, F., (2007). IP spoofing. *The Internet Protocol Journal, 10*(4), 1–9.
5. Al-Saleh, M. I., Al-Sharif, Z. A., & Alawneh, L., (2019). Network reconnaissance investigation: A memory forensics approach. In: *2019 10th International Conference on Information and Communication Systems (ICICS)* (Vol. 1, No. 1, pp. 36–40). IEEE.
6. Ananin, E. V., Nikishova, A. V., & Kozhevnikova, I. S., (2017). Port scanning detection based on anomalies. In: *2017 Dynamics of Systems, Mechanisms and Machines (Dynamics),* (Vol. 1, No. 1, pp.1–5.
7. Andrea, I., Chrysostomou, C., & Hadjichristofi, G., (2015). Internet of things: Security vulnerabilities and challenges. In: *2015 IEEE Symposium on Computers and Communication (ISCC)* (Vol. 1, No. 1, pp. 180–187). IEEE.
8. Audin, G., (2004). Next-gen firewalls: What to expect. *Business Communications Review, 34*(6), 56–61.
9. Baitha, A. K., & Vinod, S., (2018). Session hijacking and prevention technique. *Int. J. Eng. Technol, 7*(2.6), 193–198.
10. Bhuyan, M. H., Bhattacharyya, D. K., & Kalita, J. K., (2011). Surveying port scans and their detection methodologies. *The Computer Journal, 54*(10), 1565–1581.
11. Bilge, L., Kirda, E., Kruegel, C., & Balduzzi, M., (2011). Exposure: Finding malicious domains using passive DNS analysis. In: *NDSS* (Vol. 1, No. 1, pp. 1–17).
12. Borisov, N., Danezis, G., Mittal, P., & Tabriz, P., (2007). Denial of service or denial of security? In: *Proceedings of the 14th ACM Conference on Computer and Communications Security* (Vol. 1, No. 1, pp. 92–102).
13. Butun, I., Österberg, P., & Song, H., (2019). Security of the internet of things: Vulnerabilities, attacks, and countermeasures. *IEEE Communications Surveys & Tutorials, 22*(1), 616–644.
14. Chandler, J. A., (2003). Security in cyberspace: Combatting distributed denial of service attacks. *U. Ottawa L. & Tech. J., 1*, 231.
15. Cormack, G. V., (2008). Email spam filtering: A systematic review. *Foundations and Trends® in Information Retrieval, 1*(4), 335–455.
16. Cranor, L. F., & LaMacchia, B. A., (1998). Spam! *Communications of the ACM, 41*(8), 74–83.
17. Curtin, M., & Ranum, M. J., (2000). *Internet Firewalls: Frequently Asked Questions* (Vol. 19, p. 48). In Date.
18. Dabbagh, M., Ghandour, A. J., Fawaz, K., El Hajj, W., & Hajj, H., (2011). Slow port

scanning detection. In: *2011 7th International Conference on Information Assurance and Security (IAS)* (Vol. 1, No. 1, pp. 228–233). IEEE.

19. Dada, E. G., Bassi, J. S., Chiroma, H., Adetunmbi, A. O., & Ajibuwa, O. E., (2019). Machine learning for email spam filtering: Review, approaches, and open research problems. *Heliyon, 5*(6), 1–20.
20. De Vivo, M., Carrasco, E., Isern, G., & De Vivo, G. O., (1999). A review of port scanning techniques. *ACM SIGCOMM Computer Communication Review, 29*(2), 41–48.
21. De Vivo, M., De Vivo, G. O., Koeneke, R., & Isern, G., (1999). Internet vulnerabilities related to TCP/IP and T/TCP. *ACM SIGCOMM Computer Communication Review, 29*(1), 81–85.
22. Delany, S. J., Buckley, M., & Greene, D., (2012). SMS spam filtering: Methods and data. *Expert Systems with Applications, 39*(10), 9899–9908.
23. Ehrenkranz, T., & Li, J., (2009). On the state of IP spoofing defense. *ACM Transactions on Internet Technology (TOIT), 9*(2), 1–29.
24. Fonseca, O., Fazzion, E., Cunha, I., Las-Casas, P. H. B., Guedes, D., Meira, W., & Chaves, M. H., (2016). Measuring, characterizing, and avoiding spam traffic costs. *IEEE Internet Computing, 20*(4), 16–24.
25. Gadge, J., & Patil, A. A., (2008). Port scan detection. In: *2008 16th IEEE International Conference on Networks* (Vol. 1, No. 1, pp. 1–6). IEEE.
26. Gomes, L. H., Cazita, C., Almeida, J. M., Almeida, V., & Meira, Jr. W., (2004). Characterizing a spam traffic. In: *Proceedings of the 4th ACM SIGCOMM Conference on Internet Measurement* (Vol. 1, No. 1, pp. 356–369).
27. Goodman, J. T., & Rounthwaite, R., (2004). Stopping outgoing spam. In: *Proceedings of the 5th ACM Conference on Electronic Commerce* (Vol. 1, No. 1, pp. 30–39).
28. Greene, T., (2007). Next-gen firewalls will need wide variety of features. *Network World Canada, 23*(22), 1–20.
29. Guo, F., & Chiueh, T. C., (2006). Sequence number-based MAC address spoof detection. In: *Recent Advances in Intrusion Detection: 8th International Symposium, RAID 2005, Seattle, WA, USA, Revised Papers 8* (pp. 309–329). Springer Berlin Heidelberg.
30. Householder, A., Manion, A., Pesante, L., Weaver, G. M., & Thomas, R., (2001). Managing the threat of denial-of-service attacks. *CERT Coordination Center, 10*, 1–20.
31. Hussain, A., Heidemann, J., & Papadopoulos, C., (2003). A framework for classifying denial of service attacks. In: *Proceedings of the 2003 Conference on Applications, Technologies, Architectures, and Protocols for Computer Communications* (Vol. 1, No. 1, pp. 99–110).
32. Jindal, N., & Liu, B., (2008). Opinion spam and analysis. In: *Proceedings of the 2008 International Conference on Web Search and Data Mining* (Vol. 1, No. 1, pp. 219–230).

33. Jung, J., Sit, E., Balakrishnan, H., & Morris, R., (2001). DNS performance and the effectiveness of caching. In: *Proceedings of the 1st ACM SIGCOMM Workshop on Internet Measurement* (Vol. 1, No. 1, pp. 153–167).

34. Kabachinski, J., (2004). Network firewall basics—Part 1. *Biomedical Instrumentation & Technology, 38*(5), 375–377.

35. Karim, A., Azam, S., Shanmugam, B., Kannoorpatti, K., & Alazab, M., (2019). A comprehensive survey for intelligent spam email detection. *IEEE Access, 7*, 168261–168295.

36. Kaushik, A. K., Pilli, E. S., & Joshi, R. C., (2010). Network forensic system for port scanning attack. In: *2010 IEEE 2nd International Advance Computing Conference (IACC)* (Vol. 1, No. 1, pp. 310–315). IEEE.

37. Kessler, G. C., (2000). *Defenses Against Distributed Denial of Service Attacks* (pp. 1–20). SANS Institute–2002.

38. Krüger, A., Kates, R. E., & Edwards, D. R., (2010). Avoiding spam in the proteolytic internet: Future strategies for anti-metastatic MMP inhibition. *Biochimica et Biophysica Acta (BBA)-Molecular Cell Research, 1803*(1), 95–102.

39. Lagraa, S., & François, J., (2017). Knowledge discovery of port scans from darknet. In: *2017 IFIP/IEEE Symposium on Integrated Network and Service Management (IM)* (Vol. 1, No. 1, pp. 935–940). IEEE.

40. Lau, F., Rubin, S. H., Smith, M. H., & Trajkovic, L., (2000). Distributed denial of service attacks. In: *SMC 2000 Conference Proceedings; 2000 IEEE International Conference on Systems, Man and Cybernetics;' Cybernetics Evolving to Systems, Humans, Organizations, and Their Complex Interactions'* (cat. no. 0, Vol. 3, pp. 2275–2280). IEEE.

41. Long, N., & Thomas, R., (2001). Trends in denial of service attack technology. *CERT Coordination Center, 648*(651), 569.

42. Lynch, H. M., (2000). Firewall fundamentals. *Information Systems Security, 9*(5), 1–11.

43. Marin, G. A., (2005). Network security basics. *IEEE Security & Privacy, 3*(6), 68–72.

44. McDermott, P., (2000). Personal firewalls… One more step towards comprehensive security. *Network Security, 2000*(11), 11–14.

45. Mirkovic, J., Dietrich, S., Dittrich, D., & Reiher, P., (2004). Internet denial of service: Attack and defense mechanisms (Radia Perlman computer networking and security). *Prentice Hall PTR, 1*(1), 1–20.

46. Moore, D., Shannon, C., Brown, D. J., Voelker, G. M., & Savage, S., (2006). Inferring internet denial-of-service activity. *ACM Transactions on Computer Systems (TOCS), 24*(2), 115–139.

47. Nacht, M., (1998). The spectrum of modern firewalls. *Computers & Security, 17*(1), 54–56.

48. Needham, R. M., (1993). Denial of service. In: *Proceedings of the 1st ACM Conference on Computer and Communications Security* (Vol. 1, No. 1, pp. 151–153).

49. Needham, R. M., (1994). Denial of service: An example. *Communications of the ACM, 37*(11), 42–46.

50. Nikiforakis, N., Meert, W., Younan, Y., Johns, M., & Joosen, W., (2011). SessionShield: Lightweight protection against session hijacking. In: *Engineering Secure Software and Systems: Third International Symposium, ESSoS 2011, Madrid, Spain, Proceedings 3* (pp. 87–100). Springer Berlin Heidelberg.
51. Nixon, K. A., Aimale, V., & Rowe, R. K., (2008). Spoof detection schemes. In: *Handbook of Biometrics* (Vol. 1, No. 1, pp. 403–423). Boston, MA: Springer US.
52. Pan, J., Hou, Y. T., & Li, B., (2003). An overview of DNS-based server selections in content distribution networks. *Computer Networks, 43*(6), 695–711.
53. Pelechrinis, K., Iliofotou, M., & Krishnamurthy, S. V., (2010). Denial of service attacks in wireless networks: The case of jammers. *IEEE Communications Surveys & Tutorials, 13*(2), 245–257.
54. Ranum, M. J., (1993). Thinking about firewalls. In: *Proceedings of Second International Conference on Systems and Network Security and Management (SANS-II)* (Vol. 8).
55. Rattani, A., Scheirer, W. J., & Ross, A., (2015). Open set fingerprint spoof detection across novel fabrication materials. *IEEE Transactions on Information Forensics and Security, 10*(11), 2447–2460.
56. Robertson, P. D., Curtin, M., & Ranum, M. J., (2004). *Internet Firewalls: Frequently Asked Questions, 1*(1), 1–20.
57. Rowan, T., (2007). Application firewalls: Filling the void. *Network Security, 2007*(4), 4–7.
58. Schuba, C. L., Krsul, I. V., Kuhn, M. G., Spafford, E. H., Sundaram, A., & Zamboni, D., (1997). Analysis of a denial of service attack on TCP. In: *Proceedings. 1997 IEEE Symposium on Security and Privacy (Cat. No. 97CB36097)* (pp. 208–223). IEEE.
59. Schultz, E. E., (1995). A new perspective on firewalls. *Network Security, 1995*(10), 13–17.
60. Shah, M., Ahmed, S., Saeed, K., Junaid, M., & Khan, H., (2019). Penetration testing active reconnaissance phase–optimized port scanning with Nmap tool. In: *2019 2nd International Conference on Computing, Mathematics and Engineering Technologies (iCoMET)* (Vol. 1, No. 1, pp. 1–6). IEEE.
61. Shaikh, A., Tewari, R., & Agrawal, M., (2001). On the effectiveness of DNS-based server selection. In: *Proceedings IEEE INFOCOM 2001. Conference on Computer Communications. Twentieth Annual Joint Conference of the IEEE Computer and Communications Society (Cat. No. 01CH37213)* (Vol. 3, pp. 1801–1810). IEEE.
62. Shields, C., (2002). What do we mean by network denial of service. In: *Proceedings of the 2002 IEEE Workshop on Information Assurance and Security* (Vol. 4, pp. 1–20).
63. Shiravi, H., Shiravi, A., & Ghorbani, A. A., (2011). A survey of visualization systems for network security. *IEEE Transactions on Visualization and Computer Graphics, 18*(8), 1313–1329.
64. Spirin, N., & Han, J., (2012). Survey on web spam detection: Principles and algorithms. *ACM SIGKDD Explorations Newsletter, 13*(2), 50–64.

65. Sridharan, A., & Ye, T., (2007). Tracking port scanners on the IP backbone. In: *Proceedings of the 2007 Workshop on Large Scale Attack Defense,* (Vol. 1, No. 1, pp. 137–144).

66. Tang, W. X., Zhang, H. C., Ma, H. F., Jiang, W. X., & Cui, T. J., (2019). Concept, theory, design, and applications of spoof surface plasmon polaritons at microwave frequencies. *Advanced Optical Materials,* 7(1), 1800421.

67. Tomar, Y. S., & Bhile, N., (2021). First line of defense: Firewall. *Asian Journal of Research in Computer Science, 12*(3), 25–32.

68. Tupakula, U. K., & Varadharajan, V., (2003). A practical method to counteract denial of service attacks. In: *Proceedings of the 26th Australasian Computer Science Conference* (Vol. 16, pp. 275–284).

69. Viet, H. N., Van, Q. N., Trang, L. L. T., & Nathan, S., (2018). Using deep learning model for network scanning detection. In: *Proceedings of the 4th International Conference on Frontiers of Educational Technologies* (Vol. 1, No. 1, pp. 117–121).

70. Weber, W., (1999). Firewall basics. In: *4th International Conference on Telecommunications in Modern Satellite, Cable and Broadcasting Services. TELSIKS'99 (Cat. No. 99EX365)* (Vol. 1, pp. 300–305). IEEE.

71. Wilson, J., (2005). The future of the firewall. *Business Communications Review, 5*, 28–32.

72. Wood, A. D., & Stankovic, J. A., (2002). Denial of service in sensor networks. *Computer, 35*(10), 54–62.

73. Yaseen, Q., (2021). Spam email detection using deep learning techniques. *Procedia Computer Science, 184*, 853–858.

74. Zaroo, P., (2002). A survey of DDoS attacks and some DDoS defense mechanisms. *Advanced Information Assurance (CS 626)*, 1–20.

75. Zhang, X., Cui, W. Y., Lei, Y., Zheng, X., Zhang, J., & Cui, T. J., (2021). Spoof localized surface plasmons for sensing applications. *Advanced Materials Technologies, 6*(4), 2000863.

76. Zhang, Y., Yin, Z., Li, Y., Yin, G., Yan, J., Shao, J., & Liu, Z., (2020). Celeba-spoof: Large-scale face anti-spoofing dataset with rich annotations. In: *Computer Vision–ECCV 2020: 16th European Conference, Glasgow, UK, August 23–28, 2020, Proceedings, Part XII 16* (pp. 70–85). Springer International Publishing.

77. Zhauniarovich, Y., Khalil, I., Yu, T., & Dacier, M., (2018). A survey on malicious domains detection through DNS data analysis. *ACM Computing Surveys (CSUR), 51*(4), 1–36.

CHAPTER

8 Web Application Security

LEARNING OBJECTIVES

After studying this chapter, you will be able to:

- Different threats targeting web applications.
- Common vulnerabilities prevalent in web applications.
- Various attack techniques used against web applications.
- Preventive measures to secure web applications.

INTRODUCTORY EXAMPLE

The widespread availability of web applications has completely changed the way individuals engage with information and services in the digital world. Undoubtedly, the extensive use of these applications, including social networking sites and e-commerce platforms, has simplified accessibility and connectivity. However, this extensive integration has also exposed vulnerabilities, raising pertinent questions about the security of these web-based systems.

Let us consider a prominent social networking site that attracts millions of users daily. This platform effortlessly connects individuals from all corners of the globe, yet it remains a constant target for cybercriminals. Exploiting flaws in the platform's code, malicious hackers gain unauthorized access to user profiles and private information. This incident not only compromises user privacy but also undermines confidence in the platform's security protocols. In this context, the delicate balance that online applications must maintain between security and accessibility becomes evident. Due to their user-friendly nature and widespread availability, protecting online apps from a wide range of potential threats is a challenging task.

UNIT INTRODUCTION

Throughout the last five years, web technology has changed. Due to this progression, businesses are creating Web-enabled applications, and most applications now use browsers as their preferred user interface. Significant progress has been made in the banking, insurance, manufacturing, and telecommunications sectors. Due to business imperatives, organizations must now use Web interfaces to expose their core applications to partners, customers, and vendors across public networks. As a result, Web apps, or applications that run in a browser, are now utilized for high-value transactions and business-critical tasks. Because of this, Web applications become appealing targets for hackers who take advantage of the anonymity provided by the Web to obtain financial gain by breaching these systems.

Attackers' usual focal points were unsecured network devices and operating system vulnerabilities. The underlying systems are now harder to hack thanks to increased knowledge, robust operating systems, and better security measures. Recent observations suggest a shift in the attacker's domain from the internet to the application layer. Therefore, developers and security experts must understand Web application security more deeply (Li & Xue, 2011).

This chapter will discuss the threats that Web applications are currently facing, the origins of these threats, the various types of vulnerabilities responsible for these threats, and the methods that attackers employ to exploit these flaws. The reader will gain a comprehensive understanding of the risks associated with specific vulnerabilities and the exploit methodologies employed by attackers. This will be achieved by drawing on research that evaluates the security of Web applications, including online banking applications, sales force automation software, financial trading applications, and other similar applications. Additionally, the necessary steps to incorporate security into the development lifecycle of web applications will be addressed (Curphey & Arawo, 2006).

8.1. WEB APPLICATIONS THREATS

→Learning Objectives

- Identify various threats targeting web applications.
- Recognize the impact of threats on web application security and their potential consequences.

Web applications are vulnerable to numerous attacks. They utilize the HTTP protocol and are accessed and displayed through an online browser, such as Internet Explorer, via the Internet. Unlike client/server applications that rely on private networks, web applications are globally accessible through a web browser. This broad accessibility increases the user base but also opens up the possibility of misuse. Attackers can exploit web apps by taking advantage of the relative anonymity of the Internet. Malicious actors, including disgruntled workers, industrial espionage operatives, and anonymous attackers, can utilize web apps to target organizations and steal corporate secrets (Abusaimeh & Shkoukani, 2012).

To better understand the security risks faced by web applications, let's consider the example of an online banking application. What are the potential risks that an ordinary online banking application might encounter? There are five possible ways in which a hacker could harm the bank or its customers:

a) Impersonate a customer or a bank employee and execute fraudulent transactions.

b) Illegally transfer funds from another customer's account.

c) Steal financial and personal information about the bank's customers.

d) Open fake accounts for money laundering.

e) Deny access to the application to the bank's clients.

These factors have a significant impact on the bank's operational safety. The realization of these threats may be attributed to a vulnerable Web application. Therefore, let us explore the origins of vulnerabilities in Web applications (Sadqi & Maleh, 2022).

Did you know?

Well-established computer firms such as Google, Facebook, and Microsoft provide bug bounty programs to reward ethical hackers who identify and disclose security vulnerabilities in their systems, rather than exploiting them.

8.2. ORIGIN OF THE RISKS

Like any other software, web applications often have vulnerabilities in their code that can be used by an attacker to gain control of the system. These vulnerabilities can range from basic omission errors to more intricate logical problems. In Web applications, the impacts of these vulnerabilities are typically far more severe. First of all, why are Web apps more vulnerable? What is the source of their insecurity? (Wang et al., 2013). Three causes for the insecurity of many Web apps have been demonstrated.:

a) **Lack of Threat Awareness:** Application designers and developers frequently lack awareness of the threats that a Web application may encounter. While developers often receive training in a new programming language or technology, they are rarely instructed on the security vulnerabilities inherent in that language or technology. This lack of knowledge leads to a disregard for security concerns, resulting in the creation of insecure applications. It is a common mistake for developers to assume that firewalls and encryption alone are sufficient for security. While encryption and firewalls are necessary components, they are only part of the overall security plan. They are unable to defend against applications that are designed insecurely (Deepa & Thilagam, 2016).

b) **Testing Methodologies are not Advanced:** While web application testing has benefited from adapting functional testing approaches over the past 30 years, there is currently no comparable paradigm for security testing. The field of security testing is still developing and will take some time to mature, particularly for web applications. Insufficient security testing of applications in production is mostly attributed to the absence of powerful automated testing tools, the inherent complexity of certain tests, and a shortage of competent professionals to conduct these tests. Many software programs neglect security testing due to the need to achieve deadlines (Sudhodanan et al., 2019).

c) **Reverse Engineering is Simple:** The unencrypted HTTP protocol sends application-layer inquiries and responses between web applications. Web applications employ instructions and variables that are simple to reverse engineer. By observing how requests and replies move through a web site, an attacker might anticipate potential security vulnerabilities in the application (Rudman, 2010).

Did you know?

The most important security threats to online applications are compiled in the OWASP (Open Web Application Security Project) Top 10 list. It is a widely accepted awareness document that should be used as a guide for deciding which web application security initiatives to prioritize.

8.3. VULNERABILITIES IN WEB APPLICATIONS

→Learning Objectives

- Identify common vulnerabilities in web applications.
- Comprehend the potential risks associated with each vulnerability.

Let's examine common vulnerabilities that impact Web applications. These vulnerabilities enable attackers to exploit a Web application and cause harm.

a) **Insufficient Input Validation:** If the application fails to validate user input, it may inadvertently allow lengthy inputs and special characters where they should not be permitted, resulting in unexpected and potentially harmful consequences. The most severe attacks arise from developers neglecting to thoroughly validate specific inputs (Sun et al., 2011).

b) **Reliance on Data Provided by the Client:** Web application developers often place implicit trust in query-string variables, cookies, and hidden variables because these variables were initially established by the application. However, the application must verify the integrity of the data received from the client, as it could have been altered during transmission, even if it is stored in a hidden variable. If the application accepts the client's data without verification, an attacker could modify certain variables and cause harm (Di et al., 2004).

c) **Insecure Cryptography Usage:** Occasionally, when solving a problem, developers may select the incorrect choice of cryptographic algorithms. There may be situations where using the highest grade of encryption is not the most suitable course of action. Insufficient understanding of the advantages and disadvantages of a cryptographic solution can lead to incorrect and insecure implementations. For instance, there have been cases where the password is transmitted from the client to the server during the log-in process using a robust one-way hash method. While this approach works well for password storage, it is not secure for password transmission as it is vulnerable to replay attacks (Dahse & Holz, 2014).

d) **Inappropriate Use of Page Caching:** The cache-control tags, which are set by the application during the delivery of the page to the client, determine the duration for which HTML pages are stored in the client's browser cache. When a legitimate user utilizes an application and caches sensitive sites on the browser, unauthorized users can access those pages. Developers may employ incorrect cache-control directives, resulting in pages remaining accessible in the cache beyond the intended timeframe (Shar & Tan, 2012).

e) **Incorrect Selection of Variable Types and HTTP Actions:** The client may submit GET or POST requests over HTTP in its requests. Since the server-side programming language can equally understand both requests, developers occasionally use the two actions interchangeably. However, caution should be exercised when handling sensitive information submitted using a GET request, as the request will be recorded in the Web server's access log and the browser history. Using hidden variables that are POSTed to the server can pose problems in situations where sensitive data needs to be transmitted to the server instead of being included in the query string (Khalid et al., 2019).

f) **Inadequate Output Sanitization:** Web applications can fail to verify the data being placed into the HTML template before serving HTML to the browser. Because the data comes from a trusted system, such as a database, developers assume it must be secure. That being said, there is a good chance that information in the database came from a hostile user. Therefore, when a contact's email address is shown in a browser, it may have embedded JavaScript that runs on the victim's computer (Scholte et al., 2012).

g) **Insecure Web Server Application Configuration:** Despite careful development efforts, certain applications are occasionally deployed unsecured. This typically occurs due to inadequate documentation of the application's secure deployment environment. For example, a program on the Web that needs a file system folder to let users "write" access may mistakenly be granted "execute" permissions, compromising the system as a whole. Therefore, Web applications are vulnerable due to improper configurations (Li & Xue, 2013).

h) **Authentication Procedures:** Web application log-in sections frequently have security flaws. Sometimes, poorly designed log-in systems lead to high-risk vulnerabilities. For example, take the authentication system which blocks the user for twenty-four hours after three unsuccessful attempts to log in. An attacker might exploit this feature by devising a script to make three login attempts for every user, resulting in the indefinite blocking of all users. After authentication, the application should adhere to log-in best practices and redirect the browser to a new location before proceeding. Nevertheless, several programs transmit websites directly via redirection. An attacker might utilize this to obtain the password of a previously logged-out browser window (Kals et al., 2006).

i) **Ineffective "Forgot-Password" Systems:** Poor password-forgetting methods are also a common vulnerability. Attackers commonly exploit the forgot-password scheme and employ social-engineering techniques to illicitly acquire legitimate accounts. Applications that employ hint questions with a limited range of answers (such as selecting from 12 frequently guessed colors for one's favorite color), as opposed to those that send a new password to the user via email in plain, unencrypted text.

j) **Browser Vulnerabilities:** Applications often face vulnerabilities due to constraints in the browser. Certain commonly used web browsers store all the variables uploaded during a session in plain text within their memory. This creates the potential for a hacker to extract passwords from the browser's memory. If the software fails to implement measures against this browser vulnerability and properly configures its log-in mechanism, an attacker may be able to obtain credentials (Kumar et al., 2017).

k) **Security Flaw of Server Hosting an Application:** Another source of vulnerability is the Web server hosting the Web application. If the Web server is hacked, an attacker may be granted high permissions on the application and database. Popular Web servers' default configurations have recently become more secure. However, these servers still require regular patches to address newly discovered security flaws. If the server is not patched, it poses a significant threat to the application (Fonseca & Vieira, 2008).

Did you know?

Web users are familiar with the HTTP status code "404 Not Found," which indicates that a requested website cannot be located. The term "404" was derived from Room 404 at CERN, the location where the World Wide Web was first developed.

8.4. ATTACK TECHNIQUES

→Learning Objectives

- Differentiate between various attack techniques
- Comprehend the methodologies used by attackers to exploit these vulnerabilities.

After becoming acquainted with the broad category of vulnerabilities, let us now delve into the specifics of particular exploit techniques that target these vulnerabilities. These exploits can allow an individual to bypass authentication or gain unauthorized access to sensitive data within vulnerable applications (Bherde & Pund, 2016).

8.4.1. SQL Injection

A widely utilized and highly detrimental attack on web applications is SQL injection. SQL injection is an exploitative technique where dynamically generated SQL queries are manipulated through specially crafted inputs, enabling the attacker to achieve their objectives (Halfond et al., 2006). The majority of web applications operate on data that is stored within a database. The significance of this data for the organization is substantial. SQL injection is utilized to exploit weak points in web applications to gain unauthorized access to sensitive data. This approach involves the attacker sending harmful input that alters the SQL queries generated by the application to communicate with the database. The execution of these modified SQL queries can lead to detrimental consequences (Boyd & Keromytis, 2004).

Examining the results of a successful SQL injection attack can offer valuable insights into the associated hazards:

a) SQL injection allows the attacker to bypass the authentication mechanism, avoiding the authentication procedure and enabling users to gain access to the application without a valid login and password.

b) SQL injection can lead to unauthorized access of data, allowing the retrieval of data that is not owned by the currently logged-in user. As a result, a malicious individual could acquire unauthorized access to confidential information of others.

c) SQL injection enables the manipulation or removal of sensitive data stored in the database, potentially resulting in irreversible data loss.

What is the mechanism behind SQL injection? To gain clarity, let's examine a handful of key principles (Shar & Tan, 2012).

The majority of SQL queries often involve the collection of data from a database or the modification of its contents. The data is acquired from the selection criteria provided in the SQL query. The criteria are clearly stated in the "where" clause of a "Select" query. An example could be the subsequent SQL query, which collects information from the User_Details table for a user identified as "SAM":

Select * from User_Details where User_Name = 'SAM';

The value in the User_Name column of the User_Details table determines the selection criteria used by the query. It establishes the standards for choosing which records must be retrieved from the database. A malicious user might attempt to alter or access more data by providing an input that essentially changes the SQL query that is already in place. The query can be modified by providing an input that modifies the WHERE clause's selection criteria. Another tactic would be to provide an in-depth response to a valid query (Wei et al., 2006).

It should be mentioned that depending on the type of database being utilized, different input is required for different SQL injection scenarios. Despite the possibility of database misuse in any case, it is essential to modify the input according to the specific database being utilized.

8.4.1.1. SQL Injection—Bypass Authentication

When attempting to hack an application, the first barrier is usually authentication. Let's consider an example that demonstrates how SQL injection can bypass authentication and gain unauthorized access to an application. For this example, we will use a banking application called www.SampleBankApplication.com. To access the banking program, the user needs to enter a username and password on the log-in screen. The user's information is stored in a table called User_Login_Details in the database, as shown in Table 8.1 (Balasundaram & Ramaraj, 2011).

Table 8.1. Representation of User Login Details (Source: V Rao Vemuri, Creative Commons License)

User_Id	User_Password	User_Age	User_Sex	User_Role
Anderson	Qaz123	21	M	Admin
Trinity	Wsx098	25	F	User
Morpheus	Edc456	36	M	User
Smith	Rfv765	40	M	User

(The username and password entered by the user on the login display are stored in variables called strUserId and strUserPassword.)

Upon receiving the user's credentials, the application server executes an authentication process. Typically, this process involves a SQL query to retrieve user details and then compares them to the input provided by the user. The SQL query representation is as follows:

"Select User_Id, User_Password from User_Login_Detailswhere

User_Id = ' "&strUserId& " ' and User_Password = ' "

&strUserPassword& "';"

The goal of the SQL query is to verify whether the user-submitted username and password exist in the User_Login_Details table. If the query returns at least one entry, authentication is considered successful. Conversely, if no rows appear, authentication is deemed unsuccessful (Ali et al., 2009). For instance, if the user inputs the necessary information, the query will successfully authenticate and retrieve Anderson's set of entries in the User_Login_Details table.

strUserName = Anderson strUserPassword = Qaz123

However, the attacker lacks knowledge of an authentic username or password. SQL injection refers to the ability of an attacker to gain unauthorized access by manipulating the SQL query using specific combinations of special characters. For example, let us assume that the user provides the following information on the log-in page:

strUserName = ' or 1=1-- strUserPassword = <blank>

(The password box is optional and can be left blank or filled with any valid input; it is irrelevant. Replace the data provided by the user in the SQL query, as shown in Figure 8.1 (Shrivastava & Pathak, 2013)).

The initial inquiry will be repeated as shown in the following text after the substitution:

Select User_Name, User_Password from User_Login_Details where User_Name = ' ' or 1=1-- ' and User_Password = ' ';

The double hyphen (--) serves as a comment indicator in a SQL query. Any content that follows the -- symbol is treated as a comment and will be ignored when executing the query.

"Select User_Id, User_Password from User_Login_Details where User_Id = ' "&strUserName& " ' and User_Password = ' " &strUserPassword& "';"

Therefore, the ultimately modified query will be completed efficiently, as stated in the subsequent text:

Select User_Name, User_Password from User_Login_Details where User_Name = ' ' or 1=1

After a thorough analysis of the WHERE clauses [User_Name='' or 1=1], it is evident that despite the absence of a username in the column, the query will execute successfully and retrieve all the information from the User_Login_Details table. This is due to the fact that the second condition in the WHERE clause [or 1=1] is always true. The authentication will be successful if the query returns one or more rows. Consequently, the user can gain access to the application by logging in. Additionally, it is important to note that the specific value of the password field is irrelevant, as it is included in the comment segment that is disregarded (Kindy & Pathan, 2011). However, the question arises as to whose account the attacker will be logged into. Typically, the user will be logged into the account associated with the first record in the query's result set. However, this may vary depending on the specific application.

8.4.1.2. SQL Injection — Bypass Authentication, a Variation

Let's now examine an updated iteration of the previous exploit. What would occur if a malevolent assailant intends to execute a focused assault in order to obtain unauthorized entry to a specific user's account? It is solely feasible to access an individual's account if one possesses knowledge of their user ID, particularly if the software is susceptible to SQL injection (Dasmohapatra & Priyadarshini, 2022). Taking into account that the malevolent individual inputs the following data on the login page:

strUserId = Trinity'-- strUserPassword = <blank>

Replace the user-provided data in the SQL query, as shown in Figure 8.1.

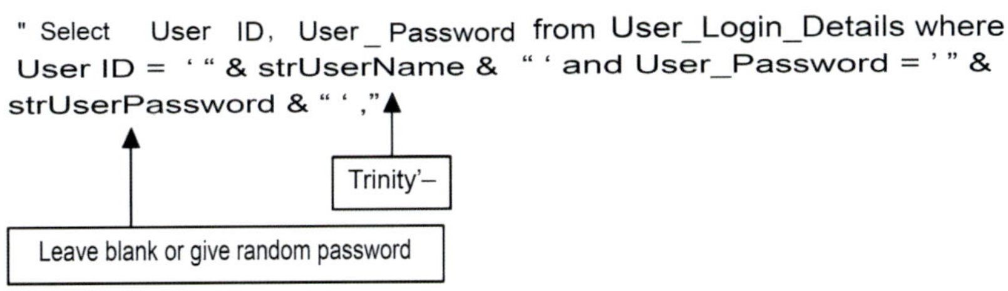

Figure 8.1. Illustration of SQL injection query (Source: Roshen Chandran, Creative Commons License).

The original query would be modified after replacement:

Select User_Id, User_Password from User_Login_Details where User_Id = 'Trinity'--' and User_Password = ' ';

After that, everything would be commented out by the --. Consequently, the last altered query would be run as:

Select User_Name, User_Password from User_Login_Details where User_Name = 'Trinity'

Even if a valid password is not provided, executing this query will allow a user to log into Trinity's account. Now, an attacker can access an administrator's account and gain administrative privileges if they know the administrator's username (Kaur & Kour, 2015).

8.4.1.3. SQL Injection — Unauthorized Access to Data

Generally, customers only need to input their account number in banking tools to access account information. User account information is stored in columns of the banking application. Review the supplied table, Account_Details, outlined in Table 8.2.

Table 8.2. Representation of user account details (Source: V Rao Vemuri, Creative Commons License).

Account_No	Acc_Balance	Account_Type	User_Name
10006245	57676	Current	Trinity
10006789	4656	Current	Anderson
10002459	19873	Current	Morpheus
10001456	236990	Current	Smith

A user-provided account number serves as the foundation for a SQL query that the program uses to retrieve account data from the Bank_Details table. The SQL query might look something like this:

Select * from Account_Details where Account_Number = ' "&accNumber& " ' ;

The variable "accNumber" contains the account number provided by the user (Buehrer et al., 2005).

Suppose a user called Anderson logs into the application and requests account details by providing the account number 10006789. In this case, the application will conduct the following query:

Select * from Account_Details where Account_Number = '10006789';

By entering random account numbers, a malicious individual may attempt to obtain the details of another user's account. Due to the typically long and randomly chosen nature of account numbers, this process could prove challenging. Furthermore, it is highly unlikely that a malicious user could utilize random account numbers to access the details of a specific user's account.

However, SQL injection can extract information about a specific user as well as multiple users simultaneously. Let's consider a scenario where the attacker provides the following information while requesting account details:

Account Number = ' or 1=1--

Replace the user-provided data in the SQL query, as depicted in Figure 8.2 (Lawal et al., 2016).

Following the change, the original inquiry would be formulated as follows:

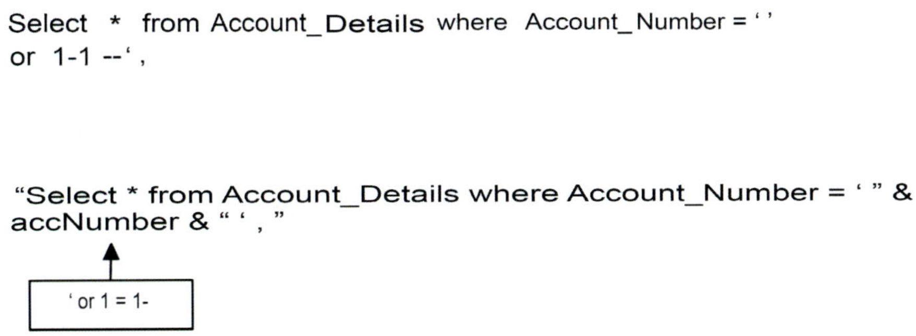

Figure 8.2. Illustration of another SQL injection query (Source: Ajith Abraham, Creative Commons License).

The modified query would retrieve the account information of all individuals listed in the Account_Details table. This is achievable because the WHERE section of the query consistently evaluates to "true" due to the subclause 'OR 1=1.'

Now, one can demonstrate the SQL injection attack using an actual web application. They utilize WebGoat, an application designed by the OWASP organization, to demonstrate prevalent vulnerabilities in web applications. This software is freeware and can be obtained from the website www.owasp.org. The SQL query that was carried out is:

Select * from user_data where userid = '101'

SQL injection is a problem that can modify a previous SQL query to the following one in the account number column:

Select *from user_data where userid = '101' or 1=1'

The execution of the altered SQL query retrieves all the entries from the user_data table (Nasereddin et al., 2023).

8.4.1.4. SQL Injection — Unauthorized Data Access via the "Union" Operator

An SQL query can utilize the "union" operator. The union operator combines the results of multiple SQL queries into a single set. It is important to note that the union operator can also be exploited for SQL injection attacks. By using the union operator, an unethical user can retrieve data from a table other than the intended one.

Now, let us revisit the banking application. This application allows users to access and modify their personal information (Bandhakavi et al., 2007). The provided SQL query is used to retrieve and present user information based on the user ID provided by the user:

Select * from User_Login_Details where User_Id = ' "&strUserId& "';

Instead of entering a valid user ID, a user may use the following input to perform an SQL injection in place of the supplied value:

' union select a username, password from DBA_USERS where '1'='1

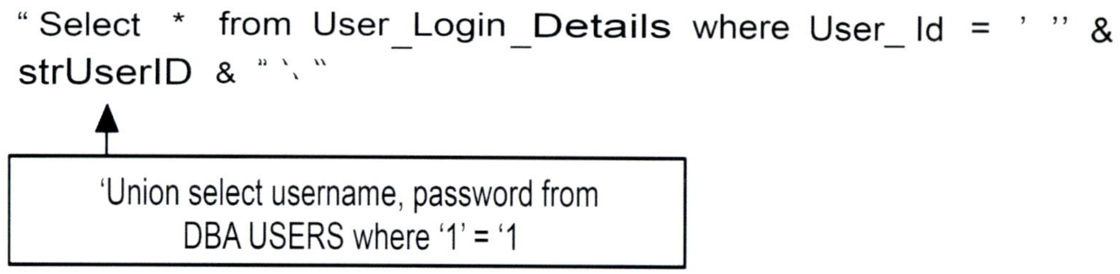

Figure 8.3. Illustration of SQL injection query with user supplication information (Source: Yihua Liao, Creative Commons License).

(The username, password, and other information for users created in the database are contained in the DBA_USERS table.)

Assuming, as shown in Figure 8.3, that a malicious user replaces the data entered by the user in the SQL query.

Following the replacement, the query would be formulated as:

Select * from User_Login_Details where User_Id = ' ' union select username, password from DBA_USERS where '1' = '1';

Because there is nothing in the User_Id field, this query will not return any data from the User_Login_Details table. However, it will still obtain the password and username entries from the DBA_USERS table. Some databases may prohibit using an empty value in a SQL query (Yeolo & Meshram, 2011). Any other value for the User_Id field can be transmitted in these circumstances, as demonstrated by the SQL injection:

Xv1yd56' union select username, password from DBA_USERS where '1'='1

The number and type of columns produced from the first table must match those produced from the second table for the union operator to function. The User_Id field is set to null or random to prohibit the selection of any record from the User_Login_Details table. Otherwise, there may be a discrepancy between the number and type of columns collected from the DBA_USERS table and the User_Login_Details table, rendering the SQL injection useless (Sadotra & Sharma, 2017).

A malicious user can input any known table name instead of using DBA_USERS. The names of tables and columns, along with other important characteristics of the database structure, are sometimes revealed in the error messages generated by the Web application. Occasionally, the application's execution of SQL queries is displayed in the error messages. All of this information can assist someone with malicious intentions in creating an exact SQL injection input and retrieving private information from the database (Medhane, 2013).

8.4.2. Cross-Site Scripting

Cross-site scripting is an innovative and interesting approach to attacking a Web service. It targets a different user who utilizes the Web application instead of the application itself. As the name implies, cross-site scripting makes use of scripts to accomplish its objective. Scripts are small chunks of code written with specific tasks. These scripts can be written in widely used scripting languages like JavaScript and VBScript (Spett, 2005). The majority of web browsers can read and execute these scripts. Due to the functionality that modern programming languages provide, it is possible to build scripts that could be destructive. The implications of a cross-site scripting attack vary depending on how the script was made. For example, a script may be written to steal a user's legitimate session ID or login credentials. The attacker must first launch the script in the victim's browser to carry out such attacks. To launch the assault, the attacker must figure out how to get the script into the target's web browser. A vulnerable program may make it easier for such a script to spread. An attacker can send a malicious script to the target's web browser via a variety of methods (Sadeghian et al., 2013). Some of these tactics include:

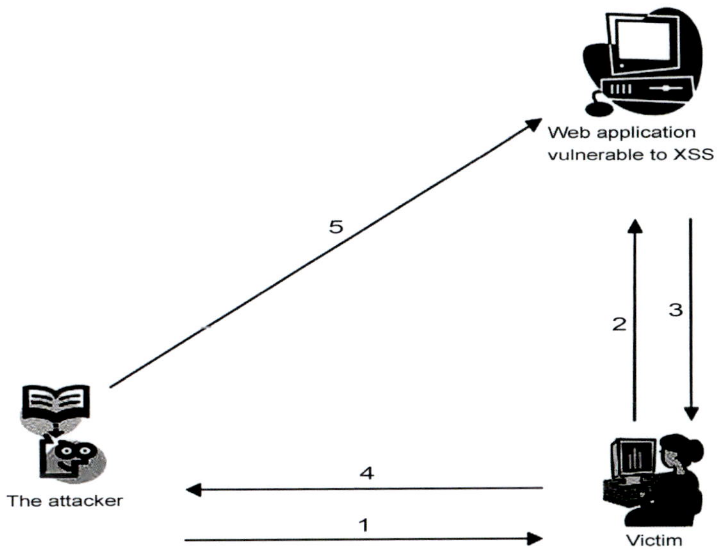

Figure 8.4. Diagram of a cross-site scripting attack (Source: Khalid Labib, Creative Commons License).

a) Several web applications offer users dynamic content in response to specific queries. The information that a user submits in a request is often sent back to the user's web browser by the server. With the help of an email message containing a malicious script, an attacker may be able to send a link to another user. The user would click on the link, unknowingly sending the script content along with a request to a web application. The input script and the response would then be returned by the server. When the server response is displayed, this script executes in the user's browser (Vogt et al., 2007). Figure 8.4 illustrates the concept with the following series of events:

i. A malicious individual creates an email with a script and sends it to the intended recipient.

ii. Upon clicking on a link, the email recipient sends the script to a vulnerable web application.

iii. The user-provided script is appropriately displayed by the online application when it runs in the user's web browser

iv. When the script executes, it sends the attacker the cookie, which may contain the targeted user's session ID.

v. By using the session ID, the attacker gains access to the target user's account in the vulnerable application.

Figure 8.5. Representing a popup message box (Source: Kenneth Ligham, Creative Commons License).

b) The user may also have the ability to upload data from the database using a web application. Subsequently, another user could view this data, similar to a Help Desk Administrator responding to a question. This functionality could be exploited by an attacker to upload a script instead of legitimate content to the server. When the victim views the uploaded content, the script executes in their browser (Wasserman & Su, 2008).

It is crucial to understand that in both cases, the application sends the malicious script to an unsuspecting user. Prior to a cross-site scripting attack, the attacker needs to determine if the application can serve as a conduit. If an application fails to properly sanitize user input and instead sends scripts to the client's browser, it becomes vulnerable and can be exploited as a conduit. This can be verified using a simple script, as shown in the following text. The script is enclosed within the HTML tags <script> and </script>

```
<script>alert(Vulnerable To XSS);</script>
```

When this script appears in the browser, it is executed and triggers the appearance of a pop-up message box, as represented in Figure 8.5 (Gupta & Gupta, 2017).

It can be used by an attacker as a test script to identify vulnerabilities in the program. The script may be sent as a form field or as an additional URL parameter. The

URL provided in the following paragraph contains the script as an additional parameter. The value of this parameter will be handled in the browser instead of being displayed if it is returned to the user for presentation:

http://SampleBankApplication.com/servlets/AccountView?Product=Current&SubProduct=</script>alert

(Vulnerable);</script>

After confirming the execution of the script, the attacker has complete control over how it is utilized (Kirda et al., 2009).

8.4.2.1. Cross-Site Scripting to Steal Session Cookie

Several online applications offer an email feature that enables organizations to communicate with their customers through an account within the service. Let's once again consider a banking application as an example, which offers web-based email functionality. The mail system facilitates communication between staff from different divisions inside the bank, enabling them to deliver information to customers. Additionally, it allows customers to submit messages to bank employees. Figure 8.6 shows the input fields found on a mail page (Hydara et al., 2015).

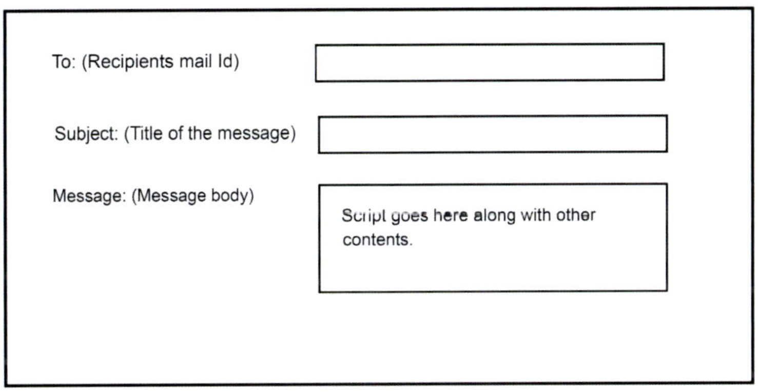

Figure 8.6. Illustration of a mail message with the script (Source: Sanjay Rawat, Creative Commons License).

Let's say an application does not validate user input. Then, it opens itself up to an attacker who may send a malicious script in the body of the email message to take advantage of this vulnerability. Users have to authenticate by logging into the application and then acquire a valid session ID to view their email. When the intended recipient views email messages, the browser displays the malicious email, which causes the script to run upon execution. This script can be programmed to get the user's session ID and send it to the attacker. The attacker would then be able to access the user's account by utilizing the authentic session ID (Bhavani, 2013).

8.4.2.2. Cross-Site Scripting to Steal Credit Card Information

Web-based applications occasionally utilize persistent cookies to store information about returning users and track their sessions. These persistent cookies are stored in the user's long-term memory. On occasion, these cookies may contain sensitive information such as credit card details and other confidential data. Even without physical access to the user's computer, an attacker can illicitly obtain the cookie containing personal data by exploiting a vulnerable application.

Now, let us examine a fictional website called www.eshopping-Demo.com. This website enables online credit card purchases through a specific mechanism. When a transaction is completed, a persistent cookie is generated, containing the user's credit card number. This data retrieval from the cookie allows the credit card number field to be automatically populated for returning users (Rodriguez et al., 2018).

Typically, an attacker would identify a webpage within the application that utilizes the URL to display user-supplied inputs. Once identified, the attacker can construct a script to generate a link to that specific page. This link is then sent to the intended victim via email correspondence, enticing them to activate the provided link.

Let's now investigate the Uniform Resource Locator (URL) that follows. Once the user confirms the purchase, an HTTP request is made to this URL (Kour & Sharma, 2016).

www.eshoppingDemo.com/goods/electronics?ItemCode=12001&Action=Yes&Delivery=Local

The server response includes the ItemCode number, which is then displayed in the user's browser. Next, the attacker creates a hyperlink containing the script encoded within the ItemCode argument, as demonstrated:

www.eshoppingDemo.com/goods/electronics?ItemCode=<script>alert(ScriptContentGoesHere);</script>&Action=Yes&Delivery=Local

The script is transmitted to the server via the ItemCode field once the victim clicks the link. The server will provide the response containing error details and the script, which will then be executed on the user's browser. Upon execution, the script can transmit the cookie to the malicious user (Sarmah et al., 2018).

8.4.2.3. Stealing Passwords with Browser Refresh

The GET and POST protocols are the common ways of sending requests to a web server. All of the information sent to the web application via a GET request is disclosed by means of the examination of the browser's history. The browser's history does not contain the URLs associated with the POST request. Therefore, it is recommended to transmit sensitive information, such as usernames and passwords, exclusively through POST requests to the web application. Still, it is possible to obtain the data linked to a POST request by utilizing distinct functionalities of web browsers (Gupta et al., 2015).

The browser stores the variables that were included in a POST request, along with the websites that the user has recently accessed. It is important to clarify that this process is distinct from preserving links in the browser's history, as it exclusively applies to GET requests rather than POST requests. Due to the application's poor design, an attacker can get confidential data that was previously transmitted by a user through the use of the browser's "Back" and "Refresh" functions. The provided information comprises the username and password (Sun et al., 2011).

To gain a more thorough understanding of the vulnerability, let us consider an example. Please visit www.SampleBankApplication.com/Login.jsp to access the login page of the example banking application. In order to authenticate and proceed, users are required to provide their login information, which includes their username and password. After the user clicks the "Submit" button, a POST request is sent to the page www.SampleBankApplication.com/afterLogin.jsp, with the username and password being sent as separate variables:

userInput = "Morpheus" passwordInput = "Edc456"

Upon successful authentication, this page finalizes the process before presenting its content (Kassim & Sujitha, 2013). Subsequently, the user has access to multiple additional pages before terminating their session. If an attacker succeeds in gaining access to the computer, they may effortlessly discover the login information and password by utilizing the Back and Refresh buttons on the browser—that is, provided the window stays open following the logout process. Users can go back to earlier pages by clicking the Back button. Users can resubmit the Web request and the POSTed data by using the Refresh button. Upon accessing www.SampleBankApplication.com/afterLogin.jsp, the attacker would begin by continuously pushing the Back button. The login information and password were shown on this page during the log-in process (Aghav & Bedi, 2014).

Any data submitted to the application via a POST request is susceptible to this vulnerability. Therefore, the "change password" page is another susceptible location to obtain a Remember password. This vulnerability only matters if the user forgets to exit the browser after logging out. Since POST request data is stored in dynamic memory, it is not preserved when the browser window is closed (Sasirekha, 2013).

Did you know?

Some hackers participate in "hacktivism," which is the use of their expertise to advance political or social issues by breaking into and changing content on websites in an effort to spread awareness or send a message.

This issue can be avoided by adding an intermediate page (such as www.SampleBankApplication.com/IntermediateLogin.jsp) that performs authentication without being delivered to the user. Instead, the intermediate page can instruct the browser to redirect to the next page if the authentication procedure is successful. Although the username and password are POSTed to IntermediateLogin.jsp, an attacker cannot access that page using the Back button because it is never shown in the user's browser (Thomas et al., 2019).

Here is a breakdown of the sequence of actions:

a) The user initiates a request for the log-in page of the web application (www.SampleBankApplication.com/Login.jsp).
b) The server responds by sending the log-in page to the user.
c) The user submits their user ID and password to an intermediate page via the log-in page (www.SampleBankApplication.com/IntermediateLogin.jsp).

d) After successful authentication, the IntermediateLogin.jsp page sends a redirect to the user, leading to (www.SampleBankApplication.com/AfterIntermediateLogin.jsp).

e) Subsequently, the user makes a request for the AfterIntermediateLogin.jsp page.

f) The server fulfills the request by sending the AfterIntermediateLogin.jsp page to the user.

8.4.3. Variable Manipulation Attacks

Let's now examine some different vulnerabilities that are more easily exposed and can cause serious damage. Web applications often transmit sensitive data to the server using hidden form fields. Consider our banking application, www.SampleBankApplication.com. With the assistance of this application, users can access account details (Kothari et al., 2011). The server retrieves account information based on the account number entered into a hidden form field. A hacker could modify the account number provided in the "hidden form" field. One such Web proxy software that enables this is Achilles. The browser can be configured to use a Web proxy tool with the application. The Web proxy then allows for the monitoring and modification of all Web requests and responses. An attacker could intercept requests for account details via a Web proxy and alter the account number before it reaches the server. The modified account number must exist in the database to retrieve records (Kumar, 2013).

PRACTICE PROBLEMS

1. An e-commerce website allows users to post comments. Explain how an attacker could perform a stored XSS attack and propose a preventive measure for this scenario.
2. A web application uses hidden fields to store sensitive information. How could an attacker perform a variable manipulation attack, and what steps can be taken to prevent it?

SOLUTIONS TO PRACTICE PROBLEMS

1. An attacker could input malicious JavaScript code into the comment section, with the intention of executing it when other users view the comments. To mitigate this risk, the website should implement input validation and encode user-generated content to neutralize or escape HTML, thereby ensuring that the execution of scripts is not possible when rendering the comments.
2. Another potential attack vector is the manipulation of hidden fields, where an attacker alters their values, such as changing the price in a shopping cart. To prevent this, the application should validate and authenticate the data received from hidden fields. Additionally, sensitive data should not solely rely on client-side manipulation and should be securely validated and managed on the server-side.

8.5. PREVENTING VULNERABILITIES IN WEB APPLICATIONS

→Learning Objectives

- Identify best practices to prevent and mitigate vulnerabilities in web applications.
- Understand the importance of secure coding practices.

The proverb "prevention is better than cure" holds true when it comes to Web application security flaws. The process of preventing vulnerabilities begins within the software development lifecycle, as this is where most application vulnerabilities originate. An application that is developed and designed with awareness of potential security flaws will be more secure than one that is not (Gollmann, 2008).

Before an application is prepared for deployment, traditional software development lifecycles go through four stages: requirements, design, development, and testing. Each phase contributes to the overall security of the system, so it is crucial to dedicate sufficient effort to addressing security concerns at each level (Scholte et al., 2012).

8.5.1. Requirements

The functional needs of the application are captured during the requirements phase, and the system designers use the specifications from this phase to guide their design work. Therefore, gathering security-related data at this stage aids in the designers' conceptualization of a more secure system.

a) Alongside the functional requirements, it is important to clearly state the application's security requirements.

b) Provide specific information about the company's risks and hazards so that the designer can gain a better understanding of the threat environment and select the appropriate technologies.

c) Specify which applicable regulatory systems the application needs to abide by. This will assist the designers in comprehending the application's minimal security and privacy requirements (Priyanka & Smruthi, 2020).

8.5.2. Design

The overall architecture of the system, the composition of each component, and the interaction between these components are all conceptualized during the design phase. Decisions regarding protocols and technologies are made at this stage. It is the most crucial phase in preventing security flaws in the system. Mistakes made during this phase can be highly costly during testing and difficult to rectify once coding has commenced. The following information provides some guidelines for developing secure software:

a) Develop a fail-safe system, one that will transition to a safe state in the event of a failure. For instance, instead of merely locking the transaction, lock the entire account if the system is unable to reconcile conflicting transactions in a bank account.

b) When constructing the protocols, take into consideration the presence of firewalls in the deployment architecture. Application-layer protocols that establish reverse connections or transmit data at the transport layer often encounter issues when passing through a firewall. The system's security is compromised when the firewall is removed to accommodate the application (Catal et al., 2017).

c) Provide as much specific information as possible about the acceptable inputs for each input. This will enable the programmers to create code that will reject any input that does not adhere to the requirements. For example, indicate that a particular input is for a name field and that only 10 English letters and numbers are permitted.

d) Select the cryptographic solution that best fits the issue. Selecting the highest encryption strength is not necessarily the best option; message digests, salted hashes, or signed messages might be more suitable for certain requirements (Noman et al., 2020).

e) Carefully consider the requirements before selecting the cryptographic system.

f) Outline the abuse-test scenarios from which the testing team should test the system.

g) Determine which distribution scenarios affect system security, and notify the application's engineers who will be delivering them in the documentation. For example, specify during the design stage that only Internet users should have write access to the file upload directory.

8.5.3. Development

An application can be made secure by implementing safe coding principles and well-designed architectures. The following are some recommendations for Web application developers to follow in order to ensure security:

a) Utilize the client's session token and, whenever possible, rely on data stored in internal session variables instead of trusting data received from the client. Only use user input when necessary. For instance, the user's account number can be directly retrieved from the session object in the database, eliminating the need to request it from the client each time. However, not all information can be obtained from the database. One example where user input is necessary is when determining the amount of money the user wishes to transfer (Vargas et al., 2019).

b) Thoroughly validate every input before accepting it. Hackers often attempt fraud by exploiting incorrect input. Validate the received data to ensure it adheres to the specified content type or format requirements for each input field, as defined in the design, whenever possible. By ensuring that all input is legitimate, exploits such as SQL injection can be prevented (Jovanovic et al., 2006).

c) Prior to outputting any data, verify its accuracy. Ensure that any scripts generated by the application are the intended scripts and not ones injected by an attacker. Sanitize the output from any scripts that the application did not explicitly include. Sanitizing the output can help prevent cross-site scripting attacks (Medeiros et al., 2016).

d) Please refrain from adding comments to the HTML that will be displayed. Although adding comments to the code is generally advisable, it is important to ensure that HTML pages intended for rendering do not contain these comments. Comment out the code that the server-side engine executes as necessary. This will prevent the comments from being included in the generated HTML and allow developers to review the application code to understand the reasoning behind the remarks (Alenezi & Javed, 2016).

8.5.4. Testing

Software security is enhanced when security testing is included in the routine testing phase.

a) Create abuse-test scenarios that mimic an attacker's behavior. While standard functional testing primarily focuses on use cases and their boundaries, it is important to recognize that an attacker may rely on fundamentally different inputs to cause harm. Identifying such inputs early on and incorporating them into the test approach makes it much easier to discover security issues throughout the testing phase (Tyagi & Kumar, 2018).

b) Verify whether the program remains secure even when intentional flaws are introduced using fault injection techniques.

c) Educate the testing team on common Web application attacks. By familiarizing themselves with the tactics employed by attackers, the team's ability to create security test cases will be enhanced (Liang et al., 2017).

d) If security is a top priority, conduct an impartial, third-party evaluation of the application. Even if the testers are highly skilled, their work may prevent them from becoming security testing experts. Expert security testing teams typically possess extensive experience with various applications and can complement the standard testing team by continuously monitoring emerging security vulnerabilities (Kapodistria et al., 2011).

SUMMARY

- Although web application security is still in its early stages, the developer community should pay greater attention to it.
- The security of Web applications is not adequate due to the volume of new attack tactics being released and the lack of knowledge about these issues.
- A combination of increased awareness and proper use of security principles across the software development lifecycle can help protect web applications.
- Inadequate input validation, unsecured deserialization, malfunctioning authentication mechanisms, exposed sensitive data, and inadequate session management are common problems in online applications.
- Web application vulnerabilities are exploited by attack techniques such as SQL injection, XSS, variable manipulation, and session hijacking.
- The process of mitigating vulnerabilities in web applications entails implementing best practices, such as secure session management, multi-factor authentication, strong password policies for authentication mechanisms, output encoding to prevent XSS attacks, and the use of security frameworks like Content Security Policy (CSP) to restrict resource loading sources.

MULTIPLE CHOICE QUESTIONS

1. **Which of the following is an example of an injection attack targeting web applications?**
   a) Cross-site scripting (XSS)
   b) Cross-site request forgery (CSRF)
   c) SQL injection
   d) Directory traversal
2. **What type of attack floods a web server with excessive traffic, rendering it unavailable to legitimate users?**
   a) SQL Injection
   b) Cross-site Scripting (XSS)
   c) Distributed Denial of Service (DDoS)
   d) Cross-site Request Forgery (CSRF)
3. **In the context of web application security, what does the term "XSS" stand for?**
   a) External Security System
   b) Cross-Site Scripting
   c) XML Secure Socket
   d) Extended Site Shielding

4. **Which of the following is an example of an insecure deserialization vulnerability in a web application?**
   a) Cookie manipulation
   b) Session fixation
   c) Cross-site request forgery (CSRF)
   d) Object injection
5. **What is the primary goal of a SQL injection attack on a web application?**
   a) To steal session cookies
   b) To execute arbitrary SQL queries
   c) To manipulate HTML content
   d) To perform cross-site scripting
6. **Which attack technique involves an attacker modifying a variable's value to bypass security controls?**
   a) Session hijacking
   b) Cross-site request forgery (CSRF)
   c) Variable manipulation attack
   d) Brute force attack

REVIEW QUESTIONS

1. Define and differentiate between various types of threats to web applications.
2. Explain the significance of input validation in preventing vulnerabilities in web applications. Please provide examples of common input validation vulnerabilities and their potential impact.
3. ompare and contrast SQL injection and Cross-Site Scripting (XSS) attacks in web applications.
4. Enumerate and explain the best practices for secure coding in web applications. How can developers mitigate security risks during the development lifecycle?
5. Discuss the role of security frameworks and libraries in securing web applications. Provide examples and explain how they help prevent common vulnerabilities.

Answers to Multiple Questions

1. (c) 2. (c) 3. (b) 4. (d) 5. (b) 6. (c)

REFERENCES

1. Abusaimeh, H., & Shkoukani, M., (2012). Survey of web application and internet security threats. *International Journal of Computer Science and Network Security, 12*(12), 67–76.
2. Aghav, S. A., & Bedi, R. R., (2014). An enhanced authentication protocol resistant to password stealing and reuse attack. *International Journal of Engineering Research, 3*(6), 1–20.
3. Alenezi, M., & Javed, Y., (2016). Open source web application security: A static analysis approach. In: *2016 International Conference on Engineering & MIS (ICEMIS)* (Vol. 1, No. 1, pp. 1–5). IEEE.
4. Ali, S., Shahzad, S. K., & Javed, H., (2009). Sqlipa: An authentication mechanism against SQL injection. *European Journal of Scientific Research, 38*(4), 604–611.
5. Balasundaram, I., & Ramaraj, E., (2011). An authentication mechanism to prevent SQL injection attacks. *International Journal of Computer Applications, 19*(1), 123–127.
6. Bandhakavi, S., Bisht, P., Madhusudan, P., & Venkatakrishnan, V. N., (2007). CANDID: Preventing SQL injection attacks using dynamic candidate evaluations. In: *Proceedings of the 14th ACM Conference on Computer and Communications Security* (Vol. 1, No. 1, pp. 12–24).
7. Bhavani, A. B., (2013). *Cross-site Scripting Attacks on Android WebView*. arXiv preprint arXiv:1304.7451, 1-20.
8. Bherde, G. P., & Pund, M. A., (2016). Recent attack prevention techniques in web service applications. In: *2016 International Conference on Automatic Control and Dynamic Optimization Techniques (ICACDOT)* (Vol. 1, No. 1, pp. 1174–1180). IEEE.
9. Boyd, S. W., & Keromytis, A. D., (2004). SQLrand: Preventing SQL injection attacks. In: *Applied Cryptography and Network Security: Second International Conference, ACNS 2004, Yellow Mountain, China, Proceedings 2* (pp. 292–302). Springer Berlin Heidelberg.
10. Buehrer, G., Weide, B. W., & Sivilotti, P. A., (2005). Using parse tree validation to prevent SQL injection attacks. In: *Proceedings of the 5th International Workshop on Software Engineering and Middleware* (Vol. 1, No. 1, pp. 106–113).
11. Catal, C., Akbulut, A., Ekenoglu, E., & Alemdaroglu, M., (2017). Development of a software vulnerability prediction web service based on artificial neural networks. In: *Trends and Applications in Knowledge Discovery and Data Mining: PAKDD 2017 Workshops, MLSDA, BDM, DM-BPM Jeju, South Korea, Revised Selected Papers 21* (pp. 59–67). Springer International Publishing.
12. Curphey, M., & Arawo, R., (2006). Web application security assessment tools. *IEEE Security & Privacy, 4*(4), 32–41.
13. Dahse, J., & Holz, T., (2014). Static detection of {second-order} vulnerabilities in web applications. In: *23rd USENIX Security Symposium (USENIX Security 14),* (Vol. 1, No. 1, pp. 989–1003).

14. Dasmohapatra, S., & Priyadarshini, S. B. B., (2022). A comprehensive study on SQL injection attacks, their mode, detection, and prevention. In: *Proceedings of Second Doctoral Symposium on Computational Intelligence: DoSCI 2021* (pp. 617–632). Springer Singapore.

15. Deepa, G., & Thilagam, P. S., (2016). Securing web applications from injection and logic vulnerabilities: Approaches and challenges. *Information and Software Technology, 74*, 160–180.

16. Devi, S. M., & Geetha, M., (2013). oPass: Attractive presentation of user authentication protocol with resist to password reuse attacks. *International Journal of Computer Science and Mobile Computing, 8*(2), 174–180.

17. Di Lucca, G. A., Fasolino, A. R., Mastoianni, M., & Tramontana, P., (2004). Identifying cross site scripting vulnerabilities in web applications. In: *Proceedings. Sixth IEEE International Workshop on Web Site Evolution* (Vol. 1, No. 1, pp. 71–80). IEEE.

18. Fonseca, J., & Vieira, M., (2008). Mapping software faults with web security vulnerabilities. In: *2008 IEEE International Conference on Dependable Systems and Networks with FTCS and DCC (DSN)* (Vol. 1, No. 1, pp. 257–266). IEEE.

19. Garcia, V. H., Monroy, R., & Quintana, M., (2006). Web attack detection using ID3. In: *IFIP World Computer Congress, TC 12* (pp. 323–332). Boston, MA: Springer US.

20. Gollmann, D., (2008). Securing web applications. *Information Security Technical Report, 13*(1), 1–9.

21. Gupta, B. B., Gupta, S., Gangwar, S., Kumar, M., & Meena, P. K., (2015). Cross-site scripting (XSS) abuse and defense: Exploitation on several testing bed environments and its defense. *Journal of Information Privacy and Security, 11*(2), 118–136.

22. Gupta, S., & Gupta, B. B., (2017). Cross-site scripting (XSS) attacks and defense mechanisms: Classification and state-of-the-art. *International Journal of System Assurance Engineering and Management, 8*, 512–530.

23. Halfond, W. G., Viegas, J., & Orso, A., (2006). A classification of SQL-injection attacks and countermeasures. In: *Proceedings of the IEEE International Symposium on Secure Software Engineering* (Vol. 1, pp. 13–15). IEEE.

24. Hydara, I., Sultan, A. B. M., Zulzalil, H., & Admodisastro, N., (2015). Current state of research on cross-site scripting (XSS)–A systematic literature review. *Information and Software Technology, 58*, 170–186.

25. Jovanovic, N., Kruegel, C., & Kirda, E., (2006). Pixy: A static analysis tool for detecting web application vulnerabilities. In: *2006 IEEE Symposium on Security and Privacy (S&P'06)* (pp. 6-pp). IEEE.

26. Kals, S., Kirda, E., Kruegel, C., & Jovanovic, N., (2006). Secubat: A web vulnerability scanner. In: *Proceedings of the 15th International Conference on World Wide Web* (Vol. 1, No. 1, pp. 247–256).

27. Kapodistria, H., Mitropoulos, S., & Douligeris, C., (2011). An advanced web attack detection and prevention tool. *Information Management & Computer Security, 19*(5), 280–299.

28. Kassim, M. M., & Sujitha, A., (2013). Procurepass: A user authentication protocol to resist password stealing and password reuse attack. In: *2013 International Symposium on Computational and Business Intelligence* (Vol. 1, No. 1, pp. 31–34). IEEE.
29. Kaur, P., & Kour, K. P., (2015). SQL injection: Study and augmentation. In: *2015 International Conference on Signal Processing, Computing and Control (ISPCC)* (Vol. 1, No. 1, pp. 102–107). IEEE.
30. Khalid, M. N., Farooq, H., Iqbal, M., Alam, M. T., & Rasheed, K., (2019). Predicting web vulnerabilities in web applications based on machine learning. In: *Intelligent Technologies and Applications: First International Conference, INTAP 2018, Bahawalpur, Pakistan, Revised Selected Papers 1* (pp. 473–484). Springer Singapore.
31. Kindy, D. A., & Pathan, A. S. K., (2011). A survey on SQL injection: Vulnerabilities, attacks, and prevention techniques. In: *2011 IEEE 15th International Symposium on Consumer Electronics (ISCE)* (Vol. 1, No. 1, pp. 468–471). IEEE.
32. Kirda, E., Jovanovic, N., Kruegel, C., & Vigna, G., (2009). Client-side cross-site scripting protection. *Computers & Security, 28*(7), 592–604.
33. Kothari, N., Mahajan, R., Millstein, T., Govindan, R., & Musuvathi, M., (2011). Finding protocol manipulation attacks. In: *Proceedings of the ACM SIGCOMM 2011 Conference* (Vol. 1, No. 1, pp. 26–37).
34. Kour, H., & Sharma, L. S., (2016). Tracing out cross site scripting vulnerabilities in modern scripts. *International Journal of Advanced Networking and Applications,* 7(5), 2862.
35. Kumar, P., (2013). The multi-tier architecture for developing secure website with detection and prevention of SQL-injection attacks. *International Journal of Computer Applications, 62*(9), 1–20.
36. Kumar, S., Mahajan, R., Kumar, N., & Khatri, S. K., (2017). A study on web application security and detecting security vulnerabilities. In: *2017 6th International Conference on Reliability, Infocom Technologies and Optimization (Trends and Future Directions) (ICRITO)* (Vol. 1, No. 1, pp. 451–455). IEEE.
37. Lawal, M. A., Sultan, A. B. M., & Shakiru, A. O., (2016). Systematic literature review on SQL injection attack. *International Journal of Soft Computing, 11*(1), 26–35.
38. Li, X., & Xue, Y., (2011). *A Survey on Web Application Security* (Vol. 25, No. 5, pp. 1–14). Nashville, TN USA.
39. Li, X., & Xue, Y., (2013). LogicScope: Automatic discovery of logic vulnerabilities within web applications. In: *Proceedings of the 8th ACM SIGSAC Symposium on Information, Computer and Communications Security* (Vol. 1, No. 1, pp. 481–486).
40. Liang, J., Zhao, W., & Ye, W., (2017). Anomaly-based web attack detection: A deep learning approach. In: *Proceedings of the 2017 VI International Conference on Network, Communication and Computing* (Vol. 1, No. 1, pp. 80–85).
41. Medeiros, I., Neves, N., & Correia, M., (2016). DEKANT: A static analysis tool that learns to detect web application vulnerabilities. In: *Proceedings of the 25th International Symposium on Software Testing and Analysis*, (Vol. 1, No. 1, pp. 1–11).

42. Medhane, M. H. A. S., (2013). Efficient solution for SQL injection attack detection and prevention. *International Journal of Soft Computing and Engineering (IJSCE), 3*, 396–398.

43. Nasereddin, M., ALKhamaiseh, A., Qasaimeh, M., & Al-Qassas, R., (2023). A systematic review of detection and prevention techniques of SQL injection attacks. *Information Security Journal: A Global Perspective, 32*(4), 252–265.

44. Nikose, B. V., Gupta, R., & Shrivastav, G., (2014). Preventing password reuse attack using authentication protocol. *IJRDET, 2*(2), 31.

45. Noman, M., Iqbal, M., & Manzoor, A., (2020). A survey on detection and prevention of web vulnerabilities. *International Journal of Advanced Computer Science and Applications, 11*(6), 1–20.

46. Priyanka, A. K., & Smruthi, S. S., (2020). Web application vulnerabilities: Exploitation and prevention. In: *2020 Second International Conference on Inventive Research in Computing Applications (ICIRCA)* (Vol. 1, No. 1, pp. 729–734). IEEE.

47. Rodríguez, G. E., Benavides, D. E., Torres, J., Flores, P., & Fuertes, W., (2018). Cookie scout: An analytic model for prevention of cross-site scripting (XSS) using a cookie classifier. In: *Proceedings of the International Conference on Information Technology & Systems (ICITS 2018)* (Vol. 1, No. 1, pp. 497–507). Springer International Publishing.

48. Rudman, R. J., (2010). Framework to identify and manage risks in Web 2.0 applications. *African Journal of Business Management, 4*(15), 3251.

49. Sadeghian, A., Zamani, M., & Abdullah, S. M., (2013). A taxonomy of SQL injection attacks. In: *2013 International Conference on Informatics and Creative Multimedia* (Vol. 1, No. 1, pp. 269–273). IEEE.

50. Sadotra, P., & Sharma, C., (2017). SQL injection impact on web server and their risk mitigation policy implementation techniques: An ultimate solution to prevent computer network from illegal intrusion. *International Journal of Advanced Research in Computer Science, 8*(3), 1–20.

51. Sadqi, Y., & Maleh, Y., (2022). A systematic review and taxonomy of web applications threats. *Information Security Journal: A Global Perspective, 31*(1), 1–27.

52. Sarmah, U., Bhattacharyya, D. K., & Kalita, J. K., (2018). A survey of detection methods for XSS attacks. *Journal of Network and Computer Applications, 118*, 113–143.

53. Sasirekha, K., (2013). Users cell phone and short message service to prevent password stealing and password reuse attacks. In: *International Conference on Engineering and Technology* (Vol. 1, No. 1, p. 102).

54. Scholte, T., Balzarotti, D., & Kirda, E., (2012). Have things changed now? An empirical study on input validation vulnerabilities in web applications. *Computers & Security, 31*(3), 344–356.

55. Scholte, T., Robertson, W., Balzarotti, D., & Kirda, E., (2012). Preventing input validation vulnerabilities in web applications through automated type analysis. In: *2012 IEEE 36th Annual Computer Software and Applications Conference* (Vol. 1, No. 1, pp. 233–243). IEEE.

56. Shar, L. K., & Tan, H. B. K., (2012). Automated removal of cross site scripting vulnerabilities in web applications. *Information and Software Technology, 54*(5), 467–478.

57. Shar, L. K., & Tan, H. B. K., (2012). Defeating SQL injection. *Computer, 46*(3), 69–77.

58. Shrivastava, G., & Pathak, K., (2013). SQL injection attacks: Technique and prevention mechanism. *International Journal of Computer Applications, 69*(7), 1–20.

59. Spett, K., (2005). Cross-site scripting. *SPI Labs, 1*(1), 20.

60. Sudhodanan, A., Khodayari, S., & Caballero, J., (2019). *Cross-Origin State Inference (COSI) Attacks: Leaking Web Site States Through XS-Leaks*. arXiv preprint arXiv:1908.02204, 1-20.

61. Sun, F., Xu, L., & Su, Z., (2011). Static detection of access control vulnerabilities in web applications. In: *20th USENIX Security Symposium (USENIX Security 11)* (Vol. 1, No. 1, pp. 1–20).

62. Sun, H. M., Chen, Y. H., & Lin, Y. H., (2011). oPass: A user authentication protocol resistant to password stealing and password reuse attacks. *IEEE Transactions on Information Forensics and Security, 7*(2), 651–663.

63. Thomas, K., Pullman, J., Yeo, K., Raghunathan, A., Kelley, P. G., Invernizzi, L., & Bursztein, E., (2019). Protecting accounts from credential stuffing with password breach alerting. In: *28th USENIX Security Symposium (USENIX Security 19)* (Vol. 1, No. 1, pp. 1556–1571).

64. Tyagi, S., & Kumar, K., (2018). Evaluation of static web vulnerability analysis tools. In: *2018 Fifth International Conference on Parallel, Distributed and Grid Computing (PDGC)* (Vol. 1, No. 1, pp. 1–6). IEEE.

65. Vargas, S., Vera, M., & Rodriguez, J., (2019). Security strategy for vulnerabilities prevention in the development of web applications. In: *Journal of Physics: Conference Series* (Vol. 1414, No. 1, p. 012017). IOP Publishing.

66. Vogt, P., Nentwich, F., Jovanovic, N., Kirda, E., Kruegel, C., & Vigna, G., (2007). Cross site scripting prevention with dynamic data tainting and static analysis. In: *NDSS* (Vol. 2007, p. 12).

67. Wang, R., Xing, L., Wang, X., & Chen, S., (2013). Unauthorized origin crossing on mobile platforms: Threats and mitigation. In: *Proceedings of the 2013 ACM SIGSAC Conference on Computer & Communications Security* (Vol. 1, No. 1, pp. 635–646).

68. Wassermann, G., & Su, Z., (2008). Static detection of cross-site scripting vulnerabilities. In: *Proceedings of the 30th International Conference on Software Engineering* (Vol. 1, No. 1, pp. 171–180).

69. Wei, K., Muthuprasanna, M., & Kothari, S., (2006). Preventing SQL injection attacks in stored procedures. In: *Australian Software Engineering Conference (ASWEC'06)* (p. 8). IEEE.

70. Yeole, A. S., & Meshram, B. B., (2011). Analysis of different technique for detection of SQL injection. In: *Proceedings of the International Conference & Workshop on Emerging Trends in Technology* (Vol. 1, No. 1, pp. 963–966).

Index

FSC
www.fsc.org
MIX
Papier | Fördert
gute Waldnutzung
FSC® C083411

Kolibri 360 GmbH
Ferdinand-Jühlke-Straße 7
99095 Erfurt, Deutschland
produktsicherheit@kolibri360.de